DANIEL O'DONNELL: MY STORY

DANIEL O'DONNELL: MY STORY

Daniel O'Donnell
with Eddie Rowley

This paperback edition first published in 2005 by
Virgin Books Ltd
Thames Wharf Studios
Rainville Road
London W6 9HA

and

The O'Brien Press ltd
20 Victoria Road
Dublin 6
Ireland

This updated edition first published in hardback in Great Britain and Ireland in 2003 by Virgin Books Ltd and The O'Brien Press Ltd

First published in Great Britain and Ireland in 1999 by Virgin Publishing Ltd and The O'Brien Press Ltd

A catalogue record for this book is available from the British Library.

ISBN 0 7535 0978 4

Typeset by TW Typesetting, Plymouth, Devon
Printed and bound by Mackays of Chatham, Kent

CONTENTS

ACKNOWLEDGEMENTS

This book is all about my life and my dream role as an entertainer, but it took a lot of people to help me produce it. There were tapes of my recorded memories to be transcribed, facts to be checked and photographs to be tracked down. I'd like to thank my family and my manager Sean Reilly for their invaluable contribution, the Ritz organisation, my co-author Eddie Rowley and researcher Sarah Hamilton. I would also like to thank my mother Julia, Sally Blake, Eoin McGarvey, Michael McDonagh, Barry McCall, Nigel Schermuly, Betty Flynn, Maxwell Photography, the Romanian Challenge Appeal and Ritz Productions Ltd for the photographs. Special thanks to my editor Jon Haynes at Virgin Publishing.

1. THE COALMINER'S DAUGHTER

It was the night I cried like a baby over a lady. Not just any lady, mind. This is a woman who has filled me with incredible feelings for as long as I can remember. Like everyone else, I have my dreams and my idols. But if anyone said to me, when I was starting out on this road I've taken in my life, that one day Loretta Lynn, the greatest female country star of all time in my book, would be my date at a dance in my own little hamlet of Kincasslagh, in my beautiful county of Donegal, I would have laughed in their face.

Imagine then, the mixture of emotions that raced through my mind and reduced me to jelly on a night in the autumn of 1997 when my ultimate dream became a reality. I just thought I had died and gone to heaven when my eyes focused on the stunning lady, in an emerald green-and-gold dress, who had crossed the Atlantic to be my surprise 'belle of the ball' at the annual Donegal Shore Festival of Kincasslagh. It's a special memory that will live with me for as long as God leaves me on this planet.

Next I experienced a terrible fright and I wanted to push this living legend away. I know I went very pale and I'd say I almost fainted. My emotions finally spilled over when we walked down to dance. I went to pieces. I just lost it completely and generally I'm not an emotional person.

I shed tears in the festival dome in front of Loretta and everyone else who was there that night. When I look back on it now and think what a show I made of myself that evening, I do get embarrassed. But I suppose under the circumstances it was a natural reaction. That experience has helped me to realise the effect I might have on some of the people who are fans of Daniel O'Donnell the entertainer. It's not something I think about very often, although sometimes, when I put my arm around people I meet at my shows, they'd be trembling. It's strange for me to think I would have that effect on someone because, after all, I'm just a normal human being myself. But the encounter with Loretta in Kincasslagh has helped me see that we do put some individuals on a pedestal and, as a result, they have a strange effect on us when we meet them. Some of the people who were present the night I met Loretta came up to me afterwards and asked, 'Now do you know how we feel?' If even one person feels the way I did, then I really thank God. I'll tell you something, it's a marvellous feeling to feel so happy at meeting somebody that you actually cry. You think, 'I'm really not worthy of this.' I feel very honoured that I've been given the ability to make people happy. It's a terrific feeling, a warm feeling, and I'll never take it for granted.

My obsession with Loretta goes back a long way. My sister Margaret had her records when I was growing up, and from the moment I heard her singing, I was hooked. Loretta became my idol. When *The Coalminer's Daughter*, a film based on her life, came out, I remember going to the première at a cinema in Dublin. It was an exciting event for me, even to hear her voice on tape thanking people for being there was quite incredible, because I had only ever heard her sing at the time.

I first saw Loretta in 1984, at the Country Music Festival which used to be held at London's Wembley Arena. I was walking around Wembley and came upon the stand where Loretta was doing a signing session and I stood there just looking at her. I suppose I was amazed that I could be so close and I watched her and watched her and when it was time for me to go I ran up and blurted out, 'I really love you.' She said, 'Thank ya, honey', we kissed, and off she went, leaving me in seventh heaven. Then I saw her perform that night and I was enthralled.

I went to Nashville in 1988 to play at the Fan Fair show and my backing group, the Jordanaires, who played with Elvis Presley, took me to Loretta's ranch, which is open to the public. I was just so impressed by the place. What I would have done if I had met her there I cannot say. I would probably have died on the spot! But at least I would have gone with a smile on my face. I couldn't believe that I was actually in Loretta Lynn's home and I searched the souvenir shop for a tape that had her speaking on it as well as singing. I suppose that is the difference between liking a singer and their songs and being infatuated. Well, I got a tape with her voice on it and sure I played it till it was worn out.

The papers around that time were full of stories saying her husband had not been good to her. I don't know if that was true or not but I remember being very, very annoyed that she would have any kind of upset in her life. I came back home and I wrote her the only fan letter I have written in my life. I told her how much I enjoyed her music. But I finished off by saying something like, 'If you ever feel down, remember that there are thousands of people like me throughout the world who have a friendly kind of love for you.' I felt bad that anything would make her feel depressed because she had given me so much joy through her music. I never got a reply and neither did I expect one. I was just happy to have the opportunity to express my feelings towards her.

In 1989, I was offered my own TV series in Ireland and I had special guests who I chatted and performed with. Loretta Lynn was among them and I was over the moon. I was really nervous meeting her, but I found her an easy person to be with. Before the show, we chatted and shared the pancakes that my mother had baked. Later, when she came out dressed for the performance, I really felt I was in the presence of a Hollywood star. John Staunton, a member of my band, often says there was magic between the two of us in the studio that night.

In 1996, I went to America for the weekend to see Loretta play because I felt I needed to see her in concert. I'd seen her at Wembley during the Country Music Festival, as I've mentioned, but I'd never seen her doing her full show. I really wanted to meet her on that trip, but I'm not the type of person who will push myself forward in those situations. Her husband was also very ill at the time, in fact he passed away the following month, so I didn't get to meet her. I was disappointed, but I absolutely loved her show.

I did meet Loretta in July 1997, just a few months before her trip to Donegal for the 'belle of the ball', when I went to see her perform at a barn-style theatre beside her home. When the show was nearly over I got up and I went to the area where she was leaving the stage, as I thought it would give me the opportunity to get her attention. Then I heard an announcement saying, 'Loretta will sign autographs on the stage.' So I ran back like a buck goat. 'For once,' I said to myself, 'you're way ahead of yourself.' Eventually I reached the head of the queue and Loretta looked down at me from where she was.

I said, 'Loretta, do you remember Daniel?'

She exclaimed, 'Honey! Oh my God!'

I was flabbergasted. I thought she wouldn't remember me because she does so many TV shows.

Loretta called to her manager, 'Lane, Daniel's here!'

Then she said to me, 'Come up, honey, come up.'

Everybody was filing by her and I was embarrassed in a way, but I thought, why should I give a hoot what they think. So I went up to Loretta and she gave me a big hug.

I said, 'I'm really delighted to see you!'

She asked, 'What are you doing honey, can I meet you later?'

I told her I was returning to Ireland. She had obviously forgotten about the secrecy of her impending visit to Kincas-slagh, as she started to ask her manager, 'Lane, aren't we . . .'

She was about to say, 'Aren't we going over to see Daniel?' I learned later that Lane, who was behind me, was ashen-faced and waving furiously at Loretta in case she let the cat out of the bag. It would have been a disaster after all the planning that had gone in to my big surprise, but fortunately Lane stopped her in her tracks and, distracted, Loretta never finished the question. I left Loretta that day, never dreaming that I would be seeing her so soon in *my* home.

Now, here I have to marvel at my sister Kathleen for the role she played in organising the event of a lifetime for me. I can only imagine how much time and effort went into it. It's Kathleen who lines up my 'belle' every year. They have included Dana, who was Ireland's first Eurovision winner, and is now a member of the European Parliament. TV and radio star Gloria Hunniford did the honours another time, and we also had Vera Duckworth (Liz Dawn) from *Coronation Street*.

There are lots of activities during the week of the Donegal Shore Festival, including the 'belle of the ball' dance, which takes place in The Dome, erected especially for the occasion at the Viking House Hotel. Other attractions include fishing, golf, card games and a heritage trail, but the mystery belle on the Sunday night at the end of the week creates the most interest. There was great speculation as to who would be that year's 'belle'. People came up and asked me what I thought and, of course, I had no idea.

As is the norm, I was blindfolded before the 'belle' was brought out on to the stage. Then Loretta was escorted out to join me and, as she made her entrance, I heard the screams of the audience. I thought, 'This is somebody incredible.' It still never crossed my mind that it was Loretta. I don't know what she must have thought of me when the blindfold was removed and I broke down and cried because I was so overcome with emotion. She must have thought I was off my head.

Loretta told the audience about my visit to her home that July and that I had promised to return in August to see her in concert again. It was an arrangement I hadn't kept due to work commitments. She said to the crowd, 'He said he would come in August. I hollered out at my show, "Daniel O'Donnell have you sneaked in here again without telling me!" ' I was astonished that she remembered how I had planned to be there.

I don't know if it's the fact I admire her so much that I think she wouldn't remember me. But sometimes I have the same experience. People come up to introduce themselves, and they start off by saying, 'Well, you wouldn't remember me, but we met . . .' And I do remember them. So maybe I'm not giving Loretta credit. I suppose I feel if she had a book of people, I would be a very small entry. So how do you remember that? Yet in my book she is the opening chapter.

What I did later that night in Kincasslagh was the first time in a public situation that I put myself first. Now I know, or I heard later, that some of the fans were annoyed and, indeed, some were thrilled. But I have no apologies to make to anybody for what I did, because if they had that opportunity, they would be selfish too. When the time came for Loretta to go – and she had to leave that night because she had a commitment to keep in America – I decided to leave the festivities early and travel with her to Dublin. I wanted to be with her for as long as I could. Loretta changed into a lovely black trouser suit and we set off. She talked non-stop from the minute we got into the car until we arrived. We got there very early in the morning and went to Jury's Hotel for breakfast, but the dining room wasn't open. I was in a panic. We went on to the Berkeley Court and I said to myself, 'Please God let someone here recognise this auld face of mine', and, fair enough, they took a look at me and said, 'OK, come in, we'll look after you.' I was so relieved because I wanted Loretta to have the best impression, not of me, but of Ireland. We had a continental breakfast and all too soon it was time to take Loretta to the airport. Then I made the five-hour journey back to Donegal. It may have been a marathon return trip, but under the circumstances I felt no pain!

I suppose if there was such a thing as the highlight of my life, I would say that was it: seeing Loretta Lynn on that stage in Kincasslagh. To think that Loretta Lynn, who I had listened to from a young age, whose music I had loved, and whose life I had studied through her movies, that she actually visited me in my village. To think that she actually sang in Kincasslagh, well, it was just perfect for me. If there's one thing that I really appreciate success giving to me, it's that special night with Loretta Lynn.

We don't keep in contact and we'll probably never become close friends as I would never push myself upon her and actively pursue regular contact. If the time came that we met on common ground, and we became friends, then I would accept that gratefully. But I will never hound her, or Cliff Richard, who is another of my favourite artists.

2. TIMES PAST

Life has many twists and turns, both good and bad. We never know what's around the corner. As a child, I never imagined the trail that would eventually lead me to where I am today. I certainly never envisaged that one day a world-famous American country star like Loretta Lynn would travel all the way to my village to give me a moment in time that will burn brightly in my mind and in my heart for the rest of my life. But then, maybe I shouldn't be surprised that she would come to see me. Loretta's family background is not so different to my own, as she too comes from humble origins. Her quiet backwater of Butcher's Hollow, Kentucky, may not be Kincasslagh, but the hardship endured by the people there was quite similar to the struggles that my parents encountered raising their family. Loretta never forgot her roots or lost her common touch and I do believe that is due to her upbringing.

My early years were spent during an era when the world seemed to revolve much slower, at least in Kincasslagh. I didn't come from the dark ages by any means, but many of the old traditions, the ancient ways of working and the social activities from a bygone era were still part of the lifestyle. Ireland was a poor country at the time, things were being slowly modernised. But it is a testament to my parents' love and dedication to their children that our childhood memories are all happy ones. The only dark cloud in our lives was the sudden death of my father Francie when I was just a wee lad of six, the youngest in the family.

My father was born in Acres near Burtonport in County Donegal and his family were known as the Donie Owens. When there were numerous families with the same name in an area, they were each given a nickname to avoid confusion. Daddy's father was Daniel and when I came along I was named after him. My paternal grandmother was Kitty Duffy, but her clan were known as the Johnny Jondies. My father was one of eleven children. He was the second youngest and a seventh son. This is significant in that there was some old man who was a seventh son and when he was dying he sent for Daddy and he passed on a cure to him. It was for some kind of lump that appears on the body. My father was often called upon to perform this cure, which involved going to the afflicted person three nights after midnight and before the sun rose in the morning. There is a woman in England who was cured by Daddy. She remembers him being only a wee boy at the time, and how they had to rouse him from his sleep and keep him awake to lay his hands on her and recite the special prayers. That lady is nearly ninety now and she comes to the concerts.

My mother, Julia, came from the little island of Owey, just off the coast of Donegal. Her father was James McGonagle and her mother was Margaret Sharkey, or Margaret Neddy as she was known. I have fond memories of Grannie McGonagle as she lived with us while I was growing up, but I don't remember my grandad as he died when I was a toddler.

My parents wed in 1948. They went on to bring five little O'Donnell's, or Bosco's as we're known locally, into the world. I was born on 12 December 1961. I have two brothers and two sisters. John, the eldest, is thirteen years my senior. A memory I have of John is of him going to dances when he was in his twenties and me wishing I was big enough to go with him. I don't know what it was about country dances in those days, but it seems there was always some trouble at them. The first question that was asked of John the following morning was, "Were there any fights last night?" There would always be at least two. John is quiet, but he has a great sense of humour. He can be very comical and great craic [fun]. When my sister Margaret (Margo) became a singer, he used to be her driver. Later he worked in a bakery in Kincasslagh. John and his wife Brigid have two sons, Frankie and Joey. Margaret is the eldest after John. I remember a lot about her in my childhood as she was a singer from a very young age and was, as a result, well known. I recall how she'd come home from school and go off to sing – one time even taking a plate of food with her! What she did had a big influence on our lives.

We'd always be introduced to people as Margo's brother, sister or mother. I loved what she was doing and I occasionally accompanied her to dances. From the age of ten upwards, whenever I was brought along to a ballroom where Margo was the star attraction I'd get up to sing with her. She would introduce me as her 'little brother' and the crowd always seemed to enjoy my minor contribution to the night's entertainment. I remember one time the excitement I experienced waiting for Margaret to return home with her first car. My brother John was driving it and in those days you had to 'run in' a car, so it had to be driven at a snail's pace. It took forever to arrive and while it wasn't a flashy car, it was a big deal to us at the time as there weren't many cars in the area. My sister Kathleen is six years older than me and she is a mother figure in the family. Kathleen and her husband, John Doogan, have four children, John Francis, Patricia, Fiona and Daniel. My brother James is four years older than me and he left home at the age of fourteen to work in Dublin as a chef. He's very outgoing and a very entertaining person. You'd have to censor the jokes he tells. He works in the Portobello bar in Dublin, he has a word for everybody and a huge circle of friends. I rarely go anywhere that I don't meet somebody who knows James. His wife is called Eileen and they have three children, Paul, Christopher and Margaret.

My first home was a lovely old house across the road from where I used to live in Kincasslagh. I used to sleep in a wee room off the kitchen and it was a busy house, there were always people in it. There were pots hanging from a crook over the open fire in the sitting room, bubbling away before mealtimes. It was a big, two-storey house, although there was nothing upstairs at the time. Mary Brown, my mother's cousin, who owns the house, has it all done up. There was no water and no toilet when we lived there, which is quite incredible considering it's not all that long ago. In fact, there was only one house in our area that I recall having a flush toilet when I was a kid. So that was a real novelty. Our toilet was across the road – a tin hut! Like most families at that time, we didn't have a daily shower or bath. In those days

Saturday night was bath night and we'd have a scrub up in a tub in front of the fire.

We moved in to a new council house in 1967, a year before my father died. It was a bungalow on the site of our current dormer home. With the council house came a bath and hot water and that was a whole new experience!

My father's death was a terrible shock. He was the youngest of the boys in his family and he must have been very good as a person, as when you hear people speak about him, it's almost in saintly terms. People used to come and ask him to pray for them. His mother, my grandmother, was still living when he died. His father died from throat cancer, he was only in his sixties and cancer must have been a terrible thing then as medicine wasn't as advanced as it is now.

Although I was six years old when my father died from a heart attack at forty-nine, the only memories I seem to have are of him going away and returning home. When he came back I used to be put out of the bed I shared with my mother, so I wasn't too happy about that! He had a very tough life. Like many family men in our area, he was forced to emigrate in order to provide for the family, because there wasn't enough work in Kincasslagh and the surrounding districts to meet everyone's needs. When I reflect on it now, it must have been a terrible wrench for both himself and my mother when he had to leave everyone behind for months on end. He worked on farms in Scotland. It was hard, manual labour and a far cry from my own lifestyle today.

When he died, my mother lost her partner in life and was left alone to shoulder the responsibility of rearing us. That must have been a frightening prospect for her. Even though my father had worked away from home, he would have been there whenever she needed him. The love and admiration I hold for my mother knows no bounds because she ensured we never wanted for anything. She was our rock and we took comfort from that. It's sad that she doesn't have a partner to share her twilight years, but I hope that myself and the rest of the family help to fill that void for her.

There's no doubt that the loss of a parent does cause trauma and have a lasting effect. But how it has affected me, I cannot really say, as I don't know. All I do know is, I find it very difficult to talk about my father and his untimely passing. Whenever I'm asked about him, I answer very quickly, because one time I went to pieces when the subject arose during an interview with an Irish newspaper. To his credit, the journalist never wrote about the incident. But I remember that it was like somebody opening up a raw wound and I became an emotional mess. I broke down and cried. It was dreadful. But I cannot explain why that happened. I've never felt that I've missed anything by losing my Dad, although I do wonder what it would be like if he had been there in my life. I wonder what influence his presence would have had in shaping me as a person. I suppose I feel it was unfair that I was deprived of having a father. I'd look at friends and they'd have their fathers with them at special events and I'd feel self-conscious that I didn't have a father to share those occasions. On the other hand, I didn't have the bother that some fellows had with their fathers, so I suppose you always long for what you haven't got, and sometimes you wish you didn't have what you have!

I have never tried to get to know him through other people, and as a family we never speak about him. I don't actually like dwelling on my father and his death. What is the point in finding out more about him? You can't rely on what somebody else tells you. I don't remember speaking about him with the family, maybe because it would be upsetting for everyone, particularly my mother. I would shy away from it anyway because I wouldn't handle it very well.

My mother had the greatest input as to how we were brought up, as we only had her to obey. If my father had been around there might have been a different set of rules, but it was my mother who ruled the roost, and she was always firm, but reasonable, in the way she dealt with us. I never once thought, 'If only my father was here.' I wasn't as conscious of his absence in our lives back then as much as the older children would have been, because they knew him and were closer to him. It was obviously more painful for them when he passed away.

One thing success has given me is the opportunity to give my mother a good life by sharing what I have with her. She's been to my shows at home and abroad, participated in TV specials, and loved every minute of it. I always make sure that I introduce her and put the spotlight on her because I know she enjoys being thrust into that position. Sure she's like the Queen Mother on occasions like that, giving everyone the royal salute!

I keep in constant contact with my mother and she keeps me up to date on what's happening around Kincasslagh. I make sure I call her regularly when I'm away or I'd get a right good telling off. You see, she'd be worried that something was wrong with me. Now the strange thing is, my brother James could be away for six months without calling home and there wouldn't be a word said about it. If I missed three days, she'd have the army out searching for me. It's the habit you give.

As a kid, I would have been afraid of my mother hearing that I had done anything wrong and, as a result, I never got into much trouble. Even in school, I never got into a lot of bother. The threat of a walloping kept me on the straight and narrow and it never had to be administered, not as far as I can recall.

Mrs Logue, one of the teachers in Belcruit national school, where I started my education as a child, also had a big influence on me. It wasn't that she ruled her pupils with an iron rod, but we held her in such high esteem that we didn't want to do anything to lose her respect. It was a case of not letting her down. I attribute a lot of my qualities today to Mrs Logue's influence as well as my mother's. Mrs Logue instilled manners in us as well as teaching us. Even to this day, if I met her at home I'd address her as Mrs Logue. I wouldn't be able to bring myself to call her by her first name, Mary, out of respect. Today, teachers don't have control over classes at all because kids know they can't be disciplined. They can sit back and stick their tongues out and they know there's nothing that can be done. In my day, you put the teacher on a pedestal. As a child, if I was out around the locality and I saw Mrs Logue, I'd be on my best behaviour. You wouldn't dare do things like laugh at Mass in case she heard about it. She probably had an awful lot more sway over us kids than she ever realised. Having said that, I'm sure she gave me the odd clip around the ears, although now, if people asked her, she'd say that I was a model pupil.

Thinking back, my first day at school in 1967 doesn't stand out as being a traumatic experience for me. I don't recall any hysterics, or having to be torn away from my mother. There would have been other children there that I knew, neighbours from around about. The school was a mile-and-a-half from my home, so it was a long walk. Margaret McGarvey, who lived nearby, started the same day. We were always in the same class and we would walk home together. There was a turf fire in our school for heat. It was a big stove. And I remember the school without electricity. Now, why they built the school in 1964 without any electricity, I don't know. But the school had none and we had tillies [lamps] in the early morning during the winter months to light up the rooms. I don't recall that there were any big traumas in the school when I was there, apart from one incident involving a girl who put her hand through a glass door and then drew it back. She suffered a dreadful injury and was off school for ages. It was a very basic school in those days with no mod cons like computers. We had the old ink-wells on the desks, and it was a frightening affair when we had to progress from writing with pencils to negotiating with ink and nibs. You weren't allowed biros. You practised your handwriting with a pen and ink to get it perfect, and I have anything but perfect handwriting nowadays!

I had friends like Leo Bonner and I spent a lot of time up at his house, even though he was totally different to me. Leo was very physical and he had a flair for mechanical work and woodwork and building, whereas I was useless with my hands. Michael Doogan was another friend who lived further down the road and I used to go over to play. I recall that we got up to devilment one day when we disturbed his sister Noreen's playhouse and she was none too happy about it.

I suspect people have the impression that my mother kept me hanging on to her apron strings when I was a kid, but that couldn't be further from the truth. She wasn't at all over-protective. I had great freedom, a terrific childhood the same as everyone else in our area.

I was always in and out of neighbours' houses when I was a kid and I was full of news. I was like a newspaper on feet. I'd sit listening to people talking and I'd carry all the gossip of the neighbourhood. And you know, now, I have no time for gossip or for people who spread gossip. I remember one incident back then involving Tessie Doalty, a cousin of my mother. Her husband, Brian, died and she had a son called George, who is a cousin of mine. Tessie also tells the story of how I went and said to her that I was sorry about Brian dying.

I added, 'But sure you still have George, although he's not very good lookin' either.' Poor old Tessie thought I must have heard someone saying there was something wrong with George's health and got it garbled. I gave her an awful fright.

There were some wonderful characters in my area when I was growing up. Nora Dan was one of them. She was a tall, strong woman and she had a welcome for everyone. But Nora definitely wasn't houseproud. There were hens in the house, cats, all kinds of animals. There would be food on the table and hens on it too. Nora would be shushing them off. 'Who invited you?' she would say. But she was a lovely person and she used to visit our house every Tuesday and Friday without fail. I remember how she always brought sweets called 'barley sugars'. Then there was John Phil, the best-natured man you'd ever meet, although his good intentions often backfired. Like the time my mother had sown grass seed for a new lawn in our garden. We were away for the day and when we returned there was John Phil sowing vegetables in it for us. In my mother's new lawn! John, of course, thought he was doing us a good turn. Pat Neil Pat was another neighbour who was always guaranteed to raise a laugh. The phone service in those days, when it finally arrived, was quite basic. We had a turn-handle phone and the service was operated through the local post office. After ten o'clock at night you had to share what they called a 'party line'. There were normally four people on the same line and you knew by the number of rings if it was your call. Pat Neil Pat was on our line. He had three rings and we had five. The priest and the doctor were two and four respectively. You wouldn't pick up the phone if it wasn't your call, although you could do it and listen in to your neighbour's conversation. One night Pat was waiting impatiently on a particular call. The phone rang five times, so it was ours but when my mother answered it she heard a man talking.

'What's your number, sir?' asked the man.

'One seven,' a voice replied. It was Pat Neil Pat.

'How many rings did you hear?' asked the man.

'I heard five, but it should only be three,' a frustrated Pat replied.

Josie McGarvey, the village blacksmith, lived next door with his daughter Annie. I remember him as an old man who was very stiff. 'Come, come, now laddie!' he would say if you were being smart with him. He was eighty-six years old when he died. They had a lovely thatched house and I was always visiting. I would sit with Annie playing cards at night. She was a great card player. She'd show me how to win particular tricks and how to read other people's hands. I certainly sharpened my card playing skills with Annie. Cards were a very, very big pastime in our area.

From about the age of nine I went to work in the Cope, which is a general store in our area, and I earned a weekly wage of £2. I got to know everyone around the district through the Cope. When I think back on it now, those were great days. I used to go out in the Cope van to all the country areas and we'd buy eggs from people. They were free range, the best kind, not those battery eggs you get everywhere nowadays. Then we'd go around selling them and people would ask, 'Are those battery eggs?' No, you'd reply, they're so-and-so's eggs! People from Owey Island would come over with fish and dulse which we'd sell. Dulse is seaweed that you dry and eat, it's lovely, as is carrigeen moss, which is like seaweed. Carrigeen moss is full of iron, it's good for people with colds and they still take it.

I loved working in the Cope, but if there's one chore I hated as a kid, it was cutting turf in the bog [peatland], to be used as fuel for the fire. I'm sure many Irish children shared my feeling about it, as it was boring, hard work. Most families in rural Ireland would spend a couple of days every year harvesting the peat from the ground. It was cut into small chunks and left to dry out in the sun before being taken home and stored for use as winter fuel. But a day in the bog was a nightmare to me as I never got to grips with the skills required. It meant a team effort, and I have to work at my own pace. I wasn't into manual jobs. I was the same at school. If there was a subject I liked, I could learn about it no problem, and if I didn't, I couldn't. I hated geography, and history. I suppose there was concern in the family about how I would earn a living when I grew up. I wasn't even good at setting tatties [sowing potatoes]. I used to set a few flowers, but you couldn't eat them!

I'm not sorry to be done with the bog today. I don't care what anybody says about nostalgia, there's none in it for me. My brother John used to say, 'If Kitty Wells [a famous country singer] was out there you'd be off in a flash.'

There were lots of pets around the house when I was growing up. We had numerous cats and then we had Rover the dog. Rover was a lovely dog and very intelligent too. He picked up lots of tricks. He would limp when my mother put a bandage on his leg, even though there was nothing wrong with him! Poor old Rover eventually died of old age and then we got a wee Rover, one of those Scottish Terriers, the one on the whiskey bottle. The strange thing about this fella was that our James arrived at the house with him the night old Rover died. You'd think he'd had some kind of premonition that the old fella was about to pass on. There was a bit of crying done over Rover Snr because people do become very attached to animals and sometimes you treat them like they're humans and part of the family. So when they die, it's like a death in the family.

We had a wee white rabbit and I had a pigeon called Jacko. I clipped his wings so he couldn't fly. Rover and the rabbit and the cats used to sleep together by the fire.

Back in those days, going in to Dungloe was a major outing, even though you could throw a stone into the town because it's no distance at all. It's only six miles from where we live. But it was a major affair going to Dungloe back then, you had to stay for the day and come back on the bus. The people from Dungloe were a lot smarter than we were, or at least we thought they were. To us, they were like city slickers. It's only a country town, but it seemed they were a lot more advanced than us fellas.

For a long time we didn't have a car to get around, but sure where was there to go to? There was only school or church and if it was a bad morning you'd get the bus to school for a couple of pence. You'd walk to Mass or one of the neighbours would take you in his van.

I remember that in those days everybody had a television, so we weren't that primitive, and you rented your telly from John Joe's in Dungloe. I'm sure it was the same all over the country. Nobody owned televisions, they were all rented. I remember I wrote to Miss Helen in *Romper Room*, a programme on UTV a bit like *Blue Peter*. I told her that me and Granny, who lived with us, were watching. I don't think she ever answered. I also watched programmes like *Wanderly Wagon*, *Bonanza*, *The Big Valley*, *Batman and Robin*, *Joe 90* and the *Thunderbirds*. They were brilliant.

After we had first got the television, a local man called Joe Doalty visited our house one night. Joe was normally very well spoken. 'Lovely God' was one of his sayings. While he was in our house, there was an advert on the telly for a floor cleaner called Flash. A woman known as Supergran was showing a girl how to use it. The advert came on three times and Joe would stop to look at it each time. Eventually he turned to us and commented, 'God, isn't that a stupid young wan, there. That's three times that woman is after showing her how to clean that floor and she doesn't know how to do it yet.' He thought it was for real!

These days I don't watch a lot of television, although I do like to keep up with what's happening in *Coronation Street*. But I love comedy shows like *One Foot in the Grave* and *Keeping Up*

Appearances. I think *Mr Bean* is just hilarious. I never watched it until I was on a plane one time. If I had seen it on the television prior to that, I would probably have switched over. But it was part of the in-flight entertainment. I had to take the headphones off because I really felt I was laughing so much. I thought I was just going to die it was so funny. I like television, but I would never watch it if I had something else to do, even if there was something very special on. I don't use the video much either because I'm not all that bothered about sitting down and watching things. I'd rather play a game of cards.

We used to amuse ourselves as kids with simple things. A branch of a tree would become a gun, or the Lone Ranger's horse, Silver. A see-saw was just a plank on a stone, which is probably still in the garden today. We'd spend hours amusing ourselves with those simple pleasures. I remember we had a swing, which was a piece of rope, just beside the chapel. Sure that was great too. I can still see that swing.

Christmas, of course, is a great time of the year when you're a child, and it was no different for me. All we'd be wishing for was snow, so that we could get a sleigh out. The big thing at Christmas when we were growing up was Santy. The most impressive present I ever got was a Scalectric set. I don't know what age I was when that arrived, but I do recall that I was pretty big – Santy came to me for a long time!

Christmas, for me, also centred around the church as I always sang in the choir, even as a child. I always feel a real closeness to people in church and Christmas Eve in the chapel was something special. We also used to go out on the Mummers, which is a tradition in some parts of Ireland. You put on fancy dress and go from house to house or pub to pub singing, or presenting little sketches, and people give you money. Myself and some friends – Anne Sharkey, Ann Hugo, Kathleen Sharkey and Ann Teresa – used to do a Nativity play on the Mummers. We were very giddy and sometimes just one person would do the whole performance because nobody else could speak for laughter. I recall going to one house and the lady asking, 'What charity is this for?' We named *two* charities on the spot, so that she'd give us double the money. When I think back on it now, we were dreadful.

Religious occasions like First Communion and Confirmation were among the highlights of our childhood years. They were special occasions, not just in the religious sense but also as events to be celebrated. Mind you, they weren't as commercial back then as they are now. When I received my First Communion, there was no family outing to a posh restaurant. We went home after church and had the normal family meal. The suit I wore was the same one my older brother John had worn for his First Communion *thirteen years* previously, there was no waste in those days! My Confirmation held great expectations for me. I thought I was going to experience something amazing, that I would feel whatever I was going to receive coming into my body. But it was a big anti-climax. I never experienced anything at all. It was later that I came to realise the significance of that sacrament.

Those were great days, a time when the sun always seemed to shine in the summer and you always had a white Christmas, a time when we didn't have a care in the world. Now, whether those memories are the result of time playing tricks, I don't know. But when I recall those early days, I can't honestly say there was any cloud hanging over them.

3. ISLAND DAYS AND MY EXCURSIONS

The little island of owey is uninhabited now, but it was a big part of my life when I was growing up. I used to spend my summers there. As I have said, I can't remember the weather being bad when I was small. I'd wake up in the morning on Owey Island and I'd hear the sound of fishermen going away to haul lobster pots or nets. The island was lovely. It had gravel roads and there wasn't a blade of grass growing on them. Everywhere looked so tidy and all the fields were worked on. The islanders grew all their own crops and everyone had a cow. If somebody's cow was dry, they'd get milk from one of their neighbours. They had their own potatoes and also baked their own bread. They really were very self-sufficient. Sometimes I wonder if islanders were better off than us on the mainland because they seemed to have everything. While fish was plentiful, meat was something that was a bit of a luxury and they'd usually only have it for their meals at the weekend. They had hens which they'd kill for their meat. They cooked their fish on a griddle, which was like a grill that hung on a crook over a fire. They'd roast crab toes in the fire and the taste of them! Och, it makes my mouth water thinking about the delicious variety of tastes from that wonderful food.

There were a few houses you'd go to at night to pass the time and have the *craic* [a Gaelic term meaning fun]. Maggie and Micky Dens' house was one. The acting that used to go on in those houses! Maggie would be cooking something on the open fire and someone would throw a piece of turf on it for devilment. You'd always find Maggie sitting by the fire reading cowboy books. Then they would be telling ghost stories and you'd be rattling with fear on the way home. I can't remember a restriction on time when I was on the island. No one was watching the clock.

I also remember the dances that took place on Owey. If there was a party, it would be held in the school. One such occasion was to celebrate Dominic McDevitt, my mother's cousin, coming back from America on holiday. Whenever someone came back from the States, it was a big occasion and everyone on Owey would go out to meet them off the boat. If someone was leaving for foreign lands, then everyone would go and see them off too. Those were emotional occasions, as the pain of emigration cut deep into the community in those days.

The views from Owey were fantastic. You could sit for hours just marvelling at the world around you. There was no phone on the island, so if you wanted to go over by boat you'd have to stand on the mainland shore and wait to be spotted. All the islanders had their own mark for waiting, like Uncle James, my mother's brother. He would know if somebody was waiting for him to collect them in his boat because that person would be standing on his 'mark'. Wasn't that a wonderful system! Granny was always there on the island.

Granny eventually came over to live with us in Kincasslagh until she died in 1971, but she always went back to the island in the summer. She was in great health, apart from being terribly stiff. If it was today, a hip or knee replacement would have rectified her problem. She was the real old-fashioned lady, with the wee round glasses, her hair tied up in a bun and dressed in dark clothes and a shawl. She had a noise about her, her feet didn't rise, they shuffled along to the corner where she sat. She told stories to me, children's stories about bogey men that were frightening. Granny used a lot of Gaelic terms and phrases, particularly when she was chastising you. She was a lovely old woman and then she took a stroke around January in 1971, and she died in July. She was ninety-three on 15 March, which is the same birthday as my sister Kathleen. I can still vividly remember her sitting in the corner of our home.

Ours was the only house in Kincasslagh where an island woman lived, so the islanders would stay with us whenever they came to the mainland, and men from Tory Island would sometimes stay too. They would roast fish over the fire – mackerel and herring – and there would be great sing-songs. Eamon and Anton were two of the characters I recall. I'd peep out of my room to see them sleeping in chairs by the fire.

In addition to holidaying on Owey, we also used to go to Derry. I remember going off with my wee case and probably nothing in it. We stayed with Leslie Harkin in Westland Avenue off the Lecky Road. That's the first place I would have seen swings, see-saws and a roundabout. And I remember too a man in a van selling lemonade and that was new to me. I loved going up to Derry. Those were the places I went to as a wee boy, Owey and Derry.

In 1972, after my Granny died, my sister Margaret, who was then a very successful singer in Ireland and known by her stage name, Margo, sent my mother and myself on a holiday to relatives in the States. That was a fantastic experience for a young boy of eleven. So, I suppose I had more holidays than most in my childhood. What other child at that age, that long ago, would have got there? Not many, I'd wager. I remember going to the States on the plane, landing at John F Kennedy airport and people meeting us that I didn't really know. We stayed with my mother's Aunt Mary in Bayonne in New Jersey. Her house was in a retirement complex and it was full of people and relations. We were in the States for three weeks. We also spent time with Margaret and Bill O'Donnell in New Jersey. They had a lovely house and two children, John and Bridget Mary, who were around my age. Margaret was so good to me, she bought me clothes. It was over the Easter period and we had a great time. They had Easter bunnies and we had never had them back in Donegal. We had to go around the house trying to find the bunny filled with chocolate. I went to school with my cousins for a day and I recall enjoying being the centre of attention as 'the Irish guy'. We went there on one of those yellow buses you see in the films.

The Americans would ask, 'Gee, would you speak for us?' Of course, I duly obliged and they loved the Irish accent. 'Isn't he cute!' they'd say.

I loved it all. Why wouldn't I? Little girls going, 'Gee, you're cute!' It was another world to me. The houses were so nice. There was a bathroom with two sinks in it. One for John and one for Bridget Mary. Margaret and Bill had a bathroom off their bedroom. We visited people all the time and my mother refused nothing, everything she was given, she took. We came home and you couldn't see us for the trolley. I was quite Americanised when I came back. I would say things like, 'Yeah, no kiddin'!' It was a wonderful experience, that trip to the States.

We used to go on bus trips to places like Knock Shrine in County Mayo where the Blessed Virgin is said to have appeared. I'd sing the whole way there, and it's a long journey from Donegal to Mayo. It took a long time in those days as the roads were bad. You'd be away at seven or eight in the morning and travelling all day. We'd stop along the route in Sligo and you'd see the old ones going off to the shops. You'd know they wouldn't be used to carrying their handbags because they'd have them stuck out in front of them! It was more an outing than a pilgrimage. There were some among the group who were very religious and the rosary would be recited along the way. But I know that all that many of them wanted was the stop off in Bundoran where there were slot machines. We used to have a great time.

Another pilgrimage I used to do was to St Patrick's Purgatory in Lough Derg, near Pettigo, County Donegal. It's an island where people go to do penance or to atone for their sins. Saint Patrick is said to have gone there on a pilgrimage to pray for sinners. I started going in 1979. Like most people, I was always asking for something or saying thanks for something. You had to spend three days on the island, fasting and praying, and there was a one-day vigil without sleep. You had to go barefoot for your entire stay on the island. So you did the stations of the cross walking on sharp rocks and cold, stone floors. For me, the significance of it was that it was a great leveller. Whatever you had in the outside world, you didn't have it on that island.

As I have said, I worked in the Cope every summer till I was fourteen years old and I got a weekly wage which I saved up for my holidays at the end of August. Then I'd head off on the boat alone to Scotland, where I stayed with relatives in Glasgow, Edinburgh, Perth and Callendar. Wasn't I a brave young lad? I would stay for a period with Mary Brown and Bridie Sharkey, two cousins of my mother from Bath Street in Glasgow. And then I'd take the train to Edinburgh and stay with Auntie Mary in Morrison Street. She's my father's sister and my godmother. She's a great character and a wonderful storyteller. Mind you, you'd need to have the time because she'd start at the very beginning and no detail would be omitted along the way. All her stories are a bit of a marathon. Mary's own personal story is truly amazing. When she was seventeen years of age, she told her family she was off to the shop to buy some sugar. Little did they know that she had bigger plans in mind and nobody noticed the hat she had concealed underneath her coat. Mary and her boyfriend John, who was twelve years older than her, had decided to marry in secret.

When she returned home, Mary said to my father, 'Do you know what I'm after doing?'

He asked, 'What did you do now?'

She said, 'I got married.'

Naturally my father was shocked and it was left to him to go and announce it to the clan. Their mother sent for Mary then and John was fetched up to the house too and they were both given the blessing of the family. That was the start of their marriage. There was no diddling about back then.

I loved my holidays with John and Mary. There were always lots of goodies to be had and I remember what I called the 'iced tops'. I just loved them. They were buns with icing on top of them, and Auntie Mary used to get iced tops for me every morning. I enjoyed going down Prince's Street and marvelling at the clock with the cuckoo in it. People always gathered to look at it and for ages I always thought that the cuckoo was a real live one! The innocence of a child.

I would then go and stay in Callendar with Peggy O'Donnell, who is no relation, but a very good friend. And next I would go to Perth and I would stay between my Uncle James and his wife Nellie and Angela White. There was a park with a lake there called The Inch and it had boats which you could paddle with your hands. I found great freedom there as a thirteen or fourteen year old.

4. MY TEENS AND SUMMER IN DUBLIN

My interest in music and fashion really started to develop when I became a teenager. It's a time when you begin taking notice of your appearance and you cast an eye at the opposite sex. Like the other boys, I wore the clothes that were popular at the time, trousers with wide bellbottoms and big platform shoes. My shirts had collars with wings so wide our elders must have thought we were from another planet! I recall wearing one of those necklaces which had your name on it. They were awful, but you had to have one because they were all the rage. Buying the latest clothes and accessories was part of the fun of those teenage years.

There were dances at the village hall and I was allowed out to them, but all the old ones would be at them too. There was a sort of youth club in the area, but I can't remember much activity at it. One of the songs I recall from that period was 'Hello Darlin' '. It was a hit for Roly Daniels, who was then a big singing star on the Irish scene. One of the boys, Charlie Sharkey, used to get the *Evening Press* and Roly's picture was always in the entertainment pages. I have since recorded 'Hello Darlin' ' on the *Love Songs* album, so it has that connection with my adolescence.

I had girlfriends, but we were fierce innocent, not like the ones nowadays. They're jawin' [kissing] as soon as they get on the dance floor today. We were a lot more pure. When I was in secondary school I was friendly with a girl called Colette in a boyfriend/girlfriend kind of way. But, as I have said, it was all innocent in those days. Mind you, I nearly got my nose broken one time over another girl and all I was doing was dancing with her. An ex-boyfriend of hers gave me a clip for it anyway. I wonder if he still remembers it?

The *céilí* [traditional dancing] was another very popular form of entertainment in our area when I was growing up.

There was a certain magic about it, although I suppose some would consider it a very old-fashioned thing for young people to be doing. I enjoyed it. It was better than an ordinary dance, because you could go and dance with anyone in a 'set' without asking first. The people who invented that dance had their heads screwed on the right way. It was a great opportunity to slip in beside someone you fancied. You would also have tea at the *céilí*, which gave people in the community the chance to sit and chat. It really was a very sociable event and to this day I attend the *céilí* whenever it's on in our area.

As far as a career was concerned, I was good at maths in secondary school – this was The Tech in Loughanure near Dungloe – and consequently I thought about the bank as a career. I was interested in teaching, but singing was a possibility. It was no great effort, and I always really enjoyed it. I didn't do as well in my Leaving Certificate as I should have done because I really froze when it came to exams. I didn't even get my honour in accountancy, when I should have got one with no bother. I had some great teachers at secondary school. There was Miss Dolan for English, and the French teacher, Evelyn O'Donoghue, was super. The accountancy and economics teacher, Breege Boland, was absolutely excellent. They stand out in my mind, as I had them over a long period. I never disliked school. It was never a case of not wanting to go and I didn't find learning difficult. I wouldn't have been a genius, but I had the ability to learn. I suppose I was average as people go, intelligence-wise. School took nothing out of me really.

P.J. Sweeney and Patrick Kyles were among my friends when I started second-level education. They were great at the practical subjects like woodwork, but, as you can imagine, I was a complete disaster. The woodwork teacher was known as Cundy. I recall how one time I thought I had turned out a fine dove-tail joint. I gave it to Cundy for inspection. He said, 'Mmm, mmm', and handed it back to me.

I asked, 'What'll I do with it now, Sir?'

He leant over to me real close and replied, 'Throw it in the fire.'

I was always slipping into the domestic science class where I'd join my friend Anne Sharkey and the rest of the girls. Their teacher, Miss Keady, used to turn a blind eye to me being there. I didn't actually participate in the class, I just helped to scoff all the goodies after they were cooked! Anne and myself were great friends, and to this day I'd go to the ends of the earth with her. I used to spend more time with Anne than I did with the fellas and, consequently, I got a lot of slagging from the boys. I would get picked on because I wasn't into the rough-and-tumble of boys' stuff. I wasn't the type to use swear-words, or *focal mór* as we called them. I was considered 'soft' and you know what guys can be like if you show any weakness like that. I disliked them for taunting me. If you weren't involved in causing trouble you'd be called a 'sissy' and that kind of name calling was something I had to endure. But Anne and I were so close that I think everyone thought we would eventually marry. She was a class ahead of me, but whenever I had a free period I would slip into her classroom and have the *craic* with her and her friends. They enjoyed my banter and I was considered a great laugh.

The teachers in my school were wonderful. I have nothing but good memories of them. I still blush when I think about poor Miss Breslin and how she caught me one day mimicking her. This was a woman who thought the world of me. P.J., Patrick and myself were the only boys in her book-keeping class and I feel we were the pets in her class. We were good at her subject, so that helped, too. She'd always be holding us up as an example to the girls. 'It's a wonder you wouldn't be like these great boys here,' she'd say. I'm sure the ladies in the class were none too pleased with us. One day she went out of the room and left her headscarf behind her, so I went up, took her place at the teacher's desk and put on her scarf. Then I proceeded to mimic her. 'Draw a red line, skip a blue line . . .' Well, if she didn't come in and catch me. I was mortified. But she ignored me and what I had done. It was as if I wasn't there. That was her punishment.

After secondary school I went on to Galway Regional College, but I couldn't relate to it at all because there was no relationship with the teachers or the lecturers. You had to take responsibility for your own education and I wasn't used to that. I don't know if city children do better in that situation, or do all country people feel the way I did? I thought the lecturers didn't give a hoot about me, and that they had no regard for me at all. I was very unhappy at the college and I longed for home. I used to hitch home every weekend or take the bus. I remember when I cycled into Galway one time, I had to get off the bike and walk the whole way because I couldn't negotiate the busy road at all. It was the first time I'd cycled in traffic, and you'd think to look at me that I was on a highway in the States. That was the last outing that bike got from me.

The summer before I started college, I had a great time when I went down to Dublin to work. There's a song called 'Summer In Dublin' by an Irish band, Bagatelle, and it always reminds me of Dublin back in 1980. We used to go to dances every night and the Irish Club on Sunday afternoons. It was a marvellous time. I was eighteen-and-a-half and I really was as happy as Larry. So the fact of being away from home was not really the problem in Galway. Even though I was staying with my brother James in Dublin, I was still away from home. I stayed with Pat and Sean Nugent in Galway, and they and Mary Teresa, Sean's sister, were really good to me.

But anyway, that summer I went to Dublin and James, who was working as a chef in the Central Hotel, got me a job in the kitchen washing dishes. The first evening a tour group must have come in as I remember fifty soup plates arrived at the same time. And then there were fifty bloody dinner plates on top of them!

I remember Margaret Coyle coming in – she was the head supervisor – and she said, 'Come out of there, you're far too slow!'

I thought, this is no joke. And at the end of it all we turned out to be the best of friends, Margaret and myself. Although I don't see her much nowadays, when I do it's like I've only seen her yesterday. When Margaret got married I was at her wedding in Birmingham and I actually gave a speech at the wedding reception. There were three of us that hit it off that summer, the other person being Maura Cullinane, who was a waitress in the hotel. It was Maura who taught me how to drive a car, a blue Fiesta. Maura was a mighty driver, but one day she let me in behind the wheel on a journey from Dublin to Glendalough in County Wicklow. And sure I wasn't fit to drive! But Maura had great faith in me. God forgive me, but I had no driver's licence. It was between God and her, and off we went. I remember taking off and landing back, thankfully without coming to any kind of harm. The chances we took back then, you wouldn't do it nowadays. I didn't actually take a test until I was in my thirties. I took one in Dublin very early on, probably in 1987, but I failed it. I was under the impression that the three-point turn had to be done in three goes. I didn't get off on a good footing with the driving instructor. We had an argument before we went out, over my provisional licence, which was from Donegal, even though I was living in Dublin. That caused some confusion, and when he raised his voice to me that was the end of him as far as I was concerned. I had no time for him. So away we went, the two of us, with him rustling papers. When it came to the three-point turn I turned three times and I was no closer to facing in the opposite direction! So I thought, 'That's that!' and I proceeded to drive up on to the kerb. I said, 'Oops!' on my way down and just drove on. When the test was over, he got out of the car and said, 'I needn't tell you that you have failed.' 'Failed!' says I, as if I had been expecting to pass.

I took a test in England once and that was a disaster as well. I didn't fail it as badly as the one in Ireland, but I failed all the same. Eventually I did one in Ireland, in 1993, and passed it fine.

So there I was, driving around that summer in Dublin without a driving licence. That experience driving to Wicklow was all part of the fun we had during those carefree summer days.

I remember, too, going horse-riding that summer in Phoenix Park. I could ride horses then, but I'm allergic to them now. Myself, Maura and Margaret went off riding and afterwards, you'd think Margaret was scalded from the way she was walking after being on the animal all afternoon. Maura loved horses. She rode with no difficulty at all. But sure I was useless at it, as I hadn't seen a horse at all growing up at home, never mind ridden one. Honest to God, I could hardly walk that evening.

There were some great characters in the Central Hotel. There was Mary, one of the ladies who cooked breakfast every morning, who had a funny walk which we all copied behind her back. Margaret, Maura and myself all ended up walking like her after our experience that afternoon. And then there was Teresa Gaynor and I'll never forget the pantomime on the day she lost her coat or somebody stole it. If she only knew how we laughed over her panicking. God, we were terrible. We were all looking for her red coat.

'Ah this is terrible!' she would say. 'Me good coat.' I had to go into the freezer to laugh because I was in convulsions.

'Ah listen, lads, for God's sake, I'll have to go home without a coat,' she would say. I don't know where she is now, poor Teresa, she was lovely. I don't think the coat was ever found.

While working in the Central Hotel that summer, I had to go down to Galway to do an interview for the college. I told Margaret the day before that Maura would take me in her car, if she got the day off. So Margaret said later in front of the rest of the staff that Maura could have the day off for a special family event. Margaret was off that day too, and she said she'd come with us. So the next day we all headed for Galway and I did the interview and got my place in the college. We took a detour on the way back and enjoyed an evening at the famous Rose of Tralee Festival in County Kerry. We ended up at a dance and the Jersey Rose was there. I'll never forget her, a blonde one. She was probably way older than me. Anyway, I thought she was the greatest thing since sliced loaf and sure I couldn't believe my luck when I ended up dancing with her. But that's as far as it went!

After the dance, anyway, we headed back to Dublin. It was 6.30 a.m. when I got to bed and I had to be up an hour later for work. I was sick from tiredness when I arrived at the hotel, and I told Miss Fitzgerald, the manageress, that I was 'terrible sick'. I couldn't tell her the reason for my sorry state because Margaret, Maura and myself weren't supposed to be away together.

Along the route between Galway and Kerry there's a ferry crossing from Killimer to Tarbert. Our James came in the next day and asked, 'Does anybody have the times of the ferry from Killimer to Tarbert?' How he knew about our escapade I don't know to this day. Margaret, Maura and myself just looked at one another because nobody knew that the three of us had been in Tralee and there he was, alluding to it. And that was all that was said. Nobody said yes or no, or I don't know. But we really had a great day. It stands out in my memory and Margaret turned out to be somebody I will always remember. Whenever I play at the Point in Dublin, she's always at the show. She's a lovely person. And poor Maura, God rest her, is no longer with us but she has left us wonderful memories.

That summer in Dublin, I went out every night to see all the big bands of the day. There was Big Tom, Philomena Begley and Susan McCann, Two's Company, The Indians, everybody who ever played. There was the Irish Club on Monday nights, the TV Club on Tuesday nights, the Irish Club again on Wednesdays, the Ierne on Thursday nights, Friday nights might be the Irish Club, Saturday night you'd go to the National or the Olympic, and on Sunday afternoons there was the Irish Club *céilí* where poor Big Joe would be calling the dances. He'd make sure nobody got too close on the dance floor. He'd be tapping you on the shoulder and that was only 1980! He'd have his work cut out for him in the nightclubs nowadays!

Con O'Mahony ran dances in the Irish Club and the *céilís* used to be brilliant. Con used to do the records from three to six in the evening and you would dance around like it was late at night. There was always a crowd at it and not a drink in sight.

I didn't have a girlfriend at the time. You'd make dates with girls and sometimes they wouldn't turn up at all. Sometimes in the clubs you'd get up the courage to go and ask a girl you fancied to dance, and you'd suffer the embarrassment of getting refused. All modesty aside, I have to say I was a good dancer and as a result, I had no shortage of partners on the floor. There were some super dancers and it was like a race track, especially in the Irish Club. The outside track was for the really good dancers, and they would be spinning around, going like the hammers of hell. I met one of my first serious girlfriends in the Irish Club when she asked me to dance. Teresa Ward and Annie Eddie from home and my friend Josephine Burke all used to be part of that scene and we had a ball.

Everyone has one good summer in their early years and that was mine. The summer before that was good too. I was working on a local scheme. Me on a scheme! That was the biggest injustice that ever was. Out digging drains. My brother-in-law John Doogan's father got some kind of grant to do cleaning-up work in the area and he employed a gang of us locals. We were working on different things. We might be painting the school. But sure I could do nothing, I was just hopeless.. I ended up in a graveyard cleaning graves. A local lad called Vincent Molloy was with me and I'll tell you, whatever Vincent did, I did less and he didn't do much! I was getting good money, too, maybe about £40 or £50 a week.

After that summer in Dublin I headed off to college life in Galway where I was doing a course in business studies. I had planned to go on to university and maybe take up teaching. But I just didn't fit in. As I have said, I couldn't get used to having to take responsibility for my own education, and I never settled down. I was lonely there too, even though Pat and Sean Nugent, the people I was lodging with, were very good to me. I found that a lot of the socialising centred around the pubs in Galway and I didn't really like that scene. Now, when I reflect on my time in Galway, I don't remember many people from the college as I never really forged great friendships there.

While I was in Galway, the show *Up With People* came to town and I was very taken by it. I would love to have joined them, but I wasn't outgoing enough at the time. In fact, I was quite shy. I found it to be a very inspiring show and that also influenced my decision to become an entertainer. Before the first Christmas in college, I met my sister Margaret in the local Flannery's Hotel and I told her that I was unhappy and that I wanted to leave college to become a singer. Then I sent her a Christmas card and I put on it, 'I want to sing now', underlining 'now'.

Margaret had already established a very successful singing career. As I have mentioned earlier, she was known the length and breadth of Ireland as Margo, she was a household name.

The first time I recall being conscious of her as a singing star was hearing her big hit, 'Dear God', coming out of a radio somewhere on the road between our house and the turn above Annie McGarvey's home. I remember thinking, 'That is my sister!' Margaret started singing professionally when she was only twelve. I was born in 1961 in December, and Margaret was born in 1951 in February, so Margaret is nearly eleven years older than me and I was only a year old when she first started singing with a group called The Keynotes. But she didn't start performing on a regular basis until she was sixteen. She had been going to school and singing in the band. Then eventually she gave up school to go full time with the band.

My father died when she was seventeen, so he saw a little bit of her success. He wrote down the words of 'The Bonny Irish Boy', which was her first single, but it was to be released the week he died, and he never actually heard her record.

Everybody in Ireland knew who she was. There wasn't much in her time that she didn't do. Back then, she was as well known as Cliff Richard is in the UK. She had the same level of success in Ireland then that I would have now. Anywhere that she did a show, it was packed. I remember that you literally wouldn't be able to move in the dance hall because there were so many people there. You wouldn't be able to see the floorboards and you certainly wouldn't need to worry about what shoes you had on! It was through Margaret that I developed my interest in the music of the showbands. Groups like The Royal Showband, The Miami, Larry Cunningham and The Mighty Avons, Joe Dolan and The

Drifters were our pop stars in the sixties and seventies. Margaret had a huge amount of record sales, number one records and albums, and two TV series. Her first number one was 'I'll Forgive And I'll Try To Forget'.

But while she had tremendous success, Margaret has had a lot of trouble in her own life, too. As she has openly admitted, Margaret is an alcoholic and everybody knows about her struggles in coping with that illness. And it is an illness, a very common illness. It just ruins your life. Anyway, when I decided to leave college, Margaret agreed that I could join her band.

5. ON THE ROAD

The Christmas of 1980 was a momentous one in my life because I made the decision to leave college and become an entertainer. One of the people I went to seeking advice was the Irish country singer Philomena Begley. If I was putting singers in order, I would put Philomena next to Loretta Lynn as my favourite female country singer. I loved her singing back in my youth and I still do. So when I was starting out I went up to her house to get her views. She was baking bread when I arrived and had flour up to her elbows. I eventually plucked up the courage to break the news that I wanted to become a singer just like her. There was a pause and I nervously plucked at my jumper as she pondered the question.

Eventually, the words of wisdom came pouring forth. Philomena's advice to me was, 'Stick to the books, Daniel.' It wasn't what I wanted to hear, but I suppose she was being realistic because it's just so hard to become successful in the music industry.

I think she was saying what I have said about other people coming on the scene for the first time. I wouldn't like to be starting again. But having said that, I would never discourage anybody. My advice would be: if you want to do it, it's a wonderful life, but it's not going to be easy.

I wanted Philomena to encourage me to pursue my dream, but in the end it didn't matter what she said. I knew in my heart and soul it was going to be the life for me. I always felt that I would be happier in life and be more fulfilled if I could survive as a singer and entertainer. And that is part of the reason why people achieve in whatever career they select for themselves. It's about having a true love for what you're doing, believing in yourself and being prepared to work hard at it. But, as I've often said, it's never work when you love what you're doing.

I don't know whether you would call it ambition, but I certainly had a huge determination to succeed. I got very little encouragement when I started out because people thought that my music was from a bygone era and had no relevance or place in the world today. I felt they were wrong and that I was right. And I was right, because I have succeeded in doing what I wanted to do.

Years later, after I became successful, I actually had the honour of crowning Philomena the Queen of Country Music at a ceremony in Barry's Hotel, which has always been a great dancing venue in Dublin. That was a funny night. The Irish company Tyrone Crystal made a crown for me. It had four balls on top like a decanter and before the ceremony didn't one of them break off in my hand! By the time I crowned her, two of the balls were off. We laughed so much about that on stage and it was great fun. We had the audience in stitches when I said to Philomena, 'Come here, the balls are in my hand.'

Bridie Gallagher from Donegal is another female singer that I love. 'The Voice Of The County Down' was her big hit and some of my other favourite songs of hers include 'Mother's Love Is A Blessing' and 'The Girl From Donegal'. I love her voice and her records. Whenever I perform in Belfast I always have Bridie at the show as a guest. I always think that Bridie is somebody I should salute because she was one of the first singers who really made it from Donegal. She was the one who paved the way for a lot of us. If there is such a status as star, Bridie has all the right qualifications.

Anyway, between the jigs and the reels it was decided that I would leave college and join Margo's band. On 28 January 1981, I stepped out on stage with an electric guitar that wasn't plugged in! I had some neck to do the likes of that! When I think back, I must have been the biggest fool there ever was anywhere. But I was doing what I wanted and that gave me a start, even though I was a bit of a cheat to begin with. People do all kinds of things while they work their way up the ladder in their chosen field. Some serve in bars or restaurants, I pretended I was a guitarist! I spent two years doing that. Ray Doherty, who was a member of Margaret's band, used to give me guitar lessons. But there was never a chance that I was going to master it. I had the feeling that if I learnt to play the guitar, I'd always be playing it. I didn't want to be a guitarist, I wanted to be singing. I always had it in my head that I wasn't going to be in a backing band. I felt I could do it and nothing less was going to be good enough for me and that was what I was striving for. I learned a lot about the business in Margo's band. I saw what was involved and it was the type of experience you couldn't learn from a book. Eventually, I was ready to go out on my own and, although it was a major step, I had gained the confidence and the ability to do it. I could have stayed where I was because it was a comfortable set-up, working in a very successful band with a singer who was well-known in Ireland, but I felt I had to go forward. I was allowed to sing out front sometimes in Margaret's band and when we played a club called St. Francis in Birmingham and I sang 'Donegal Shore', there was huge applause at the end of it. I mean *huge*, so much so that I sang the chorus a second time and I knew that night that I wanted that applause. It was like a drug and I was hooked. I suppose there are worse ways to get your thrills. There comes a time when you take a gamble at whatever you're doing, and gamble I did. I told Margaret I was planning to leave her band and become a singer in my own right.

I decided to make my own record in 1983 and I had nothing at the time. I had saved enough money to make a record and that was it. On 9 February 1983, I went into the studios owned by the Irish country singer Big Tom in Castleblaney, County Monaghan, and I recorded four tracks: 'My Donegal Shore', 'Stand Beside Me', 'London Leaves' and 'Married By The Bible'. It was a big undertaking and I felt very apprehensive because the recording end of things was a whole new experience for me. I was entering an unfamiliar environment and I didn't know if the studio people would think I was good enough. So I went in with a mixture of emotions.

But the producer, an English musician called Basil Hendrix, gave my flagging confidence a real boost. His eyes lit up and he turned to the other people in the studio and said in a surprised tone, 'This boy can sing!' I'll never forget those words. They were what I really wanted to hear at that time. I remember when I was recording my album *The Two Sides Of Daniel O'Donnell* I went into the recording booth with a packet of sweets and I didn't come out for the day. I only appeared when I was told to, because I felt so inferior.

My brother-in-law John Doogan and my sister Kathleen drove me up to Castleblaney to do the recording. In the evening, my friend Josephine Burke arrived to bring me back to Dublin. Josephine is a lady who is very special in my life. I first met her in 1973, when I was eleven years old. She was a fan of my sister, Margaret. As the years passed we became close friends and, like my manager Sean Reilly, I trust her and depend on her to a great extent. I would be lost without those two wonderful people. I just can't imagine how my life would have been without them. Josephine is my confidante and my psychologist. I always get an honest opinion from her. She's not a Yes person. I will get her view whether I want to hear it or not. She would make me stop and think and, by times, I would do the same for her. It's not a one-way friendship. I've heard it said that if you have a friend you have a fortune, so I'm a rich man in that respect. No matter what my trouble might be, I can go to Josephine with it. Anyway, on the journey back to Dublin, we started having trouble with the car. We could only travel at thirty miles an hour. It finally stopped at Chaplelizod in Dublin. I was so tired, sitting there with my wee tape, which was all I had to show for my efforts. Josephine went to phone the guards [police] because we were stranded. I was lying down when she came back.

Josephine shouted, 'Get up or they'll think you are on drugs. Get up and get out of that car!'

The guards came and gave us a lift to Josephine's house. That night John Burke, Josephine's husband, lent us his car to get me to a dance where I was playing with Margaret, but his car broke down as well. We ended up hitching a lift into the city.

When it came to releasing the single, I went for 'My Donegal Shore' and 'Stand Beside Me'. It was certainly humble beginnings because I sold every one of those records myself. The recording cost £600 and it was a further £600 to release the single, so I decided to charge £1.50 a copy. I travelled on the bus one time with the people making the pilgrimage to Knock Shrine in County Mayo, and I sang all the way there and back, and then sold my records to the other pilgrims. The thousand records I sold covered my costs. Then I proceeded to look for people to play with me. Scotland was the first place I started performing in my own right. I went over to Glasgow for a weekend in May 1983, staying with my friends, Kathleen and Eugene Sweeney, and it was arranged that I would sing in the Claddagh Club, the Irish Centre and the Squirrel Bar. I got up and sang with the resident bands and Kathleen sold my records. Out of those nights I got more work. The Irish Club asked me to come back and sing with their band. They advertised the show, and so when I went back in July of that year, there was a great crowd in the venue.

In July 1983 I formed my first group, Country Fever, which featured Patrick Gallagher, Peter Healy, Dim Breslin and Joe Rogers. We started off very low-key, playing a few dates around home that summer. I remember the first night we played, I had the entire set of songs finished by one o'clock in the morning and we were booked to play till two o'clock. So I started again with the first song and sang the whole lot a second time! Patrick Gallagher and Dim Breslin left the group after a short period and they were replaced by brothers Joe and Peter Rogers and my old school friend P. J. Sweeney. P.J. and I are still close pals. We once went on holidays together to the Greek isle of Crete. I was his best man when he married and I'm godfather to his daughter, Sharon. Our early outings in Country Fever were in Dungloe, Burtonport, Gortahork and on the island of Arranmore. Arranmore was the most important booking because we always got a great reception there. We played in Early's pub, owned by Andrew and Mary Early. It's called the Pier Bar, but it's known as Early's. There are about 500 people living on the island and in the early days there were no laws. You started at one o'clock in the morning and finished at half past four. Now you start at eleven and finish at half past two and it's still unreasonable hours! But it's always terrific.

To this day I go back to Arranmore to perform every year and, please God, I always will. We've never had a bad night there. Our first outing was on 14 August 1983, and in the early years we went back three or four times a year annually.

Arranmore at that time was a difficult place to get to. You'd go down to the pier, take everything out of the van, and put it on the half decker [a small boat] and then you'd be frightened out of your wits on the crossing. You'd land at the pier on the other side, lift everything out and load it on to a tractor to take it to the hall. Afterwards, you'd take the equipment out of the hall, put it on the tractor, take it down to the pier, on to the boat, out of the boat, on to the pier on the mainland, and into the van. And sometimes there would be a car with you on the half decker, on two planks! Honest to the good Lord, a car sitting on the half decker! When I think of it now, I might have gone down and never have been seen again! Wouldn't that have been a terrible loss to the world? No Daniel. How would the human race have survived at all!

Andrew's son and daughter, Gerry and Pat, now run the pub. The new ferry has made it so much easier. Now we drive on to the boat and the lorry goes on. God save us and bless us when I think of the small amount of equipment we had in the early days, you could have taken it out of the boot of a car. Now we have a lorry not a van, sound checks, and all kinds of stage equipment and technology.

In June 1984, after Country Fever, I formed a band called The Grassroots. It featured Gerard Gallagher, Larry Gallagher, Gerry Flynn, Roy Campbell, Jimmy Hussey and Tommy Shanley. I also got myself a manager called Nan Moy, who had managed Margo. Nan is from home, although she was living in Scotland at that time. She wasn't doing anything after finishing with Margo and that's when she decided she would get involved with me.

We had so many bad nights to begin with where we wouldn't get paid. You wouldn't get any money because nobody turned up for the dances. You'd be taking the door, as they termed it, and that meant what people paid to get in was your fee. But there were times when you'd be better taking the door that was hanging than what you got, because it would be worth more.

I played anywhere and everywhere. Poor Nan would be travelling somewhere and she'd see a venue and wonder if they would do 'a door job', and sure anybody would do a door job, but it didn't mean you'd get a crowd. The biggest crowd was on the night we played at a Christmas party down in the Glue Pot in Ballingarry, County Tipperary. The only reason people came was because it was advertised that they'd get something to eat! But it was a great night. My friend Josephine Burke was with me another night and she was taking the entrance fee at the door in a venue called the Sportsman's Arms at Ballyhay outside Charleville, County Cork. The exit was a long way from the stage, but I could see Josephine because there were so few in the place. We spent what we made on chicken and chips in a takeaway on the way back and that wasn't much. There were a lot of nights like that.

In the time we were together, The Grassroots didn't achieve anything on the Irish scene, but things were happening for us in England. We'd play ballrooms like the Gresham and the National in London, and they would be packed. We were playing a lot in England then but still we weren't making much money and it was a hard struggle. I used to drive the van myself (and me with no licence!) and I recall travelling around England during the early hours of the morning, driving from London to Birmingham or Manchester or even to Glasgow.

Although we did a lot of travelling in those days, and I frequently drove through the night, I never had a crash in a van, thank God. I've only ever been in one bad crash, but, again, I was lucky to escape without serious injury, although my then girlfriend was badly hurt. I was going back to Dublin from home. We weren't going fast because there were people with me and I was pointing out to them where Philomena

Begley lives. I could see a little Renault van coming towards us overtaking a lorry and I could see he wasn't going to get past us unless I took some action, so I moved on to the hard shoulder. But he did exactly the same thing as me and we crashed, head on. Ach, it was a bad crash, terrible!

I had been talking about the car I was driving, an Omega which I had on trial from a car sales firm. Everyone had been saying to me, 'You really need a stronger car', so I was trying this one out for the weekend. I had just commented that it needed to be cleaned as I was taking it back. And when I crashed, I remember I was holding on to the steering wheel. Joan, a friend I stay with in England, was in the passenger seat. And I looked over at Joan and I said, 'Now!' As if to say, isn't it a good job I didn't bother cleaning the car.

Then the madness started. The alarm was going off in my car and the other car was on fire. Joan's little daughter was with us and she was screaming. My girlfriend was hurt and I thought she was dead. We got out of the car and I felt I had to lift her out, even though you shouldn't do the likes of that. The lorry had stopped at the scene and it towed my car away from the car that was on fire. The police came then. The ambulance arrived and took my girlfriend and the other driver away. When I went up to the hospital to see my girlfriend, I had this idea in my head that they were going to take me into a wee room, like you see on television, and tell me she was dead. Fortunately, she had no life-threatening injuries but her face was badly cut and she had stitches. She was eventually moved to an Ulster hospital in Dundonald, as I suppose the standard of surgery was better there, because they had more experience of all kinds of injuries, due to the Troubles.

The day of the accident, I was in the police station. The guy who crashed into us came up to me. He was very upset and asked, 'What happened?'

I said, 'There just wasn't enough room for you and me on *my* side of the road!'

Of course, news of the accident was all over the radio at the time. It really was dreadful. Luckily my girlfriend made a full recovery.

At one point our van was repossessed because we couldn't afford to keep up with the repayments. I was in Donegal when Nan rang and told me. I said, 'We'll just have to hire one.'

She said, 'The gear is gone too.' It had been in the van at the time.

Then it wasn't funny at all. We had shows to do in the UK, so band member Ronnie Kennedy and myself went over with just an accordion and we told the venue owners that the back axle had fallen out of the van! We played the Irish Centre in Manchester and there was a resident band there, so they backed me. In Newcastle the only song the backing band knew was 'It's A Long Way To Tipperary'. However, we got by on a wing and a prayer.

We got back on the road again with hired vans that were rigged up not to go very fast. It was probably to save petrol or something. Or the van, I don't know. Jesus, Mary and Joseph, it used to take us an hour longer than it should to go everywhere because you could only press down the accelerator so far!

There was another night we were going to Glasgow and we stopped at a service station. When I got out I heard a kind of a bang and I thought, goodness it will blow up here. But anyway, I looked around and couldn't see any holes. So I put in the petrol or gas. Well, we weren't far down the motorway before the red light came on. There was no water in the radiator. We hadn't any water with us and we had no vessel to carry water from a stream. The band were all looking at me. As if I could fix a radiator! I could hardly locate it, never mind mend it. But I was the one in control of this operation. I thought, God save us, what are we going to do? The only person I could think of who might do any work for me was St Anthony up above. At the time people used to put money in the St Anthony collection box and it was used for good causes. You'd be looking for a favour from him in return.

I said, 'Listen, you'd better get to work here and do something if you want my little retainer to continue.'

We stopped the van and it cooled down, then we drove on very slowly until we came to roadworks. I saw this workman's hut in the distance and I said, 'Drive up to that.' Two of us got out, and we went to the door and there was a big padlock on it and it was hanging open. We went into that hut, and I'm telling you, there was a five-gallon drum of water. The only thing that was sitting in that hut was that drum of water! It was just amazing. We took the whole drum although we only needed to fill the radiator once, so I suppose there was a bit of the doubting Thomas in us. We should have known that once would be enough. That was an incredible incident to me. Even though it wasn't a life or death miracle, it was a miracle all the same. The water might have been there for six months, but it was what we needed at that moment.

I remember a funny incident one night at the Irish Club in Glasgow. We went out for something to eat. There was another band on before us. We were the star attraction, but the other band was terrific. I was wearing a duffel coat and when we came back the guy on the door said, 'The band is on and it's a full house, no room. If you haven't got a ticket you're not getting in.' I can still see him, adamant he was. He obviously didn't know who we were. People wouldn't know me to see me at that time. It took a lot of persuasion before we finally convinced him that I was also one of the entertainers that night.

One of the band members, Roy Campbell, had a dog and he loved that dog. He'd make arrangements with friends to come and let the dog out when he was away working weekends with me. But there were times when the poor dog obviously wasn't let out because you'd arrive back from shows in far-off places like Scotland on a Monday morning and you'd hear the dog crying. Roy would open the door and the dog would run and stand at a tree – and how he kept his leg in the air for so long I don't know, but he'd be there for an age. I can still see that dog!

One night we slept in a Travelodge near Carlisle with the whole band in one room. We had a family room because we were cost-cutting at the time. I went in to the reception and I asked, 'Do you mind if we have no mammy or daddy in the family room?' It was £24 and that was great value for six of us: £4 each. We couldn't afford to stay in a room each or even share one between two of us. And even if we could, the cheaper way was better. We went in and we devoured the tea and snacks in one sweep. We went in again later to see if we could get more free food. So we had great times, terrific fun, but we were going nowhere fast. Arranmore was the best place. We'd go to Arranmore and we'd get maybe £300 and that was a fortune to us back then.

Eventually the time came when I had to make a very difficult decision. I would have to leave Nan Moy and try to move up to the next level. It wasn't a decision I enjoyed taking, but we were never going to get anywhere together. We hadn't two halfpennies to rub together between us and the reality of the music business is that somebody needs to have money.

I was turned down by numerous managers in those early days. I went to a number of people and none of them could see anything in me. One of them said I'd only last six months. They didn't believe in what I was doing. I always believed in it and I'm glad they didn't, because they would never have done for me what Sean [Reilly] and Mick [Clerkin] have done. They weren't capable of it.

I played at the 1985 Irish Festival in London and my performance caught the attention of Mick Clerkin. He contacted me and said he was interested in recording an album for his label Ritz. After more than two years of struggling, it was a real ray of hope. *The Two Sides Of Daniel O'Donnell* was released in the autumn of that year, but it didn't have instant success. I felt that to progress I needed Mick to take over the management of my career as well, so I rang him that December looking for an appointment to make my case. Mick decided that the Ritz organisation would take me on and it was a huge relief as the thought of giving up my dream had crossed my mind.

As the celebrations were in full swing on New Year's Eve and 1986 got set to make its arrival in the usual razzamatazz that surrounds that night, I was engrossed in my thoughts. I was twenty-four years old and it was time for tough decisions. Life was moving on; many of my friends were in secure jobs, getting married, starting families and getting on with their lives. It seemed to me that I wasn't really going anywhere. Mick had agreed to take care of the management side of things but I had no car, no money and I was in debt. My album hadn't taken off, and I didn't know at that stage that my recording of *My Donegal Shore* was getting airplay and gaining momentum on the local radio stations. I really wanted my singing career to work, otherwise I would have to emigrate to America or Australia, like so many of my fellow countrymen and women. Everything now hung on what Ritz and Mick Clerkin could do for me.

Mick introduced me to Sean Reilly, the manager he thought would suit me. I met Sean in the Gresham Hotel in Dublin. That day certainly changed my life because Sean Reilly is a very special man and I would go to the ends of the earth with him. My first impression of Sean was that he was a man with integrity. Since then, my respect for him has grown and grown. He has tremendous qualities. He's a very family-orientated man. And when he looks at me he sees me; he doesn't see something that's making money. He wants me to survive, as a person first, and then as an artist.

I met my new musicians next. They had been in a professional Irish band called Jukebox, which had split up. We started rehearsing in the Nashville Rooms in Moate, County Westmeath. Our first night was in St Cyprian's Club in Brockley, Kent. It went well, and things progressed from there.

The whole band started to develop and the show became more professional with someone working on the sound and lighting. Bandleader Billy Burgoyne always had a big vision. He realised that good quality sound and lighting were important in order to be taken seriously as a professional outfit, and so the whole production got bigger and bigger. We weren't immediately selling out shows, but it wasn't long before there were queues outside the venues. The crowds at the dances around Ireland were huge. I am so glad I experienced that, although sometimes I can't quite remember it as well as I'd like to.

It was reminiscent of the glory days of the showband era in Ireland when ballrooms around Ireland were bursting at the joints with as many as 2,000 people nearly seven nights a week! Then disco music came along and the nightclubs with bar licences killed off the 'dry' ballrooms, bringing the curtain down on showband mania. People came out to shows who hadn't been out for years. You'd arrive at venues like the Castle in Dungiven, County Derry, and they'd be queuing to get in, maybe at seven or eight o'clock at night, and it got to the stage where if people weren't there early they definitely wouldn't get a seat. Another venue we used to play was the Ragg in Thurles, County Tipperary. The owner John Kennedy would say to me before the show, 'Don't go out, don't go out, the star is never to go out! You never see the star until the beat is hit, would you not be going out until the start!' You see, I was one of those entertainers who liked to walk around the venue before the show and I could do that then. We used to have great nights in the Ragg and in places like Ballyhaunis, County Mayo. Up to 1,000 people every night, it was incredible. We played five nights, sometimes six shows a week.

Something was happening around Ireland at that time which also helped to introduce me to the audience on the home scene. A mass of pirate radio stations began to crop up around the country and they were playing my records. Ireland's main music station, then known as Radio 2, didn't really feature the type of music I was into. Larry Gogan, a legendary DJ with Radio 2 [now known as 2FM], played me, as did Alan Corcoran later on. But in general it was difficult to get records like mine played on Radio 2. The demand was for pop and rock, because that was the flavour of the day and commercial stations have to meet the demands of their listeners. It's not easy for them to please all of the people all of the time but there was also an audience for my style of music, particularly in rural Ireland, as the pirates around the country had revealed. I was one of their popular requests. The disco scene had peaked and the pirate radio stations were supporting people like Big Tom, Philomena Begley, Margo and Daniel. People were particularly interested in me because I was the first of a new generation of singers to emerge. Today, it would probably be more difficult for me to make the same impact.

The pirate radio stations had given tremendous support to my album, *The Two Sides Of Daniel O'Donnell*. They introduced it to the public by constantly playing tracks, including 'The Green Glens Of Antrim', 'The Blue Hills Of Breffni', 'Any Tipperary Town', 'The Latchyco', 'Home Town On The Foyle', 'These Are My Mountains', 'My Donegal Shore', 'Crying My Heart Out Over You', 'My Old Pal', 'Our House Is A Home', 'Your Old Love Letters', '21 Years', 'Highway 40 Blues', and 'I Wouldn't Change You If I Could'.

The Two Sides Of Daniel O'Donnell served me well, after a slow start. It introduced my music to the people of Ireland and around the UK. But it was my second album, *I Need You*, which really set the ball rolling in Britain. Strange things have happened to me all along the way in this business, and there was a bizarre coincidence surrounding the song 'I Need You'. One night a fan called Anne, whom I had known for some time, came up to me at the Georgian in Ballina, County Mayo. Anne mentioned this song from the 1960s and suggested that it would really suit me. I asked her to send it to me and a tape arrived in the post. The moment I played it I knew that I wanted to record the song. And here's the strange coincidence. When I took the song to Mick Clerkin to suggest recording it, he had already got it and was going to ask me to do it!

Along with 'My Donegal Shore', 'I Need You' is one of the most important songs in my career. It helped to introduce me to a wider audience around England, Scotland and Wales, more than it did in Ireland. It was played on all the radio shows and it's one of the songs that will always be a part of my live show. I recorded the album, *I Need You*, towards the end of 1986.

Television also opened up for me around that time and I vividly recall my first TV appearance. I've done a lot since, but the first show was tremendously exciting because I felt I was moving up the ladder and getting recognition at national level. We were on an afternoon show called *Live at Three*. I sang 'I Need You'. The night before we had been performing in a Community Centre in Ballyhaunis, County Mayo. We came back to Dublin and it was incredible to be doing *Live at Three*. I still remember what I wore: grey trousers with a light grey sweater.

In 1987 I did my first major festival in the UK when I appeared at the Peterborough event and that was another major step up for me. It was later in the same year that I did my first major concert tour of the UK and I felt great apprehension going into it. It was a huge step into the unknown for me and I can remember looking at the tour dates and seeing places like the Beck Theatre in Hayes, where I was doing two nights, and not knowing where Hayes was. I didn't know what the Beck was like. I thought two nights anywhere was too many. I was concerned that people wouldn't come, so you can imagine the relief I experienced when I was told that sixteen of the twenty-two were sell-out shows. When I think back on all the concerns I had starting out and look at how much we have done, how many places we have played, and the number of people we have met, I am amazed at the level of success we have achieved.

In 1988, I was so proud to get a place on the bill at the Wembley Country Music Festival, where all the legendary country music stars from America had performed down through the years. I first went to the Wembley Festival in 1979 to see one of my idols, Kitty Wells, perform. Kitty was the first female country singer in the States to sell a million records with her hit, 'It Wasn't God Who Made Honky Tonk Angels'. I finally made it over to Nashville, the home of country music, in 1988 when I represented Ireland at Fan Fair, the showcase for international country music artistes. I sang 'Take Good Care Of Her', 'Don't Let Me Cross Over' and 'Don't Be Angry', backed by Elvis Presley's legendary band, The Jordanaires. The 15,000-strong crowd gave me a very warm and enthusiastic reception. One of the highlights of the trip was an appearance on Nashville's famous Grand Ole

Opry. The following day I took the stage at Summer Lights, Nashville's annual four-day street festival, when I performed outside the Nashville Courthouse, sharing a bill with George Hamilton IV, Lorrie Morgan and Ricky Skaggs.

The American audiences were just like any other. Although every audience is different, every audience is also the same in a way. Different, because I could play four or five nights in the same place and every audience in that theatre would be different because every night is different. That is something I realised very early on in my career. You can't judge one audience against the next; you have to take the audience that you have before you and relate to them as they are. As regards audiences being the same, well, people are the same the world over. I think people want to enjoy themselves. They don't demand too much, but they do want to have a good time, and I think that's the common factor wherever you go as an entertainer. The most important thing as an entertainer is to relate to people; that's certainly number one for me. Obviously the music is the primary reason why I should be there, but what I get out of it is the relationship I have with the audience. Whatever happens on the night, I think it's very important to have that rapport, that one to one, with the people. It may be difficult as the shows get bigger, but it's something I strive for all the time. I think audiences are different in the way they respond. In places they are very expressive and in other places they are more reserved.

When I returned to Nashville six months after the Fan Fair in 1988, I recorded there for the first time and worked with producer Allen Reynolds, who is one of the men behind the success of Garth Brooks, Don Williams and Crystal Gayle. I was very apprehensive about going to Nashville; I didn't really know what to expect. When you go somewhere like Nashville to record, you're taken out of the environment you're used to. But the people out there are very warm. I thought I would be like a fish out of water, but I was never made to feel that way; I always felt that I was right to be there. Initially, I thought they would have had reservations about a guy from Ireland singing country music, particularly as I do it in my own way.

But I wasn't in the place too long before I felt at home and recording *The Last Waltz* album there was a good experience for me. I also enjoyed the freedom that not being known over there gave me. I revelled in the quiet time I had to myself and it gave me the chance to reflect on the whirlwind that had whipped me up and carried me along since I joined the Ritz organisation. When *The Last Waltz* was released it repeated the success of my other albums, going straight to number one in Britain's country chart, as well as entering the pop chart.

My career continued to grow and grow and it became more and more demanding. When we started doing the concert tours in England, it was six nights a week, every week. It really was too much. It would have been all right if I was going on stage, doing an hour-and-a-half, leaving without meeting anybody, but I was doing two-and-a-half hours, maybe more, and meeting everybody who would wait afterwards. I was the type of person who just couldn't say no. I did everything I was asked to and more. I could see that all my hard work was yielding results, from the success of albums like *The Last Waltz*, which was my eighth for Ritz. But eventually, the pressure of all the commitments began to take its toll on my health. I knew within myself that I was heading for a slippery slope. I didn't feel well and it was becoming such a struggle. It was a very worrying time for me and by the end of 1991 I realised that I couldn't go on.

6. THE ROAD TO RECOVERY

On New Year's day in 1992 I went to my manager Sean Reilly and I told him that I needed to take a break.

'How long do you need, Daniel?' he asked.

'Six months,' I replied.

At that time, I would hazard a guess and say we probably had between forty and sixty shows sold out. Another manager might have put pressure on me to keep going and fulfil my commitments because there was money at stake. But as I said earlier, Sean puts my welfare first and business second.

'That's fine, Daniel. Leave it with me,' he said.

Mick Clerkin and Ritz Records greeted the shock news with the same reaction. I was treated with nothing but support and understanding. Their response once again made me appreciate the quality of the people I have around me. It must have cost a lot of money cancelling all those shows, but there was never a word said to me about it.

At the time, I was near to cracking up from doing too much work. It was literally too much. I kept saying 'yes, yes, yes', to everything. Apart from the shows, I was visiting people who were sick or disabled, calling here, there and everywhere. Now this was a pressure I brought upon myself, because I really don't have to do all those things. I wanted to do them, and I thought I could handle it all, but at the end of the day, the human body can only take so much. I had to realise that there are things that I can do and things that I can't. As a result of the number of things I committed myself to undertaking, I was feeling the strain. It got to the point where I had difficulty singing. I felt a terrible pressure in my chest and my throat was hoarse. I literally couldn't speak during the day. At no time did I not enjoy the singing, but I felt I was dragging myself up all the time.

A whole series of factors and events aided my recovery over a period of more than two years, although I was able to return to the stage after a break of three months. One of the people I went to see initially was an Irish herbalist called Sean Boylan and he gave me some degree of relief. I saw a Dublin throat specialist called Tom Wilson for a few months, and he taught me to sing from the diaphragm and not just the larynx, and that was very beneficial. I had never been trained as a singer, so his advice really helped. I started singing again at the end of March, but I still didn't feel one hundred per cent. One day I heard about a healing priest called Father Peter Rookey. The Irish broadcaster Pat Kenny's show was on the radio when I turned it on as I was driving along in my car, and Father Rookey had almost finished his interview. I learnt how Father Rookey was blinded in both eyes by a firecracker as a child in Chicago. After being told that doctors could do nothing for him, he made such a miraculous recovery that he does not have to wear glasses. He's in his early eighties now, and his reputation as a healer extends around the world. I felt I would like to see him, but I didn't pursue it at the time. I was treated at the Blackrock Clinic in Dublin and put on all sorts of inhalers and tablets. In September of 1992, I was on steroids and became a little bloated, so for a period I looked heavier than I normally am, my face moon-shaped and wider.

I played in Brentwood in January 1993 and a nun called Sister Aidan was there. During the show I spoke about the problems I'd experienced with my voice and I told the audience about my time off and how I was delighted to be back. After the show, Sister Aidan wrote to me and also to my mother and in those letters she spoke about Father Rookey and said that I should really try to see him. I don't know what happened, but I either lost the letter or mislaid it. I read my mother's letter, but there were no details of when or where Father Rookey was going to be in attendance. So I decided to track down Sister Aidan, who was based in a convent in Clacton-on-Sea in England. Being from Donegal, I thought, why don't I ring the police, because if you rang the guards at home they would know the convent. They didn't entertain me at all. Then I thought of ringing Patsy Sharkey, who lives in Clacton and used to be a neighbour. As luck would have it,

Patsy knew Sister Aidan well, as they both went to my shows together! Now that, in my book, was another strange coincidence – as I have said, there are many of those in my life. I explained my predicament to Patsy and she put me in touch with Sister Aidan.

I learnt that Father Rookey was saying Mass in Acton Town Hall, so on a Saturday morning I headed over to London with my friend, Josephine Burke. We were there early, so we could have got a front row seat, but I thought it would be better to be a bit further back. We met Sister Aidan and she was extremely religious. I'm sure she's in heaven now, God rest her, because she has since passed on. Father Rookey eventually landed out on the altar. He had a bit of a crying voice. I had heard him on the radio and I knew he was like that, and he said the Mass and it was lovely. Then everybody went up to get blessed and a lot of people were collapsing on to the ground when he touched them. We got talking to a woman in front of us and you could predict that she was going to fall down because she had that kind of personality. There were a number of people there like that, who were going to go down. It was that kind of atmosphere. I saw the ridiculous side of it and I saw the sincerity and I saw everything about it, and I knew why I was there, but I didn't quite feel comfortable.

The time came for me to go up to Father Rookey and I can tell you that I had no intention of falling because of the embarrassment of it. But when Father Rookey touched me on my forehead, down I went. I thought it took me ages to go down, and when I was down I thought I was a long time trying to get up, and I felt a fright inside me. I went back to my seat and I glanced around to see if anybody had seen me falling. I don't know if Josephine was embarrassed or not. I remember there was a young girl, whose name I later learnt was Ruth Flanagan, and she cried all the time. I found out she had cancer of the bone, and she wasn't much more than twenty years old. I remember I had a pair of beads with me and I thought, I must give her these beads. So I gave them to her, and I jotted down my address and I said, 'Let me know how you get on.' And eventually I had a letter from her telling me she got the all clear. I've never heard from her since. I would love to know what she is doing now.

So Mass was over and I sat back and Sister Aidan was talking, and I got up and didn't I see this other friend, a nun called Sister Philomena from Donegal (you'd think all my friends were nuns and priests, but they're not). I had first met her through Nan Moy. She asked me what I was doing there and I said I felt the need to come, that I wanted to see Father Rookey, and I explained about my health. She put her hands in her bag and she said, 'I had to put these prayers in my bag today. Something told me to put them in and I know now that they are for you.' So I took them and she said, 'You know, there's a healer in Dublin called Joe Dalton and he's a wonderful man.' And she gave me his number.

I went home and I called Joe Dalton and I really felt I had to see him. I said, 'Joe, I am doing a show on Wednesday. I really need to see you before that.' I must have felt very desperate in myself. And Joe was very busy but he relented and said, 'Come on Tuesday.' So I went out to his house near Stillorgan on the south side of Dublin. We sat in the sitting room and Joe proceeded to tell me his story about problems he had in the past. I don't know if I was really listening all that closely, I was to a point, but I was very preoccupied with myself. I wanted Joe to tell me that I was going to be fine. And then Joe said: 'I spent my time questioning and saying why am I like this, why have I got this turmoil, why can I not do what I want to do. And then one night I sat down and said, "Right God, if you want me to do something I'll do it. If I'm not meant to work at what I am doing then I'll happily stop it, but I need to know."' And I could hear what I needed in that statement.

I thought, 'If I have to not sing, I need a reason for not doing it. I'm giving it over to God to be sorted out, because I can't handle this.' I left Joe's and I didn't feel anything, nothing happened. I didn't see any lights, didn't hear any voices. I did shows on the Wednesday and Thursday and I went to Belfast to do the Gerry Anderson TV show on the Friday night. I was staying in the Europa Hotel in Belfast on the Friday morning and I got up and remember walking a few steps from the bed. Now I can't tell you if I said this, or if I thought it, but I remember the words, 'I feel better today'. I didn't feel physically better, but it seemed that whatever was affecting me wasn't as important or it wasn't holding me as much and I felt better. I felt that something had released me.

A friend, Dolores Corcoran, also told me about a homeopath called Kevin Barrett from Castlebar in County Mayo. I had been told about other people and other things, but for some reason I felt I really needed to get in touch with him. We met and talked – this was in the autumn of 1993 – and he later sent me some bottles containing medicines. Almost immediately, I stopped using my inhalers. About two years after that, I stopped using the medicine Kevin had put me on, and I steadily got better. I gradually got rid of the feeling of tightness in my chest. I think all those people and events that I have described contributed to my healing. First there was my experience with Father Rookey. Joe Dalton released me from whatever was wrong with me mentally, and Kevin healed me physically. Today, I never go on stage without saying the miracle prayer that Sister Philomena gave me and it's the one Father Rookey uses:

'Lord Jesus I come before you just as I am. I am sorry for my sins. I repent for my sins. Please forgive me. In your name I forgive all others for what they have done against me. I renounce Satan, the evil spirits and all their works. I give my entire self, Lord Jesus, now and forever. I invite you into my life, Jesus. I accept you as my Lord God and Saviour. Heal me, change me, strengthen me in body, soul and spirit. Come Lord Jesus, cover me with your precious blood. Fill me with your holy spirit. I love you Lord Jesus. I praise you Jesus. I thank you Jesus. I shall follow you every day of my life. Jesus you live in me. Jesus I live in you. Jesus we both live together. Mary, my mother, Queen of Peace, all the angels and saints, please help me.' I bless myself and out I go.

I talk more than I pray, but I suppose that is praying. I don't say the formal prayers as we learnt them. I would say to God, 'Now listen, I'm not really ready for this, but I am going to do it, and it would be better if you can come with me.' I do often feel that I am not as good as I should be. At times when I'm feeling insecure, or anything like that, I sit and say, 'I do ask very strongly for Jesus to come into my heart.' I would like to know that I'm doing all I can.

The Gospel show that I do is a religious experience for me. When I first staged it at The Point in Dublin, at the end of 1996, I honestly felt that the stage rose up and if I had kept rising without the stage, I wouldn't have been surprised. It was the most wonderful feeling that I've ever had on stage. As I finished singing the Gospel choir continued and it was glorious, I felt so good. For me, God certainly came into my life that night. If ever he was in it, he was in it that night. I have often experienced a feelgood factor on stage, but nothing like that. I love singing the Gospel songs and I would like to do a series of gospel evenings in churches. I just think it would be wonderful.

During the time that my throat was affecting me, a friend of mine called Angela died, and I really wanted to sing at her funeral because we had been such close friends. There was no music and I prayed that I would be able to do it. Angela lived in Perth in Scotland, but she had also lived near us for a time. She was brought up with a woman we called Moinie. When Moinie was old, Angela came home to look after her and brought her children with her. So our family were the same age as those children. We just loved Angela so much, she was such a great character. Later, she came to my shows and I feel she was proud of what I achieved, although she would always play it down, so there was no chance of me getting a big head.

We'd be backstage and I'd say, 'Are you going out to see the show?'

She'd reply, 'What would I be going out to sit listening to you for?'

But every so often I would see her at the side of the stage. She would bring apple tarts and buns with her, as if my waistline needed them! Angela died in 1993, very suddenly. She had an aneurysm. She had been due to come to a show, and I got a call to say that she had died. Then a very strange thing happened. I very rarely flew home to our local airport at Carrickfinn. It was just a novelty, it wasn't something I had got used to, but I decided two weeks prior to the show that I would fly home this time. Well, by sheer coincidence, Angela's body was on the plane. I was really, really upset about Angela. She was just terrific and she would laugh and laugh. We'd get into the greatest pickles laughing, not so much at people, but at situations. I'd be in a café with her and the two of us would be in stitches. She'd had a stroke a number of years before she finally passed away. She was very ill and she shouldn't have recovered, but she pulled through. I remember a night in Dundee, somebody had got the singer Dominic Kirwan to give her flowers. She said to me, 'That's more than you have ever bloody given me!' So when she next came to my concert, I pulled the heads off two roses I had been given and presented her with the two stems. We have a picture of us laughing, my mouth is open and the tears are running down her face. The funny thing about it was, I took flowers to the funeral and I left them on the grave, but just as the coffin was coming out of the church I remembered that we hadn't got any roses for the family. They were really distraught over Angela's death. Her family were all grown up, but sometimes you are not ready for people to die. I went over to a wreath and I broke off the heads of the flowers, leaving part of the stems behind. I gave a rose each to her husband and her brother and the rest of her family. We were turning away and I looked back and there was this bouquet, a headless thing, and when I went back to check, it was the one I had left. When I was pulling the roses out, I never thought that it was my own one and I thought of the significance of that moment, as I reflected on the night I had given her the headless roses in Dundee. It was another funny moment for Angela and myself. There was this terrible looking bouquet, no flowers, only a lot of green things sticking up. As I said earlier, I prayed so hard that I would be able to sing at her funeral Mass and in fact I was able to. A lot of the time these things are in your head as well.

As I've mentioned, the lure of the stage became too strong for me and I made my return after a few months – on 1 April 1992. Although physically I didn't feel an awful lot better, I felt well enough to sing again. But I was very nervous before my first show, which took place at The Civic Centre in Halifax. I had some real panic attacks before that event, and then on the actual night I felt weak as I waited in the wings to go on. When the time came for me to go out in to the spotlight, my legs refused to carry me to the centre of the stage. I supported myself by leaning on a speaker, but as I burst into song and heard the sound of my voice, my confidence began to soar again and I was back.

My official return to the stage was at The Point in Dublin. It's recognised as the premier concert venue in Ireland and everyone from U2 to Bruce Springsteen and Celine Dion has performed there. It's the one to do, and you know you have made it when you get there. There may be bigger venues, but to have your name up in lights at The Point carries a lot of prestige. Now, I never imagined that I would ever perform there. It's a venue that just didn't seem to be within my reach. But Sean Reilly and an Irish promoter called Kieran Cavanagh had other ideas. They discussed it and they felt it was something that would work, so Sean came to me with the idea. Like everything else, I left the decision up to Sean. If he thinks I can do something, then I'll go along with it. He's never been wrong yet. I may be nervous about it and I may be a 'doubting Thomas' at times, but I'll go with it. So we decided that Daniel O'Donnell was going to perform at The Point on Saturday 11 July 1992.

It does take a lot of people to fill the Point, so the promotion wasn't just confined to Ireland. Sean and Kieran organised package deals from England, Scotland and Wales and people travelled in their droves. I was amazed by the reaction to the show. It was a big undertaking from a production point of view as well, as we had never played that size of theatre before, so extra equipment had to be brought in. I was coming back with a bang! I was nervous though, and, like a husband-to-be on the morning of his big day, I was up with the larks. I couldn't sleep and I remember thinking that I should have gone out to a dance the previous night, as Irish country singer Mick Flavin was playing in Barry's Hotel, which is one of my favourite haunts in Dublin. If I'd been out late, I would have been able to sleep on. The Point turned out to be my biggest show so far at that stage of my career, with over 6,000 people turning out to see me perform. It was also the first time that an entertainer, singing Country and Irish songs, had performed at The Point. Since then, I have played concerts to more than double that number of people, but back then it was a huge undertaking for me. I was on cloud nine, as it was a turning point in my career. I was so proud to be bringing my style of music and entertainment to The Point, which had been primarily a rock venue until then.

There were many people there that night who had never seen me perform before – some of them were probably there under duress! But for whatever reason they came, and I hope they were impressed by what I had to offer. I think people who see me for the first time are surprised by the amount of energy in my show. I don't stand in one spot crooning all the time, as many believe. One woman who came to praise me afterwards said that she'd never seen me before in a way that suggested she was asking herself, 'Why?', and that was a lovely compliment to receive. Many were surprised by the rock 'n' roll aspect of the set, particularly features like the medley of Elvis hits, 'That's Alright Mama', 'Love Me Tender', 'Are You Lonesome Tonight' and 'Don't Be Cruel'. So The Point was a good showcase for me as well as being a tremendous night.

By the end of it I was shattered, really exhausted from the whole experience, the build-up to it, the size of the place, everything. I went out to meet people after the show. The Point had never seen a performer come out to meet the fans afterwards, so that was a new experience for the staff. But it became a bit of a crush and a little chaotic, as people surged forward to meet me, and eventually the bouncers took me away. There were a lot of people backstage that were obviously very pleased that the concert had been such a huge success. They were all on a high, but I remember that I just wanted to get away. I remember at one stage I got presented with some award and when I got it, I remember asking, 'Can I go home now?' I was like a child. I suppose there were people there who thought I should stay and enjoy it, and savour the thrill of the big night, but I wanted to go home. A lot of the time I want to do that, if it is a big occasion. I like to go and be calm on my own. My highs and lows are not far apart. Sometimes I don't like any kind of hysteria around me at certain points, and at a time when people expect it, I don't want it. After shows it's different because I'm going to meet people.

That first Point concert and the first Christmas show in Ireland in 1996, which was a mixture of Gospel songs and Christmas numbers, were quite demanding. In both cases, I was doing a show that I had never done before and it was so different. And the evening of that first Christmas concert, the stage was supposed to rise, go down and swivel around, but it blew up! Sean came in and he was very irritated and I asked him, 'Sean, what's wrong?' Sean and I would never be annoyed together, because one of us always has to be calm. The problem was that the stage hydraulics had just collapsed. So I said, 'Well, at least we still have the stage.' Because of the timing, so close to show time, my feeling was, there is nothing that can be done about this now. Just rise above it. When I'm expected to throw a tantrum, I stay calm, and when it's not expected, I go mad. We're all unpredictable at times, I suppose. Everyone is human at the end of the day. But by and large, I get through life without too much drama. It's easier that way.

7. FESTIVAL TIME

It's a well known fact that the Irish love to party, so annual festivals in villages, towns and cities around the country are a common feature of our culture. A big gala in my area every year is the Mary From Dungloe, which started in 1968. Although it's a week of entertainment, the origin of this event is based on the terribly sad story of a local girl called Mary Gallagher, which dates back to the 1860s. Mary was a very striking, blonde, six-foot tall woman from Dungloe. She fell in love with a young man from the Donegal area of Gweedore who had returned from America after making his fortune. The couple decided to wed and initially they had the blessing of Mary's parents. But malicious gossip later turned them against the young man and they persuaded Mary to end the relationship. Although heart-broken, she carried out their command. She later emigrated to Auckland, New Zealand, where she married Daniel Egan, a man she met on the emigrant boat. They had a son, but Mary died from illness four months later and her little boy also became ill and lost his life at the age of nine months. Mary's tragic story inspired the song, 'Mary From Dungloe', which gave its name to the festival.

It's a week of fun and frolics that runs through to the August Bank Holiday Monday in Ireland. It's one with which I have become very closely associated through my career. I find it strange and exciting when I reflect on that now, because I grew up with the Mary From Dungloe, never thinking that one day it would become associated with me on a very large scale. I remember the first festival, all the floats and the big group of the time, Emmett Spiceland, singing the 'Mary From Dungloe' ballad in an open-top car. They released it as a single and had a huge chart success in Ireland. Their treatment of the song was gorgeous.

The festival started very small and it generated a lot of excitement every year for families who turned out to enjoy the fun fair, the floats and the bands. It was definitely the most exciting part of the year as I grew up. As a teenager, I enjoyed other aspects of it, like the dances and the discos. Later on there were well-known bands playing on an outdoor stage, and I got to perform there in 1985 and then in 1987. When we played again the following year, there was an absolutely huge crowd in Dungloe. We did an open air concert during the afternoon and there thousands of people on the streets. It was an incredible day. Then the organisers came up with the idea of having a dome for the entertainment, so that became a feature of the town during the festivities. For a couple of years, in 1989 and in 1990, I performed one show in the dome. It started to grow from there. In 1991 we did two, and from 1992 onwards, we've been doing three shows every year.

The 'open day' at my home in Kincasslagh then developed by sheer chance and took on a life of its own, becoming a huge occasion. I could never have imagined that it would grow into something so big. When it first came about, I was doing shows on the Monday and Tuesday and it was the first time a lot of visitors travelled to see me play. While in the area, they came up to my house, to see where I lived, where I come from and to meet me. But I wasn't there as I need my privacy on the day of a show to rest my voice. I got up on stage on the first night and I apologised for not being at home, explaining how I found it difficult to speak with people and sing on the same night. I mean, everybody thinks it only takes a couple of seconds, but it all adds up when there are a lot of people. So I said, 'I won't be there tomorrow either, but if you want to come on Wednesday, I'll make a point of being there. And sure we might even have a cup of tea.' A lot of people came and that's how the 'open day' began. It didn't start off as a publicity stunt, but in a way it turned out to be one because it got so much attention from the media. At the last one, there were people from all sorts of television station: NBC from America, Sky News, I couldn't believe it.

All good things come to an end at some stage and we eventually had to bring the curtain down on the open day. It became a victim of its popularity. It got to the point where there were too many people to cope with. Towards the end I felt I was only getting an opportunity to see a fraction of the crowd. I feared the fans were ultimately going to be disappointed with the experience.

Looking back, I find it intriguing that it interested people so much. And to tell you the truth, I rarely did an interview, especially in England, where they didn't refer to the open day and I found that repetitive because it wasn't such a wondrous thing, although it was certainly unusual. It started off with hundreds and then it became *thousands*. People came from everywhere. I suppose it was because they were guaranteed to see me outside my own home, where I was brought up, and usually some of the family were there as well. Apart from that, I think the best thing that happened on the day was that people met people with a common interest. I was the common interest, and the music was too, and then it extended to their own lives. They'd talk about me for a while, then they'd get into conversation among themselves, 'Where are you from? Are you married? Do you have children?' Through what I'm doing, I've noticed, people form friendships. If I was to be remembered in any way, I would love to be thought of as somebody who brought people together. I see it happening and I think music in general does that.

There are people who tell me that I have helped them through difficult times in their lives. That is obviously very satisfying, to think that who you are and what you do can make a significant difference to other people's lives. There are cases where people suffered from a condition called agoraphobia, which is a fear of open spaces and of going out into the world, but they made the effort to come and see my show and the experience helped them to overcome their problem. There are people who have lost loved ones and say I have helped them get through their grief, which is obviously a good feeling. I get a lot of letters from families, in cases where the mother has died, and the writer says, 'You have no idea what you did for my mother.' There have also been situations where the father died and you hear how the mother heard me singing on the radio one day and she enjoyed my music, bought the records or videos, went to a concert and 'We saw mother come back'. That is lovely to hear. That makes me feel good.

There is one Australian woman, Barbara, whose son committed suicide and, naturally, she was devastated. She became aware of me through my tours to Australia and I reminded her of the son she had lost. So I became the focus for her and she bought my records and videos and came to the show and it helped her to deal with the tragic death of her son. She has travelled to Ireland numerous times to see me and I still visit her when I'm in Australia. At the end of the day, I want people to be happy because of what I'm doing. I find it difficult not being able to do everything that people want me to do, even though I know that it's not physically possible. It's very hard for me to be all things to everybody, no matter how much I try.

One of the highlights of the Mary From Dungloe festival is the competition which involves the selection of a lady to represent the historical 'Mary'. It attracts contestants from all around the world. In 1998, I was offered the job of hosting the event and interviewing all the girls in the contest. My reaction was, I would do it if the organisers genuinely thought it would help the festival. My only concern was that the people of Dungloe would think I was trying to take over the entire event. In a small area, the majority of people will be with you, but there will always be an element who are against you. There is a little bit of that in Dungloe and there's no point in me saying anything different. I'm always aware of it and I took it into consideration when this new role came up. There was a question mark hanging over the festival in 1998 because it was in dire straits financially. I said I would be the host if it was beneficial to the festival.

The job was something I had never done before and I became a little apprehensive as the time approached for the big night. I wondered if it was wise of me to be getting involved because I wasn't sure I could do it. One day I was driving somewhere and all of a sudden as I was thinking about it I could see Irish TV personality Gay Byrne sitting in front of me. Gay, who has a holiday home outside the town of Dungloe, always did a great job hosting the Rose Of Tralee, another popular Irish festival. I said to myself, 'What am I doing this for? The fellow that's better at it than anyone will be sitting in the audience looking up at me on the night.' It was a sort of shock. So if someone had said to me before the night, 'We have somebody else to do it. Would you mind stepping down?' I would gladly have done so.

In the end, it turned out to be one of the most satisfying things I've ever done in my career. That evening I went in, and my plan was to sing a song if things started to go badly wrong for me. At least the people who had come because I was there would be happy and that would lift the atmosphere. But there was never any need for me to sing. I was a compère, I was presenting a show that meant interviewing people and that's what I did. I was not a singer that night, even though I sang the 'Mary From Dungloe' at the end, but I didn't feel the need to sing. It was the first time ever this happened in a public situation. At the end of it, I was very grateful to the committee for giving me the opportunity to host the show and interview the contestants, for having the faith in me to do a good job.

Hosting the 'Mary' contest that night made me realise that there are other things I can do and that I will enjoy doing. I do believe now that I would be capable of doing other things in that line. If the right event came up, I would happily consider it.

One of the other great events in my annual calendar is the Kincasslagh Festival, which was launched in 1995. It has turned out to be a huge success and is extremely popular with people from home and abroad. But when the organising committee first came to me and suggested it, launching a week-long series of events in the village, including my show, I thought they were mad. I asked, 'Who is going to come?' Then I said, 'You can try it.' One of the suggestions they came up with was a gala ball where they would have a 'belle' celebrity, who would be my surprise date for the night. Well, I was amazed to see how successful it was in the first year, and to see it grow and grow every year since.

It opens on a Friday evening and is launched by a senior member of the local community, someone like my mother, Annie McGarvey, Doalty Sharkey or Eoinie Sharkey. The people selected are all people in their seventies to eighties who have contributed to our area during their lifetime. It's a lovely way of paying tribute to them, the committee never look for a celebrity to open it. They rely on people that we admire among our own. Eoinie Sharkey, for instance, is regarded as very knowledgeable, and I would describe him as a local historian. Doalty Sharkey is somebody who everybody knows and he's a great character. He's a cousin of my mother's who works as a courier for the tours that come to our area and he tells anything but the truth. I don't know if they believe him or not, and I won't say he tells lies, but he certainly exaggerates the facts. And he is marvellous, he really is. He took a bus tour to Lourdes one time, and before leaving home, he got a bundle of *Democrats*, the local newspaper. They were way up in the Pyrenees on the bus and they stopped at a wee shop and Doalty got out of the bus first and put the *Democrats* on the paper stand. The crowd from home got off the bus and they couldn't believe that you could get the *Democrat* up in the Pyrenees! They all picked up a copy and went into the shop to pay and sure the man in the shop didn't know what was going on. Doalty is just a terrible case, there he was falling around in stitches. There was a time, too, when we went down to *currach* [a small rowing boat] racing in Spiddal, County Galway. Rowing was a very big sport in our area when I was growing up. Anyway, there was a parade in Spiddal at the time and we were all standing in the street watching it and one of the floats went past with Doalty sitting on it playing an accordion! You just couldn't credit how he manages to do those things. Those are the kinds of people who are chosen to launch the Kincasslagh Festival.

There are many activities centred around the Kincasslagh festival, including dances, discos, a heritage trail, treasure hunts and the whist drive card games. But the centrepiece of the festivities is the ball and that has always been a huge success. As I've said elsewhere, I never, ever know who the mystery 'belle' is going to be.

Those two festivals are close to my heart as they have given me the opportunity to be involved in the affairs of my community. Apart from the entertainment factor, they also help to boost the local economy, thanks to the huge influx of visitors. I feel it is a great honour to have been involved with the festivals and to have shared the benefits of my success with the people of Donegal.

8. HOME SWEET HOME

They say that home is where the heart is, and my heart has never left Donegal. There is just something magical about my native county, it has a grip on me and won't let go. I've been to some of the most exotic parts of the world and, while I have had my breath taken away by the sheer beauty of those places, they have never diminished the regard I hold for Donegal. I've tried living away from my little village of Kincasslagh, but in the end the magnet drew me back. So home for me was in Kincasslagh where I lived with my family until I bought a house nearby at Cruit. The council cottage where I grew up has been converted into a large, dormer bungalow. My mother lives there, as does my sister Kathleen with her husband, John Doogan, and their children. When it was redesigned, gutted and rebuilt, I had my own private quarters included at the back of the house and I loved it there. In 1992 I wanted to experience the big house and a bit of grandeur, so I went in search of my dream home and found it above the village of Rathcoole, twenty minutes south-west of Dublin city centre. I was out at my friend Josephine's house one Sunday – she lives out that way. I had been at Mass that morning and they were going in the evening and I said I'd go with them, another Mass wouldn't kill me. Very occasionally I would miss Mass, but not very often, so I said it would make up for one of the times I missed it or would miss it. Josephine's mother was visiting her and on the way Josephine passed Irish comedian Brendan Grace's house to show her mother where he lived. He's a big star in Ireland and among his admirers was the late Frank Sinatra, whom Brendan entertained during the legendary singer's visit to my homeland one time. As we drove around his area, I saw a house for sale and we stopped to have a look. It was a magnificent dormer bungalow set on a hill and it had a spectacular view of the surrounding countryside. I thought, 'God that's beautiful', and I ran down the drive. There was nobody in and I looked through the windows and thought, 'I really must see this house.' It had an instant attraction for me and I had to follow my instinct. I went out to view it the day after and I knew when I went inside that I wanted to buy it. The stairway in the hallway was the main feature I loved and there was also a balcony around the top. It wasn't well done up, or well furnished, but it had terrific potential. While I couldn't drive a nail straight, I've a great eye for what I'd like to achieve, and I felt it was a piece of property I could put my stamp on. I got quite excited about the prospect of it becoming my home. All kinds of ideas started building up in my mind and it became my obsession.

As luck would have it, I was able to acquire the house and I entered a new phase in my life. Away from the stage, my new 'baby' became my hobby and planning the renovations occupied any time off from my busy lifestyle. It was great fun. I got the builders in as I knew what I wanted to do and eventually the house became what I thought I wanted. And I did love the house. I proceeded to buy things for it and furnish it, and I thought about getting somebody in to do the interior decorating and then I thought I would rather do it myself. It became a labour of love. Navy and pink were the predominant colours throughout the house. The funny thing about that is the fact that my favourite colour is yellow, and I had no yellow anywhere. The large, open-plan hallway where there was a magnificent staircase leading up to a spacious landing, was adorned by an elaborate chandelier. The master bedroom was located off my own private, sound-proofed sitting-room which had a blue colour scheme and was designed as a library-cum-refuge suite. I'd got used to having a sitting-room off the bedroom from the hotels I stay in on tour. That was my haven, my favourite room in the house. It didn't have a telephone and I used to go up there to relax. I closed the door and shut out the world. There was a king-size bed, which had a canopy. The patio doors led on to a balcony and there was a spectacular view across the plains with Dublin Bay in the distance. I never drew the curtains. At night the twinkling lights of the capital on the distant horizon were a magnificent sight. I had a walk-in wardrobe and an en-suite with shower. The downstairs sitting-room and split-level dining room were carpeted in pink, with matching navy and pink wallpaper. The white kitchen had every mod con, all carefully concealed behind panelled doors. Outside, horses grazed peacefully in a neighbour's field bordering the property. I had no pets around the house. I suffer from allergies and I'm allergic to nearly all animals.

I didn't turn the place into a shrine to Daniel O'Donnell The Entertainer. There were no awards or discs displayed anywhere and no pictures of me with other entertainers. I wanted it to be a normal kind of house full of the things you see in other houses.

I had a granny flat converted for my mother, as I thought she would live there because she had shared a previous home with me in Dublin. I remember the first day I took her out to see my prized new possession, my pride and joy, but she didn't really like it. She thought it was miles away from everything, and she didn't spend much time there. Prior to buying the house in Rathcoole, I had a home in the Dublin suburb of Ballinteer. It was much smaller and my mother came down from Donegal and lived there with me. I don't really know why she decided to do that, to tell the truth. It wasn't as if we discussed it. She used to come and visit and then one day when she arrived, she put her coat on the stairs and stayed, and I was very happy with that arrangement. We always got on well together, we wouldn't have hassle with one another and she was happy there. Maybe she thought I couldn't look after myself. When I sold the house in Ballinteer I lived in a flat in Terenure, Dublin, for a few months. After I moved to my new abode in Rathcoole, I got a housekeeper called Brigid, so maybe my mother felt that at least I had somebody to cook for me. My mother stayed with me on and off in Dublin for six years. She had been living at home in Kincasslagh with my sister Kathleen and her husband John and their family. Then she came to live with me and, although she regularly spent time in Kincasslagh on visits, I would say if you asked her where her home was in those days, she would say she was living in Dublin. I think she was disappointed when I sold the house in Ballinteer because she loved it there. She found it very convenient but, although I don't mind people at all, I felt I wanted to move somewhere more private.

The alterations and renovations in Rathcoole took nine months to finish. You could probably have built two houses in the time it was done. I had a conservatory added at the rear and the garden was tremendous, it was really lovely with lots of features, including a pond and a pagoda. I had great fun buying bits and pieces for the house, rummaging around antique shops and the like. I got paintings done at home in Donegal by a woman called Annette Curran. Her first painting was of Maggie's Strand, the seashore where I played and swam as a child. When I saw this painting, I just needed to have it on my wall in Dublin. All the time I was bringing Donegal to Dublin, although I didn't know that was what I was doing. I had this nice house I was furnishing, but I would often say to myself, 'If I could only lift this and bring it home.' Eventually I had everything done, more or less, but there was one wall I had to finish and I needed a painting for it. I was doing shows in Telford, England, and there was an exhibition on and I saw a lovely painting and bought it. I came home and I hung the painting and when that was done, I stood back and looked at it and said, 'I want to sell the house.' It was as if I had no more to do.

By that time, it had dawned on me that home was calling me back. I turned the cottage at home into a large dormer-style bungalow and I put the Rathcoole property on the market. When it was sold, everything in it went to Donegal where the converted house was completed. It's actually very similar in appearance to the house in Rathcoole, although not quite as big. It's really lovely and it was a good move for many reasons. There was a time when it wouldn't have made any sense whatsoever basing myself in Kincasslagh from a travel point of view. But now we have a little airport not far away in a place called Carrickfinn and there's a flight once a day to and from Dublin. But I'm very content at home. People say to me, 'Do you know what you've done, do you realise you've actually taken a step back?' But I didn't move away from home to get away from home; I moved away because that's what was necessary at the time, and I moved back because I wanted to.

But I loved my time in Dublin, I loved living in Rathcoole and Saggart. The people were very nice and friendly. They never infringed on my privacy and were always pleasant. The house in Rathcoole was empty though. It rattled even when I was there, there were never enough people in it. So the big house is not the answer to whatever I thought I was going to achieve by having it. The best time I had there was when my friend Josephine and her husband and their children came to stay, after their own house burnt down. It was only then that the house became a home and all the facilities were put to the use they were invented for. I had a dishwasher and I never used it. After Josephine and the family were in residence a few days, I came in one night after a show and I went to make tea and there was only one mug and I thought, 'Where have they all gone? They can't have broken all the mugs. This is shocking!' But what I failed to do was look in the dishwasher, it just never occurred to me that they would be in there, washed! I don't think it had ever been used before they arrived and I probably didn't even know where it was. I remember Josephine laughed so much at that. So that was the best time in the house for me and I imagine now, and hope, that the people who are in it have a lovely family home because it is beautiful, and I'm sure they have made it very nice and cosy and put their own mark on it.

During my time there, I got to know many of the local people from going down to the village. I'm not the type who makes calls on house visits, I'm not into that kind of thing. At home, I would only go and see Annie McGarvey. It's not in me to visit and sit and gossip, because that's what you'd be doing. But I used to meet people out and about in Rathcoole and Saggart and they all made me feel very welcome. Eventually I would recognise the people at Mass, so it felt like I was part of the community while I lived there.

One of my neighbours was Brendan Grace, a well-known and very popular Irish comedian, as I mentioned earlier.

Brendan was a lovely neighbour, although I wouldn't have seen himself and his wife, Eileen, all that much. He's a real character off stage as well. I remember when I played the Point Theatre in Dublin, the first time the show got great reviews and Brendan Grace was up at the gates the following morning, bowing among a group of fans who had gathered there. He was so funny. Whenever he called in for a visit, my mother, if she was there, would give him the pancakes she bakes (God, they're sinful, but delicious). So my time in Rathcoole was a happy one and I have good memories from that period in my life. Moving there is something I had to do in order to find my place in life. And that place is Kincasslagh and Donegal.

I bought the Viking House Hotel in Kincasslagh because it came on the market and I felt it was a way of creating employment as well as giving the fans something to focus on when they came to the area. The hotel was not a profitable investment, contrary to what people might have thought. It's not actually big enough to be profitable. I wanted to extend it and I'm sure it would have increased the influx of tourists to the area. But it would also have meant a huge, personal financial commitment and it's something that I really didn't want to take on. I felt I had already done my bit for where I live and for Donegal in general. I feel that what I do has led to a lot of tourists coming to Ireland and especially to Donegal, having been introduced to it through my music. It came as a huge let-down then, when we applied to the local authorities for grant aid to develop the hotel and expand the business, and we were turned down. That was a big blow to me. The politicians will say, 'Ah, Daniel is a great fella, he does a lot of good for tourism, there's nobody like him.' But when it came to assisting me in making major developments, they weren't much good. They expected me to do it on my own. If the hotel was bigger, I could have done concerts there and it would have brought in a lot of extra tourism. The shows would obviously have been smaller and more intimate than what I do on a regular basis and that would attract people. But I did not extend the hotel because I did honestly feel that the authorities with the power to give the grants had not played the game with me. None of the politicians inside and outside my area had been successful in encouraging the Irish Tourist Board to provide adequate funds to expand. I eventually sold the Viking House and I'm glad to say the new owners are doing very well there. I often drop in to say 'Hello'.

9. FOOTBALL FEVER

In 1992, I had one of the most thrilling times of my life when the Donegal senior football team climbed the mountain and made it to the All Ireland Football Final for the first time ever in the history of the sport. Well, you can imagine the level of excitement and interest that generated in our county. The celebrations on the path to the final as Donegal saw off opposition after opposition really lifted the spirits of the local people and our confidence grew and grew as we began to smell the sweet smell of victory. A lot of people thought they would never see Donegal win the All Ireland. I remember when I started travelling with Margaret after joining her band, we were down in Kerry one night, a county that had won numerous All Irelands, and a man asked me where I was from. When I said I was from Donegal, his reply was, 'There'll be white blackbirds flying by the time Sam Maguire [the All Ireland football cup] goes to Donegal.'

Well, our day basking in the sunshine eventually arrived. For us, it was like Cup Final day at Wembley. I'll never forget the build-up to the big day. I spent the Saturday night in Dublin going to functions and singing 'I Want To Dance With You'. The atmosphere in the centre of Dublin was fantastic and I went in and savoured it. I remember walking up O'Connell Street and meeting neighbours from home. It was a great time for me personally because 'I Want To Dance With You' was in the charts and for a lot of people from Donegal, it was a double cause for celebration. I had been on *Top of the Pops* that week, and the day of the All-Ireland, 'I Want To Dance With You' went up from number thirty to number twenty in the charts.

I was filled with the tension and excitement of the occasion as I took my place in Croke Park [the national football stadium]. There were supporters from the Dublin opposition behind me, and their comments were ringing in my ears and getting me really annoyed. 'Show the boys from the hills now what it's like to be in the big city. Show them what to do when they come into the city.' I thought this was just shocking. But anyway, 'the boys from the hills' were getting on well, and when Donegal went ahead in the game, I turned around and took off my Donegal supporter's hat and said, 'Now, you eejit!' and I put my hat on top of one guy's head. So as the end drew near, I saw the boys behind me getting up to leave and I turned around and gave them the greatest shake hands that anybody ever got in their whole lives. We couldn't get beaten at that stage and I was just so thrilled and proud that our team proved everyone wrong and didn't collapse under the pressure of the big occasion.

When they won, I saw people getting kisses that day that had probably never been kissed before, and will probably never be kissed again. I saw auld ones crying with joy. It was an exhilarating moment. I lost the run of myself completely and there is a great picture of me with my Donegal hat raised in the air as I celebrated the victory. I wasn't aware of it being taken after the match, it's a brilliant shot and now it's proudly displayed in the Viking House Hotel in Kincasslagh. Somebody from Armagh took it and sent it to me.

We didn't want the celebrations to end. We could have wallowed in the after-match euphoria for a lifetime. I beeped my car horn all the way home to my house in Rathcoole, where I had a Donegal flag proudly flying and only the cows listened to me. That night I headed off for the Grand Hotel in Dublin's Malahide where the post-match celebrations continued into the early hours of the morning. It was mighty.

I got to experience what it's like to be part of a county that wins an All Ireland, and for the first time ever. Sam Maguire might be the name of a cup to some, but to us Sam was like a living being, and everybody met him. Mind you, he took a bit of a battering during his time in our county, he returned with more dinges [dents] than when we got him. I heard a story about how the team went to Dublin for a function, and they took Sam with them but forgot to bring him home again. How they could have let him out of their sight after waiting more than one hundred years to get their hands on him, I'll never know. But the year we had Sam was a great one for us. We had him at the GAA [Gaelic Athletic Association] dance in Dungloe and it was the most wonderful experience. Sam was touched by every man, woman and child, from the oldest to the youngest, in Donegal.

There are certain occasions in my life that were similar to winning the cup, like the day I went to see the Pope in Galway, and when I first saw the Irish show *Riverdance*. Along with Donegal's All Ireland victory, I would say those two things gave me the same uplifting feeling. Now, in what order would I put them? I do believe the All Ireland was an incredible day. *Riverdance* was the most wonderful show that I've ever seen, without a shadow of a doubt. I couldn't believe it when I saw it. It was a gasp, I was left speechless. That happened to me once at the Fan Fair show in Nashville. George Jones and Lynn Anderson were compering. Nobody said George Jones was going to sing at any time. But George landed out on the stage and his voice broke into 'He Said I'll Love You Till I Die', and the whole audience breathed in at the same time. I'll never forget it. There was just one communal, sharp intake of breath. The hairs stood up on the back of my neck.

I'll never forget Bishop Eamon Casey and the late Father Michael Cleary [two high-profile Irish clergymen] the day I saw the Pope. They were just terrific. The Pope was marvellous and we, the audience, were terrific! It was a very charismatic day. That was 1979, it was around the beginning of June. I was sixteen years old and I travelled from Donegal to Galway by bus along with all the rest of the people making the pilgrimage. The roads wouldn't have been good, but there was a string of cars and everybody was going, everybody in Ireland. It wasn't like that in England. I also went to see the Pope at Wembley in 1982. There were some people on the tube who were not going to see the Pope, but everybody in Ireland went when he was there. The whole of Ireland was united for that occasion. It was incredible. The bus broke down on the way home, but even that didn't spoil the memory of the event.

I suppose I felt great love on that day. There was great love shown to us by the Pope, and we showed unconditional love for him because we felt that being a country like Ireland, we were always small, and it was such a privilege to have a man of his calibre visit us. I don't know if we as a country had achieved an awful lot up to then, particularly in the area of entertainment. We've had a lot more success on a world scale since then. U2 hadn't made an impact at that time, Mary Robinson wasn't President, and *Riverdance* hadn't been created. It's different now. I wonder what reaction the Pope would get if he came now? I don't think it would be the same.

There are people who have been disillusioned by the actions of some clergy, but any wrong-doing by an individual of the Church has never affected what I get out of Mass. And I think that anybody who gives up Mass because they feel let down by a member of the clergy didn't really get anything out of it in the first place. You cannot base religion on a human individual. Does that mean if there is a bus conductor who's not nice, you never get on another bus again? If he insults you, you might report him, but you wouldn't stay off the buses. I very rarely miss Mass. It's very easy to give up going when you move away from home and lead a busy life. But I decided I needed that religious experience in my life.

If there's one regret I have in the aftermath of Donegal's victory in the All Ireland, it's the fact that I couldn't travel home to join in the celebrations because I was fighting my own battle to get well health-wise, as I've explained earlier. At the time I couldn't tell people why, because I didn't want anybody to know that I was struggling so much in myself. Nothing would have kept me from Donegal other than that. On the Sunday evening of the big match, I had to go to the Blackrock Clinic in Dublin for a check-up. Afterwards, I travelled on to the Grand Hotel in Malahide, as I've mentioned, for the celebrations.

I missed not going home with the All Ireland cup so much that the following year, when Derry won it, I went to Bellaghy for the experience of the triumphant home-coming. People probably couldn't understand what took me to Derry, but that's the reason. I had to live what I had missed the previous year and although I was in Derry, I was in Donegal in my mind.

As a youth, I never excelled at Gaelic games. I just didn't have the talent. I would have loved to have been a good footballer. I suppose I felt I wasn't one of the boys because I didn't master the sport. I was awkward, making myself noticed but trying not to be noticed. There were very few people as bad as I was. They nearly wouldn't allow me on the bus as a supporter I was that bad. But it didn't colour my attitude towards the game. I prefer the Gaelic football to the soccer. It feel it's more exciting because there is more happening. I also love to watch the hurling. I think it is captivating because there is a lot of scoring. You could sit all day at a soccer match and there would only be the one goal or maybe none. But at least you are guaranteed scores at the Gaelic matches.

I might have been good at tennis or ten-pin bowling, but we grew up without them. So when I say I was no good at sports, I was no good at Gaelic football and hurling, but who is to say I mightn't have been a champion at something else? However, I have no regrets. There are some who say I am good at singing, so everybody gets something.

Today, like everyone else, I enjoy the big sporting occasion, like when the Irish soccer team was doing well in the World Cup in 1990. It was beyond everyone's expectations for such a small country, and we were all caught up in national soccer fever. And, of course, goalie Packie Bonner from Donegal was one of the heroes, so there was a great sense of local pride. I heard stories of how people around Ireland sold their cars to follow the team as they blazed a trail in pursuit of World Cup glory. In the end, of course, we didn't win, but we did give our team a hero's welcome when they returned. Tens of thousands of people packed the streets of Dublin to welcome the side as they travelled from the airport to the city centre on an open-deck bus. In situations like that, a sense of national pride gets you caught up in the excitement.

10. CLIFF

While Loretta Lynn is my favourite female singer of all time, those who know me will be aware that I am also one of Cliff Richard's biggest fans. I have been fortunate to have met both of those artists as a result of my own singing career. You could say it's one of the perks of the business. I have got to know my two favourite entertainers on a personal level and, thankfully, I have not been disappointed by them as people. They both lived up to the impression I had of them. They say you should never meet your idols in case you are disillusioned by them. Thankfully that hasn't been the case where Loretta and Cliff are concerned.

I have met Cliff a number of times, and I appreciate how lucky I am to have done so. I know there are lifetime fans who will never meet him. I encountered one lady who had been following him for thirty years before she finally got to meet him in the flesh. I was actually introduced to him at the first concert I went to, and since then, I've met him on a few occasions. I admire Cliff as a singer, as an entertainer and as a person, because of the manner in which he conducts himself. I just think he is a terrific performer. He is somebody who is not afraid to take a chance with his career and he's achieved a lot of things. Nobody gave him any credit for taking on the role in the stage production of *Heathcliff*, but it was a tremendous success for him. Cliff is forty years in the business and I don't care what anybody says, that speaks for itself. And he is bigger today than he has ever been. Songs such as 'Lucky Lips' and 'Living Doll' first got me hooked on his music. And one of my favourite songs of all time is his 1976 hit 'Miss You Nights'.

I think where the media are concerned, he's really taken a battering and he just rises above it all. Having been on the receiving end of that kind of media attention myself, I can identify with Cliff. But neither Cliff nor myself should pay any attention to the critics because what they say is only their view. People are entitled to their opinions, of course. We have to accept that not every critic is going to like what we do, but some of them go over the top with their criticism. Have you ever seen a statue erected to a critic? That says it all.

I went out to dinner one night in Edinburgh with Cliff and some friends after a performance of *Heathcliff*, which was on tour around the UK, and I found him a very comfortable person to be around. The conversation was so normal. I don't know what I expected because prior to that I had just met him briefly on a few occasions after concerts. It turned out to be a lovely evening. The conversation in general was about shows, what you do, what you don't. He was talking about acting and how different it is to doing a show. When you are acting you're living a part, the audience sees the other person you're portraying. I must say, in relation to this, when I went to see *Heathcliff* I wasn't actually aware that it was Cliff up there on stage. It obviously proves that he is a good actor and that whatever they tried to achieve in the show worked, for me, anyway. I think Cliff is aware that I admire him. I'm the kind of person who would never be too shy to say I like somebody. It's not as if I wouldn't want them to know. And I do think he is interested in my work and quite aware of what I am doing too. Although he is on a different level to me, our audiences are not very different. A lot of the people who come to see me are fans of Cliff as well.

That evening in Edinburgh with Cliff, in the company of his manager Roger Bruce and Moira McKenzie, the manageress of Edinburgh's Usher Hall, was so enjoyable. Something that struck me is that Cliff is very down-to-earth and he still gets a kick out of simple things, like staying in a nice hotel. That night, Cliff took us to see his hotel and gave us the grand tour. You would think that having stayed in top hotels all around the world, and lived in mansions, he wouldn't be excited by hotels at this stage of his career. But it shows he hasn't lost touch with reality. This was three o'clock in the morning and there we were, the four of us, traipsing up and down stairs on a guided tour! It was a great night because you were with easy people to be around. We can make ourselves feel ill at ease around celebrities because we are in awe of other people and, after all, people like Cliff are just normal folk. They just happen to be doing a job that is out of the ordinary, or perceived to be so.

I'm normal, although my life is probably different to most people's. When I'm being interviewed I might say, 'I have a very normal life' and when I sit down and define what I mean by normal, it seems anything but. I get up in the morning and certainly I do ordinary things. But if I am doing a day's promotion, and I need something, perhaps from the chemist's, I find myself asking someone to fetch it. I find that people do an awful lot for me. When I'm on tour I generally don't go to the shops. Occasionally I do, but usually if I need shampoo, or this, that or the other, somebody else gets it. And that's not normal. It's not that I'm abusing my position, it's because I have other commitments and it's easier to have someone else do the shopping. But when I'm not working and I need something, I buy it myself.

My work is not normal. Doing three TV shows in England in one day with a few radio interviews in between. Probably the most normal thing I would do on that day is eat. But I would come home without telling the family or whoever that I had done those things, because it would just be a normal part of my working day. But if that sort of thing happened to me ten or twelve years ago, I would be getting ready for a month and getting over it for six weeks. So you create what's normal, I think.

I suppose it's the same with Cliff Richard. He just regards what he does as normal, and it is to him. I have always preferred Cliff to Elvis Presley, although I like Elvis too and I sing some of his songs, maybe more than I do Cliff's. But the reason I do it is because Elvis is dead and Cliff's still doing it. But I have more of a leaning to Cliff than to any of the other singers of that era. Nobody can dispute that, as a solo performer, Cliff is one of the biggest stars that Britain has produced. And you look at the audience when you go to see Cliff, there's young ones there, old ones, every age. You can't say Cliff's fans are all forty and up, that's not the case, anything but! Some radio stations said that they were banning him from their shows in 1998 because he was too old. Well, that was just like plucking mushrooms, the more you pluck them the faster they grow. All they succeeded in doing was gain Cliff more publicity and more recognition and support. What the radio stations didn't want to do, they did in abundance. Cliff's albums are going to sell anyway, whether they play them or not.

Something similar happened to me in 1991 when six of my albums were dropped from the UK Country Music Chart because they weren't considered country. People who supported me objected and objected loudly. They went out marching in some places, and in the end the controversy gained so much publicity that the people who make the rules reversed their decision. I was a bit disappointed by their initial decision, because I find it strange that people need to categorise you. It's as if you have to have a label. Maybe it's to do with the business side, and the marketing side, so that people know which shelves to put you on. I'm not really worried where I am, as long as I am on the shelves. But I do think that a lot of what I sing is country.

At a time when they wanted country music to move forward, I came along, singing a more traditional type of country. If you're trying to do something new, you don't like it when people come and say, 'I like things the way they are.' If you're building an extension to your house and somebody comes along and says, 'I'd rather it was left as it was', you'd be annoyed because you'd be thinking, This is the way to go. I suppose if you look at it like that, you can see where their frustration lay. But instead of moving along and leaving me there, they tried to remove me. My music is very hard to define and that was part of the controversy. When I started out, I never tried to define it. Certainly there are some songs that are middle of the road, but I do think I'm more country than anything else. I don't tear along the dotted line all the time!

While I have got to know Cliff, I'm not claiming to be a close friend, by any means, nor do I feel that I'm on a par with him. I would send the odd card to Cliff to wish him luck with things. I sent him one for his fortieth anniversary tour. Even if he never feels he should send a card to me, I feel the need to do it for him, as he is one of the entertainers who has given me most enjoyment.

My personal taste in music is varied. I can appreciate anything that's not too heavy. Obviously, I love country music and that is my favourite. But I like most of the popular music. I'm not very good with jazz when it gets too heavy, or when rock is sort of heavy metal, and I'm not too keen on opera. Once it's not too over-the-top, I can be in there enjoying it like everyone else. It's such a wonderful gift to be able to enjoy music because it can be so therapeutic.

11. AROUND THE WORLD

I'm in perpetual motion most of the year as I'm an entertainer who's hardly ever off the road. I play to over a quarter of a million people most years, sometimes it's more, sometimes less and it's been that way since the late Eighties. I usually have January off, but from then on it's a very full itinerary. The spring, autumn and winter periods are generally devoted to the UK where I do roughly sixty shows annually. The support I've received from people in Britain has been incredible. It's my biggest market and the concert venues there sell out six months in advance, with fans often queuing for days to get their tickets. I've been working in America since 1990, but it's only in the last couple of years that I've started to concentrate on building a following there, particularly in Branson, Missouri, where I do a two-week residency at Jennifer's American Theater. However, I've done better in Australia and New Zealand than in the US. I've been working there since 1992 and my concerts are growing with every visit. In the summertime I tour America, Canada and Ireland and I visit Australia and New Zealand every eighteen months.

My first introduction to America, as Daniel O'Donnell the entertainer, was in 1990. I thought it was going to be better than it actually was. I thought the Irish in America would support us in a huge way. Some came out, but it wasn't to the extent that you could depend on that market and we still can't. If I am to succeed in the States, I will have to cater to a general market and not just the Irish one. As a result of that early experience, I've never quite got airborne in the US, although now things are beginning to work. My experiences performing in Branson, where I've been going since 1997, have certainly given me a great boost. Even though the crowds are not huge, the reaction of the people who do come to the shows has been fantastic. I think the States could grow into a major territory for me.

One of the highlights of America for me was my performance at New York's famous Carnegie Hall in 1991. That was incredible. It was a great feeling to be there as it was another milestone in my career. I was very calm about it in the build-up to the big night. I suppose most people know that I'm kind of cool and some would say that if I was any more laid back I would be lying flat! People were saying in the months leading up to that how I must be looking forward to it, and I was in my own way. But because we work so much, there were many, many concerts to be done in the six months prior to Carnegie Hall. It wasn't until a couple of days before the big event that I felt it was going to be something special. I remember all the preparations, getting ready, walking out and the minute I did I knew it was extraordinary. I remember the rush of emotions as I introduced myself to the audience with the words: 'I never thought I'd get the opportunity to say this, Welcome to Carnegie Hall.' It was a momentous occasion, certainly, but behind the scenes there were some funny things going on. I always do a couple of changes of suits during my performance and halfway through the Carnegie Hall show I went to the dressing room to put on the next outfit. There was no sign of Loretta, who looks after my clothes. I was told, 'Oh, half of your suit is back at the hotel', and this was halfway through one of the biggest nights ever! I saw my trousers and shirt and decided to put those on. Then I went to put on the matching shoes and there were no shoes! The band had played their song and they had to be told in whispered tones with frantic hand signals to play another one. Anyway, the outfit arrived and it didn't take too long – the band only played one extra song – but I was annoyed at the time. When I look back on it now, I can appreciate the funny side of it, but it wasn't funny at the time because everybody, including myself, was so tense. Nobody knows what goes on behind the scenes at shows. If it happened to me nowadays I'd probably go on without the shoes and have a bit of fun over the cock-up. That all comes with experience. If the electricity goes down these days we just continue, Ronnie on the accordion and the acoustic guitar, and me singing something that everybody knows, so everybody can sing along with it. But it was different then, everything was so perfect and controlled. But Carnegie Hall was special, and I know it's something I'll always remember.

I know in my heart that if we get a break in the States, the Americans will absolutely love what we are doing, judging by the response we get in Branson. Some of them come to every show we do there, ten or eleven or whatever we do. I said to one man who told me he'd been to them all, 'Jesus, you could nearly do it yourself now!', and he said, 'Gee, we're just getting used to what you're doing and then you go and change the whole God damn thing!' I believe that from night to night the show should be different for us and for them, but for us primarily because I don't like structure. I love the variation, so I introduce a couple of different songs, or I will perform a request from the audience.

On our trip to Branson in 1997 we were accompanied by fans from Ireland and Britain. *Eight* flights took people out! I was absolutely staggered. I thought if we got twenty people we would do well. There were about 350 people and it was just amazing to see the seven coach loads of people arriving at Branson. I stood back and I thought to myself, "I wonder why?" And I don't know why. It's a question I've never been able to answer. But it really added to the whole atmosphere in Branson to have those people there and I did get the chance to spend time with them.

Two of the fans on that trip, a couple called Marie Fallon and P. J. Tierney from County Galway, Ireland, had planned to get married and they asked the organiser if they could do it on the trip. In particular, they were hoping that Mary Duff and myself would act as the best man and bridesmaid. Well, it's not something we would normally do. We wouldn't have had much contact with the couple, but it seemed like the right thing to do. It was their special day, the most important day in their lives, and it was an honour for Mary and myself to be asked to play such an important part in it. Apparently, Marie has always been one of my most ardent fans and whenever people chided her about getting married, she would quip, 'Get Daniel O'Donnell to be there and I'll do it in the morning.' So when she saw an advert for the tour to the States, the thought struck her that it would be her opportunity to get me to the wedding. She says the thought never crossed her mind that I might turn her down. Marie made all the arrangements and the couple kept their wedding plans a secret from the fans as they flew out from Dublin. But there was a surprise in store for Marie when she arrived – she discovered her younger sister Louise waiting for them. Louise made the five thousand mile trek from Ireland as she just couldn't miss her sister's biggest day. It was a very emotional meeting for Marie as she had regretted not having her family with her. The wedding took place in a church in Branson and we all got dolled up for the occasion. It was a lovely service. Mary and I sang. The band played and all 350 people came along to the wedding ceremony and Mass. We had a performance to do in the afternoon and the newly weds changed out of their wedding gear and came along to that. Then in the evening, they donned their wedding finery again and we took a trip on the Branson Belle Showboat. That's where we had the wedding reception and as Marie and P.J. cut the cake, I serenaded them with 'Moonlight And Roses'. Then the celebrations continued with a Cajun-style concert. It was romantic and lovely and so enjoyable. Marie and P.J. were surrounded by tour people they didn't know, yet it was like a big family occasion and I'm sure the couple will never forget it. It was certainly something different for me as well. I think the people in Branson were amazed by this singer from Ireland who brought along all his fans and even threw in a wedding for good measure! They didn't quite know what to make of it all.

I felt very insecure at first about going to the States to try and make an impression there. Why? I don't know. And, do you know, if I had to start out in my career all over again, I don't think I actually could. I just wouldn't have the confidence. I just feel I could never make it again. It would be too much of a mountain to climb. I can't say what I've done has been difficult, but I could not start again. Maybe it's because I'm aware of how much luck is involved, being in the right place at the right time, teaming up with the right people and having something that people see in you, without really knowing what it is. They say that ignorance is bliss and I think that's why people like myself go into the entertainment world with high hopes – it's because we are completely unaware of just how difficult it is to succeed. Now that I know the industry and how it works, I could never see myself making any progress within it. But I was fortunate that I was naive starting out, as I didn't have all the negative things in my mind. I suppose going to the States was like starting out again for me because I was introducing myself to people who had never heard of me. On my first day in Branson there were very few people at the show because they didn't know me from Adam. After my first experience in Branson, if Sean had said, 'I don't think we'll bother going to America any more,' I wouldn't have gone back.

I suppose in a sense I feel I can't achieve any more than I have in my career. I can do more of the same and when you play to 10,000, there's no difference playing to 100,000, because 10,000 is just huge. I remember the first time I played the Sand Centre in Carlisle, it holds 1,400 people, and I thought I couldn't see the back of that place. I was so nervous when I came out on to the stage I could see nothing. And I welcomed them all to Dundee because I was in Dundee the night before. I was so nervous with that 1,400 audience and to think now I play to crowds of up to 12,000 and more.

I know that if we gain more success in America there's no end to what might happen. Now whether I want that or not I don't know, I really can't tell you. If I was able to go to Branson for a month and fill the theatre I was in, whatever size it was, whether it be a thousand seats or two thousand, and fill it for twenty shows, I would feel that was success enough for me in America. But I do feel I can reach the people in America the way I did in Ireland and the UK. In 1998 when I was in Harrod's in London doing a signing, a youngish woman, maybe in her forties (it's funny as you get older how much younger people become!), said to me, 'You've got to come to Washington.' She said, 'We were in Ireland six months ago and we went into a record store. We wanted an Irish singer and we just happened to buy your record, you've just got to come to Washington.' I thought, well people who say you have to see a show to really experience what a performer is about are obviously wrong because this lady was never at my concert. She just bought a tape and she loved what she heard. When I see how some of the people in the States have linked on to us I think, in general, that's no different to what happened in the UK.

I normally go to Australia a week before I start doing concerts there because I find the journey so tiring. The jet lag is just incredible. And because there are days when I might do thirty or more interviews, it really can be draining. I remember one night I was doing an interview at 10.15, but coming up to 10 p.m. I just couldn't stay awake because I was suffering from jet lag, so I set the alarm clock and dozed off for fifteen minutes. I do enjoy Australia as a country. The people are lovely and I'm very grateful that my singing has taken me there because otherwise I might not have experienced it. It's a long way to go for a holiday.

My first visit to Australia was planned for 1991 and I can't tell you how relieved I was when I didn't have to go. I really wasn't well that year in the run up to my physical breakdown. I didn't know I wasn't well at the time. It's not that I was sick, but I suppose I was overworked and stressed out. My resistance was low and I didn't really feel able to fly to Australia. I couldn't face that journey, for one thing. I would be going out to people who didn't know me at all, and I just didn't have the motivation, because of the way I felt. At that time whenever I was singing I would have the most awful feeling in my chest. I went to Australia in 1992 and it was a good experience. I went to Melbourne and Sydney and only did a few things, but I did appear on their big TV show, *Good Morning Australia*. My career in Australia gained momentum in the same way it did in the UK. It's still growing and yet the man on the street there doesn't know me. It's probably because I'm not in the public eye constantly. I had the strangest experience in a shop in New Zealand – the female shop assistant said to me, 'You sound just like that Daniel O'Donnell.' I smiled and she asked, 'Do you come from here?' I just said, 'Somewhere around . . .' I couldn't believe how she could listen to me speak and connect me with myself, yet not recognise me. The fans who do know me, generally know everything about me. We didn't go to New Zealand until our second tour Down Under and now it's a regular part of the trip. One of the great memories I have from Australia is the night Judith Durham of The Seekers came to see my show in Melbourne. That was a big thrill for me because I have always been a huge fan of The Seekers. I found it difficult to absorb the fact that Judith Durham would come to see *me* perform in concert.

Some funny incidents have happened to me in places like Australia as a result of the difference in the way we Irish express ourselves. Obviously, prior to going 'Down Under' on tour, I wouldn't have been familiar with some of the terms they use to describe things and I'm sure I've made a real fool of myself sometimes as a result. One particular incident sticks in my mind. It happened one of the times I went to Australia and did a TV show the day I arrived. We landed at nine in the morning and I was on the television at one, and later, a local man said to me that he had seen me on the TV show. He added, 'You looked crook.' So I replied, 'Thank you.' Now, I had no idea what he meant and I knew by his reaction that my response had seemed strange. He didn't say anything more, he just walked away. Later during that same trip I met band member Ronnie Kennedy's brother-in-law at my show in Melbourne.

He said, 'I saw you on the TV, were you crook that day?'

I asked, 'What does that mean?'

He said, 'Sick.' And I had thanked the other Australian man for telling me I looked 'crook' on the telly! What must he have thought of me? Somebody said to me another time, 'Would you give me a cheerio on the show?' I didn't know what they wanted. What they were asking was, play a request for them. Aren't the differences in the language amazing. When I tell the Australian audiences about those incidents on stage, they get a great kick out of them.

I sometimes embarrass myself during shows by saying the wrong thing or saying something that has a double meaning. Often I realise that I've put my foot in it when I see the lads in the band laughing. I remember one night we were in Inverness in Scotland and an incident happened that made me blush. There was a request for a man who was at the show without his wife and it said, 'There'll be no need to mark the calendar tonight.' I read the request out and I said, 'I'm sure that will mean something to you, it doesn't mean anything to us.' Then I noticed that everybody was starting to laugh, the band more so than the audience. The audience sometimes don't laugh until they know it is all right to do so. And then I knew that I had made a blunder and I said something like, 'What happened?' I don't know whether Ronnie told me or I twigged for myself, but I said, 'Oh my God!' That just made it funnier because everyone knew that I was only just getting what the phrase meant. So that was certainly one of the funny ones and there have been many like that. I suppose they actually contribute to the fun of the night.

I've found generally that whenever I go to foreign parts I'm made to feel very welcome. I suppose I hardly ever meet a stranger in far-off places, there are always people waiting to greet me at airports and venues, and I really do feel like I have a charmed life. Certainly Australia has been no different. Whichever airport I arrive at in the land of Oz there are people waiting to meet me. Sometimes there are up to a hundred fans. And even when I'm leaving, they nearly always come to see me off. They are appreciative that we visit Australia, particularly in the smaller towns and I wish we could go to more. I have met a lot of Irish and Scottish people out there and very few of them have lost their accents. It's like they never left, even though some of them have been there for thirty or forty years!

I've also been to South Africa, my records are on sale there, and I feel there is certainly a market for me in that part of the world. I went there in January 1998 and I used the trip to do some interviews, but my primary purpose was to visit a friend called Sister Marietta. We met back in 1996 while she was on holiday in Ireland and we struck up a friendship. She has become a really good friend and over the years whenever she returned to Ireland I always promised I'd visit her in South Africa, and I finally made the trip. I loved my time there. I stayed in a convent for a short time. Convents are not at all like people imagine. They're great fun. The nuns have got a wonderful way about them.

As far as my career is concerned South Africa is really another part of the world I have yet to develop. I haven't done enough work there to know what kind of reaction my live show would generate. It is impossible to judge the level of success we could achieve, so it remains another challenge for the future if I want to take it on.

12. THE STAGE

I've never sung to make money. When I'm performing I never think about how much I'm making on the night. I sing because I love it and the money is just a by-product of what I do. My biggest payment is being on the stage and that is a big part of the secret of my success. Entertainers who do it for the money do not love performing as much as they ought to. You'll often hear them say, 'It's tough, the travelling is awful.' I would never say that, not even in the days when I was travelling the length and breadth of Ireland in a Transit van. I didn't hate that journey because I knew that the stage was at the end of it.

I have heard some American performers complaining, even though they have huge success. They say, we miss this, that and the other and we don't get time to spend with the family. There is nothing that I have missed and there is nothing that would have come close to what I've got and I don't think anything will as long as I live. If it all ended tomorrow, I couldn't say there is anything the world could have offered me that is better than what I have. I followed my dream and realised my dream and I never let anything distract me from that dream. I would even go so far as to say that I ruthlessly pursued my dream in that nothing or no one was ever more important to me than The Stage.

I'm not sure whether I'm comfortable using the term 'celebrity', but I suppose it defines what I have become as a result of my success as a singer and entertainer. Some people find it difficult to deal with the change in life that being a celebrity or 'personality' involves. But I do feel that I have handled it well because I haven't allowed it to change me as a person. I like to keep things as normal as possible in my life because that's just the way I am. I've moved back home to the area where I grew up and I think that's good for me. I am still lucky to be able to enjoy family life and be a part of a local community when I'm not working. I'm blessed in that regard.

I'm not saying I don't enjoy the limelight because obviously I do or I wouldn't be doing what I'm doing. But when I go abroad on holiday and meet people who don't know me, I never reveal to them what I do in life. If people know me, fine, I have no problem with that. But in situations where they don't know me, I like them to accept me for who I am, not what I am. And I think that if I said, in situations where people are meeting me for the first time, what my life involves, it would change their view of me. My life as an entertainer is not normal by any means and I do believe it changes how people react to you.

There are certain times when I feel that it's inappropriate for people to make a fuss of me and one of those is at church. I hate getting that attention at Mass, I despise it. I don't mind greeting people outside the church, but when it happens inside the building I just feel it's not right, because it is a place of worship and you have to be respectful. Not that people are blatantly disrespectful and I can understand what happens, but it makes me uncomfortable. If I'm out shopping, I don't mind seeing a lot of people, although I don't actually like creating a scene in public places like shops. So I just try to keep moving and get on with my shopping, to keep things as normal as possible.

Being well-known does bring it's own problems when you are out in public because, naturally, you're going to meet people who don't appreciate what you do. Believe me, I do meet my fair share of them, but it's something you learn to deal with. And I think I do deal with it fairly well. It seems a lot of the people who give me hassle are people who've been influenced by what's been written about me. Then, of course, you'll meet the people who just want to bring you down and my approach is generally to ignore them. There are times, though, when it's impossible to avoid a confrontation. Sometimes you win and sometimes you don't. It's the same with a pack of dogs, you need to take the dog out of the pack and see what he is like, if he is as vicious outside the pack as he is in it. I've been harrassed by a group of men on occasion, but I've also had the opportunity to confront individuals from those groups after meeting them by chance on their own. I've done that more than once and made my point. Nobody has the right to abuse or try to demean or humiliate anybody. It's just not right. What's not right is not right and sometimes you have to stand up and say it.

The way I look and my style of clothes is a great source of comment and criticism in some quarters and it's something I could never understand. After all, style and presentation are all part of being an entertainer. They're all part of my working 'tools', if you like. A carpenter loads up his tools when he's heading off for a day's work. I go out and buy clothes or get my hair trimmed for the stage, or for photo shoots and videos with my creative consultant Michael McDonagh. It goes with my work, so I think it's ludicrous that some sections of the media, make such a fuss about it.

I seem to get a lot of criticism for not having 'a hair out of place.' But the reality is, I have the type of hair that just sits the way it sits. I shake it for a bit of rock 'n' roll on stage and then it falls back to where it was. But I even have people coming up to me and touching my hair to see if it's a wig. People come to interview me and my hair might not be done at all, but they go away and write 'perfectly groomed, not a hair out of place.' I have one guy called Traolach MacAn tSionnaigh, a hairdresser from the village of Rathcoole where I used to live, who cuts it all the time. We all have someone we trust to cut our hair and he is the best hairdresser I have ever met. I do have a concern about going bald because I don't have a nice head for it. Some people do, but I don't think I do, and I do believe that whatever it takes for me to have hair, I'll have it, even if it means robbing it from someone else!

I do think style is important when you're working on stage and I can't blame anyone else for the way I look because I take care of my own wardrobe. I know what I want and I go out and select the clothes myself. I buy them, rather than have them designed and specially made for me. I buy a lot from Boutique Homme and Louis Copeland's in Dublin. I also buy some in a shop called Marmalade in London's Oxford Street. The selection of clothes is terrific and I think it's generally the black community who shop there. But I buy most of the outfits for the year from Boutique Homme in Dublin. When they go to fashion events in Europe they keep me in mind and if they think something would suit me they bring it home. Each outfit costs around £1,000. I think that's expensive, but it's not when you consider that I wear that suit maybe fifty times. So it's £20 a time and that's not much really. But I would look twice at spending that kind of money for everyday use.

You can get away with something a little bit more flash on stage. I always like a bright suit to finish the show with. Something pale grey or blue or cream. Something striking. I'm always on the lookout for clothes for the stage. I once came up with the idea of a Dickens-style look for some Christmas shows and I knew what I wanted as I had seen it on Christmas cards. It was a long velvet frock coat. I found one in a theatrical shop that hired clothes, so I got it out. A woman called Breda Nolan from Kilkenny in Ireland then made one for me just like it. She and her husband, John, come to the shows a lot and I wore the coat she made on stage several times. I buy a lot because I do a lot of television as well and I feel it's important as an entertainer to dress differently for those kinds of appearance.

While I have to stay in fairly good shape for the stage, I'm not a keep-fit fanatic and my choice of foods is not particularly healthy. I like fried onions with steak and chips. I don't like vegetables or salads at all. As I've got older I've tended to put on a few pounds easily and when I heard about a new way of losing weight, called the Nutron Diet, I thought, 'This is definitely for me.' They do a test to find out which foods your system digests most easily. I went away and got the test done and I must say I never felt better than when I was on the diet. I never ate as much and I enjoyed what I ate. I could still eat many of the things I liked if they were cooked in a special way. So I wasn't restricted that much. But while I felt really healthy on the diet, I also lost a lot of weight and it didn't really suit me. That was my reason for eventually going off it, although I still observe it from time to time. I didn't really notice any dramatic weight loss until I was in America two years ago and I had a picture taken with a Polaroid camera and I thought I had a neck like a giraffe. My clothes looked baggy, as opposed to fitting tightly, and I thought, 'I really don't look well.' My sight mightn't be the best, but I've got very good hearing, and I could hear people saying 'He's awfully thin, he's probably working too hard.' I realised then that I needed to start eating the *wrong* things again. And then I went on a binge where I thought I just had to put on some weight. I'm now around twelve stone, give or take four pounds any week. When I'm home I tend to put on weight because when you have a mother – and mothers are good and not so good sometimes – who makes pancakes and apple tarts, it's not so good. I would have two slices of tart for breakfast, followed by pancakes.

Nowadays I don't drink tea or coffee. I never liked coffee, but I loved tea and I had a reputation for drinking lots. When I was off with the voice trouble I went to a doctor in Dublin who tested me for allergies and I was put off literally everything, and that lasted for seven or eight weeks. The next thing I heard that he had dropped dead. I started eating everything as quick as I could!

On a day when I'm working I would boil the kettle and have hot water and a bar of chocolate. The morning for me is not morning, it probably starts at twelve o'clock so when I get up I eat any time from twelve to three. We would normally be within a stone's throw or a short drive of the theatre, wherever that might be. I would usually get there between half four and five and do the sound check. After a show I would normally have water and maybe a bar of chocolate, or if somebody had given in a cake I'd have a piece of that. I love chocolate – Walnut Whips, Twix bars, Mars bars – but I have to discipline myself. When I get back to the hotel I might have a sandwich. Occasionally we would stop at a motorway restaurant in the early hours of the morning and have a piggish meal, like sausage, bacon, black pudding, beans and chips. Then go to bed! So that certainly doesn't do much for the image now and then.

My manager Sean is the person I deal with more than anybody. There is nothing I do that he doesn't discuss with me. Sean will always ask, 'Do you want to do it? Are you happy with that?' It is always important to Sean that I am happy with whatever it is he is proposing. I usually follow the advice of Sean and Mick Clerkin, and I would value Mick's opinion greatly as well. I don't think anybody could achieve the success that Mick Clerkin has had without being shrewd and without making good decisions. So when things come up I kind of throw it back to them and if they are happy then I am happy to go ahead. If things were left up to me, I would not be where I am today, because I would have been too cautious. Maybe I'm afraid of failure, maybe that's why America creates that insecurity for me. Everybody is afraid of failure.

It's strange the image some people have of me, they think that because I'm working at a certain level in the entertainment business I must be living the superstar lifestyle. The reality is that I don't because I don't have extravagant needs and there are lots of things I wouldn't be at ease with. For instance, you wouldn't catch me dead in a limousine, unless, of course, there was a wooden box in the back of it. I remember one time I was performing at Birmingham's NEC and there was a limo there and people assumed it was mine. There was even one man who said he had actually seen me in it. But I wasn't even near it. We were staying in the Metropole Hotel, which is only a stone's throw from the venue, along a nice walkway with a big fountain in it. I walked to the NEC for the show and when it was over I just walked back.

I remember being really embarrassed when I did a signing at Harrod's in London and they sent a horse-drawn carriage for me. When I was getting in, I said to Ann Clerkin from Ritz, 'You'll have to get in with me, I just can't sit here on my own.' I thought to myself, 'Everybody is going to be looking at me.' We were going down through Knightsbridge and there were people staring in not knowing me from Adam. You see the thing about my success, compared to Cliff, is that everybody knows him, and I mean everybody, whether you like him or whether you don't, but not everyone knows me by sight.

I often travel by tube in London. If I don't have a car with me, I get on the tube at Heathrow. I think it's ridiculous to pay for a taxi when you can get on the tube. You see, people have this idea that if you have money there are certain things you shouldn't do, but with me that's not the case at all. I still look for the bargain. I love getting something cheap. I don't have time for people who show off what they have.

I am not obsessed with building up lots of possessions. That's not what motivates me or gives me pleasure. But, having said that, I do have a BMW. I used to drive a car which let in water. I got in the back one day and there was water coming up through the mat on the floor and I thought, 'Why am I doing this? Why don't I buy a decent car when I can afford it?' Then one day I bumped into a woman's car in Gweedore. I'm an OK driver, but I wouldn't be the best at manoeuvring in tight spaces. I did no damage at all to her car, but the front of mine was a mess. So I said, 'Right, that's the end of that!' I went to Dublin and I tried this BMW and I did think it was lovely, although I felt a little embarrassed. I sat in a Jag once and it was like being in an aeroplane, but I thought it was too flash. I thought, 'How could I go home in a Jaguar? I just couldn't do that, you know.' I probably could, but it took enough out of me going home in the BMW. It's a lovely car, but it wouldn't bother me if it was gone. I've got out of other people's cars and I've seen people looking at me and you can tell that they're thinking, 'What the hell is he doing in *that* car?'

I particularly remember somebody commenting one day, 'Surely you're not driving in that!'

And I just replied, 'It got me from where I was to here.'

I don't feel that what I have actually belongs to me. I don't feel that the hotel is mine, even though it is. Whenever I need to buy something and I phone my accountant to tell him, I'm actually embarrassed about it. It's like I'm taking somebody else's money. I'm like, 'Is it all right if I get this?' I feel nervous. I hadn't bought a car for nearly five years and I actually felt apprehensive. Isn't that incredible? I hate visits to the accountant. I really don't want to know about the business side of things. It is a pure drudge as far as I'm concerned, so I leave it to the experts and I'm confident that I have good people looking after me. I haven't a clue what I have in the bank. If you said to me, 'I'll give you a million pounds if you can tell me how much you're worth,' I just couldn't do it. When I read what they say in the papers, more often now than before the heading is 'the millionaire singer', or 'millionaire bachelor'. I just think, 'How could that be me?' All I know is that any time I want to buy something or pay for something I can always get the money. I don't know anything about the finances after that.

Now some people might read this and say, 'My God, that fella is just for the birds!' But I don't shower people with money. I don't give presents to people. It's not the way I am. As a family we are not like that. We don't give each other birthday presents. At Christmas time I would give money, but not a fortune. I know people probably think that that's miserly, but that's just the way things are. I might get a shirt from one person, a jumper from another. And probably what I give them only covers what they spent buying those presents for me. I don't buy things because I can't be bothered to go out and buy them. People will say, 'My God, he's not at all what I imagined, I thought he would be going out picking and choosing, "such and such a one would like this." ' I don't do that. I don't give my nieces and nephews lots of money. If they like me, they like me, if they don't, they don't. But I certainly don't want them to like me for what they get from me and that's not the case.

Material things don't give me any personal satisfaction. I don't wear jewellery at all. And I don't even possess a watch. I used to have a chain and a ring and I just thought, I really don't need those things. I wear nothing now. And I'm never late, even though I don't have a watch. I find without a watch you become a better judge of time. I felt I was always rushing when I had one, so I took it off. I took the ring off when I was playing golf and I thought, I don't need a ring. The chain went at the same time. But something I do own that gives me a lot of pleasure is a holiday home in Tenerife.

13. TENERIFE

I love my life for many reasons and I've never been happier since I moved home. Not that I get the chance to spend a lot of time in Donegal because my work takes me away for such long periods. But when I'm there I feel very content and very secure. I have such a lovely lifestyle and golf has become a big part of it. I've been bitten by the bug and it is now one of the big passions in my life. It's a great release for me. I feel very lucky. All my family and friends are around home and I have made new friends through playing golf. People like Carmel Bonner and Donal Gallagher. 'Carmel the Tigress' we call her, because she would fight to the last on a golf course and she plays well. I'm longing for the day when I take them all out and beat the pants off them. We have the best fun and we travel to play golf too. I would travel the world with those people. I am so comfortable with them. Carmel is funny, she would take you to task very quickly. Golf can sometimes be very frustrating because there are days when everything goes wrong and I often announce that I'm retiring, saying my clubs are bad, and Carmel looks at me and says, 'What kind of a clown are you? Chill out, chill out. Keep the head down and chill out.' She's chilling out when she's taking the £3 off us at the end of the game, that's her chilling! She's the tigress and we're the cubs.

Other than Donegal, there's another part of the world that has captured my heart and that's the holiday island of Tenerife in the Canaries. I have made it my second home in recent years and I go there whenever I can to recharge my batteries. I love the sun and always have done, although nowadays, with all the global warnings about what it can do to your skin, I tend to keep my face out of it. There's no point in helping nature to speed up the aging process! When I first went to Tenerife back in the Eighties it rained for a week and I thought it was the most awful place I'd ever been to. I certainly never imagined that one day I would actually buy my own apartment there and become a regular visitor.

My love affair with Tenerife happened through the daughter of a lady called Beatrice who used to come to my shows, Breda is her name. Beatrice was quite old and her health eventually deteriorated. I was doing Cilla Black's *Surprise Surprise* TV programme in London and I called home and there was a message from Breda saying her mother was getting worse, she was dying. That was quite strange because I wouldn't normally be in London and it was also a coincidence that I got the message on the day she phoned. So I called Breda and asked if she wanted me to come up and visit her mother and Breda said that would be great. Beatrice was kind of sleeping and waking, not in a coma, she said, but she was sort of sedated. Apparently the doctor was with her when Breda went back in and said, 'Mammy, that was Daniel O'Donnell on the phone, he is coming up to see you.' Beatrice's immediate response was, 'Where's my ear rings, get my lipstick and is there a film in my camera.' I arrived up at their home in Streatham and I could see that she was very ill. I spoke to her and she responded, but she was very tired.

During my visit that night, Breda brought up the subject of Tenerife. She owned an apartment there and she had suggested to me on several occasions that I should borrow it for a holiday. I'm always very reluctant to impose on other people or take advantage of situations. But that night Breda again mentioned it to me and taking up the offer seemed like the right thing to do at that moment. I told her when I had some time off and she said she'd book the flight for me. I left their home just before one o'clock in the morning and Beatrice died somewhere around six or seven o'clock that morning. When Breda told me the news she also had everything arranged for my trip to Tenerife and that's how I ended up back in that holiday isle.

Breda's apartment is beautiful and it was a different Tenerife that I returned to. From then on I kept going back. I loved staying at Breda's and a whole gang of us all went out together one time. One day I was sitting on the balcony and

◀ My parents in the year they were married, 1948.

▼ James and Margaret McGonagle, my grandparents on the maternal side, in 1959.

▶ A visit to my father's grave with my mother on the day of my First Communion.

▼ On my travels in Galway, with my sister Margaret (Margo), who was a singing star at the time. I was eight.

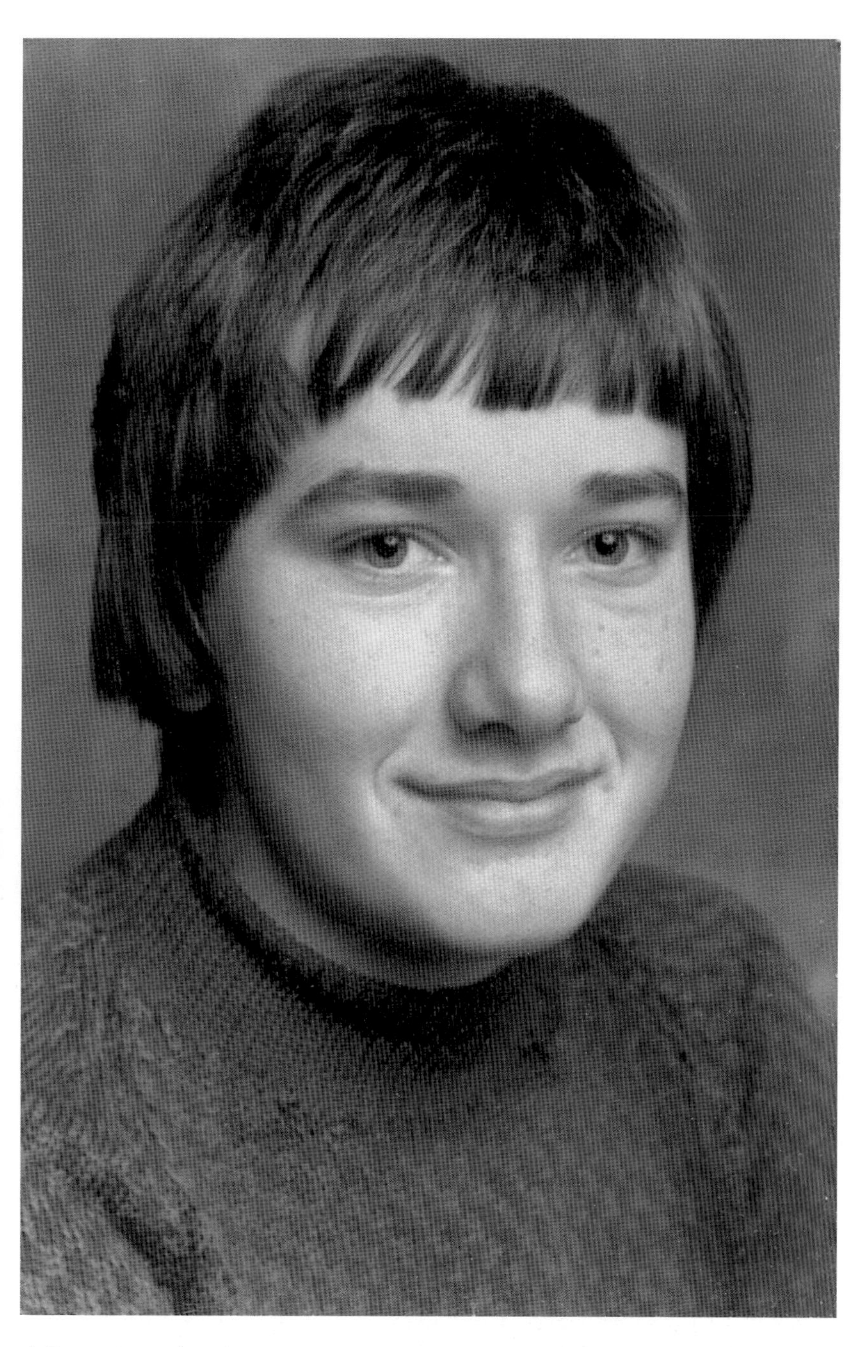

▲ Teenage years have arrived. I'm fifteen.

◀ My godchild Patricia, pictured in 1987.

▼ The Cope, where I worked as a boy.

▲ With Nan Moy, my first manager.

► Mick Clerkin, boss of Ritz Records, has given me enormous personal support over the years.

▲ My manager and dear friend Sean Reilly at the Hall of Fame in Tamworth in 1992.

▼ Josephine Burke is my closest friend and here we are meeting Irish soccer star Packie Bonner.

▲ The O'Donnell clan, pictured at the opening of my Viking House Hotel in 1993. From left to right: Kathleen, James, Margaret, my mother Julia, John and yours truly.

◀ Annie McGarvey, my neighbour, who taught me how to be a shark at cards. She also captured me on camera growing up.

◀ At home by the shore in my beautiful Kincasslagh.

▶ I started my working life washing dishes in a hotel. Later I owned one!

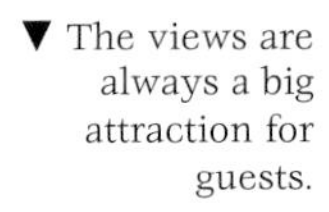

▼ The views are always a big attraction for guests.

I said, 'You know, Breda, if I wanted a place with a balcony or a terrace like this, I would look for it here, it's lovely, the privacy and having the sun all day.' Breda mentioned this to a friend called Alice and by coincidence there was a lovely place below her up for sale, a really nice apartment with a lovely balcony, and I bought it. I actually did so without seeing the inside. All I saw was the terrace from a neighbour's apartment and I bought it for that alone.

I loved the view of the sea, the openness, having the sun all day and the privacy of it. Since then I've grown to enjoy the social life around the Irish bars of Tenerife. Now I know that is not in keeping with the image people have of me, they wouldn't associate me with bars. And I was never one for going to the Irish bars, particularly somewhere like Tenerife because it's a place I go to for a break. But on one trip, I went to Mass and I met Ellen and Peter Duffy, who are from my home area of Donegal, but live in Coventry. After Mass, I went to eat with them. Ellen asked, 'Would you like to go to an Irish bar?' I reluctantly said yes because I didn't want to disappoint her as I felt she would like me to go with her. We ended up in three bars and that was the end of my rest in Tenerife! I never looked back after that night.

I would still not be a bar person, but I love the atmosphere in the bars of Tenerife. I really love it. The bars I go to all the time are the Hole In The Wall, the Irish Fiddler and the Dubliner and everything climaxes in the Dubliner. Whichever way you start out, you always seem to end up in The Dubliner. I do try to make it back home, but for some reason, whether it's a wind that just blows you into the Dubliner, I don't know, you just seem to end up there in the small hours. But I love the other bars too because they are all very different. The Dubliner is a very loud pub. I can't say it's a young person's bar, although the mix of people is varied in it. The Hole In The Wall is a nice bar and I enjoy the music, and the Fiddler is a sit-down, singalong type of place. So now I'm a regular on the bar scene when I go to Tenerife, although I can sit in for days and nights and not go anywhere, especially when I have no visitors.

Even though I don't drink I just soak up the atmosphere and it's great fun. Having said that, there was one occasion where I did have a few drinks too many and ended up in an awful state, even though they were purely for medicinal purposes. I arrived in Tenerife with a lot of friends, including nieces and nephews. We headed for the Irish Fiddler, as we normally do. I was coughing and spluttering and I said, "I feel shocking." I was in bad old form. So Noeleen, the owner, said she'd give me a hot whiskey. At home I would take one if I had a cold. I'd rarely take two. It makes you sleep and you sweat out the cold. So I proceeded to drink the whiskey and she said I should have another one. I took another one and didn't think much about it, and then when I got home I was offered another one and sure if I had any cop on at all I would have known I had enough. Unless it was going to blow things out of you, another would do no more than the two had done. But I had another one and all of a sudden I just couldn't coordinate my movements. A friend called Patsy was there with the gang and she started play acting, taking off my jumper and saying, 'We'll have a bit of nookie now.' Patsy is just a desperate case altogether! Another friend, Tess, was the only person I could see who had any sense and I remember looking at her and pleading, 'Please Tess, take them away, as I have no control.' We went to a disco then and I don't remember much about that. My mother will have a shock when she reads this. I was sick then, whether I was sick with the flu or from the whiskey, I don't know, more than likely the latter. So every time I go into Noeleen's Irish Fiddler bar in Tenerife now she asks me if I want a hot whiskey. That experience certainly solidified my thoughts about the drink.

I go to Tenerife, where I now have a new home, as often as my time allows and I love it, I really do. I like to think that in the years to come I will spend more time on the island because I do feel so at home there now. I have my favourite restaurants like the Swiss Chalet, Garibaldi's and there's a Chinese which is the best I've been to anywhere in the world. I don't walk a lot, it's not something I do. I will occasionally, depending on what humour is on me. I'm not big on swimming. It depends who is with me. If the people are pool people I will go down and swim. I haven't done much sightseeing. But I do enjoy the freedom to do whatever I want to do and there's no watching the clock. I meet an awful lot of people who would know me and I do enjoy that. Of course, I do also meet people who have no regard for me, but you get that everywhere. There are always people who try to bring you down, but you either bring them up or you flatten them and I won't say which I do most! I go to the bars and I know that for the first ten or fifteen minutes when I go in, people are going to want autographs, photographs or time to say hello, but then the fuss dies down and I can enjoy the evening like everyone else.

I enjoy meeting people who know me in those situations. It adds to my enjoyment of the night. If I want to go and sit down and talk to someone privately, there are places to avoid. But I want to be in an atmosphere that I enjoy and, whether it's good or bad for me, what I enjoy is the places where people know me. I don't go for them to know me, I go because that's where I feel comfortable. I know when I go in that I have to be prepared to accept people coming up to me, and that within fifteen minutes I am going to have met everybody. I don't actually call the people punters, I hate the word. I don't see them as them and me. I see it more as us and that's genuinely what I feel. People say, 'You must get fed up with all the fuss and attention.' But I honestly don't and I know people enjoy it and it probably adds something to their holiday. I've often made arrangements to meet people because on the night I dropped in unexpectedly to the Hole In The Wall they didn't have a camera; I would call back at a certain time the next night for them to get their picture with me. That doesn't cause me any pain whatsoever. It's a lovely position to be in and I do get a sense of satisfaction from it. Tenerife, of course, is where I met my wife Majella, as I will recount later.

14. THE FANS

There are no words to describe the feelings that I get from an audience when I perform on stage. It is heaven on earth to me. And it is a gift to me from people, the people who follow me and enjoy what I do. Without those people I would not have this life. They say that when you're doing a job you love, you never work a day in your life. Well, that is certainly the case with me. I have never worked since I became an entertainer. I just love every minute of it and I would be devastated if it was all taken away from me, if people no longer enjoyed what I do. So I have a great respect and great love for the people who follow Daniel O'Donnell the entertainer.

As I have said, not everyone appreciates what I do and some sections of the media have made that quite clear. On a personal level, I can accept that, because you have to when you're in the public eye. I might not like it, but I have to accept it. You have to take it on the chin because all personalities are sitting ducks. Some of it cannot be taken seriously, so I tend not to read stuff and just let it all pass over my head. But what really does make me angry are the attacks on the people who come to my shows and buy my records. I just cannot understand the narrow minded attitude of the media types who use the audience as some kind of weapon to poke fun at me and my style of entertainment. I've seen things written like 'blue rinsed, toothless, menopausal women'. Is that an invitation to the scrap heap if you're not young and of child-bearing age? Does that mean you don't deserve to be entertained? I remember one fellow in England who came and asked me what I thought of the audience, saying that they didn't have their own teeth. I turned around and said, 'To tell you the truth, as long as you can eat your dinner it doesn't matter whose teeth you have!'

You can't look at people in that way. I won't even mention his name, but in Ireland there was one journalist who wrote something about the audience to that effect, about menopausal women, and I have never experienced anything like the anger of some of the people who were at that particular show in Dublin's Point venue. It was the first time I performed there, in 1992. I went to play cards the next night at a Care For The Aged centre in Naas, County Kildare, and the ladies there were just seething with anger over his description. They had every right to be up in arms over it. It is a strange way to look at things, to dismiss people at a certain stage in their lives.

Another thing I find peculiar is that critics or reviewers or whatever you call them never see young people at my shows even though they are there. There have been a few articles in England where the writers have said they were surprised at the mix of ages and the mix of men and women. I don't read what's written about me now unless I'm playing a few nights in the same place and I hear that people have been upset over something that's been said about me and them in the papers. I was doing a series of shows in Cork City in Ireland and this journalist fella came in, bald as a coot, with his head shaved. Now that was fine by me, I wasn't going to judge him on his looks, just because he had a good shiny head on him. He interviewed me and I knew in my heart that this fellow wasn't a fan. Well, he went away and wrote a very unflattering piece. The next day there was so much annoyance from people I met in the hotel that I decided to get the piece and read it. He referred to the women's hair and their age, the usual kind of thing that these journalists home in on. So that night when I went out on stage and addressed the audience I referred to the newspaper article and I told them not to worry about it. I said, 'He talked about hair-dos, well let me tell you, he was here and he had a head on him like an enamel basin, and what he would have given to have one of your hair-dos!' And that just defused the whole thing. And every so often I would say, 'It's a good job the wee baldie fellow's not here tonight.' So instead of that article affecting what we do, I was able to use it to create a wonderful show. And it's the only way to treat something like that. Nowadays I'm more selective about the interviews I give because there's no point in talking to people who are just going to make fun of you and of the people who follow you.

I don't expect everyone to enjoy or appreciate what I do. If we all liked the same thing there would only be one market in one marketplace. I might go to an opera and be pulling my hair out because I wasn't able to appreciate it, but the person beside me might be in ecstasy over the whole thing. But could I come out and write rubbish about it? I don't have the right to do that. But people do it to me and they do it to others too.

While no one likes criticism and sometimes it can be very hurtful, I always take succour from the fact that it's not the people who write or comment about me in the media that are responsible for giving me a life that I love and work that I love and for which I thank God every day. I'm here doing what I do as a result of people enjoying what I do and appreciating me as a person and that's a wonderful feeling. It's the same with awards. The ones voted for by the public are always that extra bit special because they come from the people rather than the industry or the media. They are a true reflection of what people think of me as an entertainer and, possibly, as a person. I have been lucky to receive many awards, but the one I hold dearest to my heart is the 'Donegal Person of the Year.' That still rates as the best award I have received during my career. Why is it so special? Well, it's because it honours me as a person from Donegal. I love Donegal more than anywhere else in the world and I would challenge anybody to say I'm not being serious when I state that. To think that honour was mine in 1989! What is it about Donegal that has such a claim on my heart? It's the people, and it's the place too. I grew up with the people and I love being at home.

Another entertainment award that means a lot to me is the Irish 'Entertainer of the Year', which I've won three times, in 1989, 1992 and 1996. It means so much to me because it's also an award that's voted for by the people. I think it's marvellous that I love what I do and it's not such a great effort, yet it has brought me so much recognition and honour. In Ireland, the 'Entertainer of the Year' is the one everyone would like to receive and I never thought I'd get it once. And when I got it once, I certainly didn't expect it twice, never mind a third time. Awards don't generally mean that much to me. It's nice to get them, but the real award for me is when I go out in the middle of the stage and the people are there and we create something together.

I've always loved meeting people after shows, although I don't get the chance to spend as much time with everyone these days. In times gone by, I had a lot longer. Sometimes now I feel that I am meeting people too quickly and I would love to be able to say, 'We need to slow this down.' I know we can't slow it down because you'd be there all night. I do a long show and meeting people is not the norm for the majority of performers. So I know we have to keep it quick and that I can just go and say a quick 'Hello' to people and have a picture taken. Sometimes I think I'm not getting to know people as I used to. But what can I do about it? It's just how it has become. There are hundreds waiting after each show, and generally I'm there for about an hour and a half to two hours. But that extra hour is tiring, although I don't mind. If I'm tired, I'm tired. But I hate anybody telling me, 'God you look tired!' I would automatically get annoyed and say, 'God, I thought I looked great.' Joe Collum would be standing there muttering under his breath, 'Ooh, that's her finished, hmm, bad move!' It's like a film where there is a narrator: 'Bad move, bad move missus!' But I really don't like anybody saying, 'You look tired!' because when you do you don't look well, and I like to think I look well.

There was one night I ended up on the street with the fans after we were all evacuated by the police from a theatre in Middlesbrough following a bomb scare. As I got chatting with the people who had come to see the show, one woman told me that she had come specially to hear me sing 'The Old Rugged Cross'. So I decided to sing it there and then for her in the street! The police interrupted to say it would be safer if we all made our way to the local park, so we duly obliged. I got up on a park bench and sang another couple of songs. Then the police turned up again and this time they offered me the use of the loudspeaker in their panda car. I took them up on their offer and sang another few songs through the loudhailer. Now that was a night to remember!

ISLROMANIA [illegible] Then I made [illegible]
[illegible] and [illegible]
[illegible] show that the strength of [illegible]

[illegible]

Indeed, [illegible] on my hand, however, more
[illegible] with [illegible]
[illegible] I could make a difference.
[illegible] was what [illegible]
[illegible] looking for [illegible] Romanian
[illegible] spirit [illegible]
[illegible] of Sibiu. When she returned
[illegible] about the [illegible]
[illegible]

15. ROMANIA

If there is one event that has made an impact on my life in recent years, it's my visit to Romania to see at first hand the horrendous living conditions of the orphans and the young people who have been cast on the scrap heap in that part of the world. Their agonising plight would melt the hearts of the most hardened individuals in our society. To say I was shocked and horrified by what I witnessed would be an understatement. No words could adequately describe the horror that existed in the orphanages and homes I visited. But from that moment, my own life took on a new meaning and it has become intertwined with the Romanians in the Siret orphanage.

Romania is I would say probably the best opportunity I've been given in life to make a difference. There are fans who write and tell me how I've helped them cope with personal trauma. There was Ethel when her husband died and Mary when somebody close to her died and somebody else who never used to leave the house because she suffered from agoraphobia, but overcame those fears to attend my concerts. Time and time again people have written to me with stories, thanking me for bringing some joy and hope back in to their lives. It is so rewarding and fulfilling to think that I can enhance the quality of people's lives through what I do and the way I do it. It gives depth and meaning to my work. Helping people has always been in my mind, but never more so since Romania came into my life. It was then that I genuinely felt I could make a difference.

My first introduction to Romania was when Eileen Oglesby, a neighbour of mine, began working for the Romanian Orphanage Appeal charity, in the Spital De Copii Neuropsihici orphanage in the town of Siret. When she returned home on visits, Eileen talked about the situation that existed there and she showed us photographs. Sheila Mulholland, who worked with Donegal Tours, also went over to help out and she showed me the pictures she had and told me about the huge amount of work that needed to be undertaken there in order to bring some hope into the lives of those unfortunate people. While I was looking at the photos an idea came to mind and I said, 'Sheila, I have a song that seems like it's made for this.' I went out to the car and played it to her and she also felt that it was just right. It was a song called 'Give A Little Love'. It was only a demo, the writer had sent it to me and I hadn't recorded it at the time. So I then went to Sean Reilly and I discussed with him my plan to record 'Give A Little Love' as a charity single in aid of the orphanage. We then took the idea to Mick Clerkin and he gave it his blessing. So I recorded the song, and then I felt I should go to Romania to make a video to promote it and also to see who was going to benefit from the sales. At that time, in 1998, I had no intention of getting directly involved in the relief work that the volunteers were caught up in there. I thought I'd go out and make the video and promote the record and that would be it. My main aim at the time was to ensure the orphanage and the people there would benefit from the cash raised through sales of the single.

Eventually the arrangements were made and I found myself on a three-day visit to Siret where I stayed in a house with the charity workers. As I arrived at the orphanage and went through the gate for the first time, I gazed up a long avenue and saw children and young adults running towards me. I could see a lot of disfigurements and disabilities on that first meeting and the people just hugged me. They hadn't a clue who I was, what I was, what I was doing there, but they would hug anybody that came to see them and was prepared to hug them back. It was heart breaking to see people and children who'd been totally deprived of love and human warmth and kindness. But worse was to follow. We proceeded in to the orphanage and I went into one room and I thought, 'Jesus, I don't like this situation.' It's not that I personally didn't want to be there. It really was a house of horrors. All the children and young people were just sitting around vegetating. At first it seemed like there were only boys there and I thought, 'What has happened to the girls? How come there aren't any?' And then I realised there were girls, but they looked liked boys and I thought, 'It's unbelievable that something like this exists in this day and age.' They all had their heads shaved. They were sleeping about thirty to a room, and they were sitting around tables and they were all rocking back and forth. Some of them would stop rocking when you showed them attention.

I asked, 'Are all these children mentally or physically disabled?'

Monica McDaid, the Irishwoman in charge of the charity, replied: 'No, no. There are about three hundred of them who have no disability.'

'Why are they here?' I asked. Monica shrugged her shoulders, indicating that's just how it is. And she proceeded to explain about Ceaucescu, how he ordered that every family should have five children, but they simply couldn't afford to keep them and they gave them up and they ended up in these awful orphanages. When Monica arrived there in 1989, she found 1,700 children at the home I was visiting. The majority of them were actually living in the basement. It's a huge building and she said it had only eight light bulbs at the time. Most of it was in darkness. The inhabitants were living in a basement with water flowing on the ground, rats were scurrying around the place, there was no heating, and two or three children were tied to each cot. That's where many of the disabilities and deformities come from. During my time there, I realised that some of them were clever enough. There were those who would come and speak to you in English, and I discovered that they picked it up from listening to people. So many of them are very bright and they can learn if they are given the opportunity. One boy, Gheorghe, was able to play the guitar and I was amazed at that.

I went into one room and, although the place was actually done up for our benefit, it was still in a dreadful state.

Eileen tells it as it was. 'What the hell is going on here! Cushions out on the beds!' she said.

I was listening to her coming up behind me. She wasn't telling me, she was just commenting out loud, 'Jesus, Mary, cushions! I've never seen a bloody cushion here in my life.'

It was all for the cameras. The people running the orphanage there want help, but I suppose they don't want to look so bad. We were taken to an office by the authorities there and they told us not to show anything negative. I thought we weren't going to be allowed to do filming for the video of my song when we first arrived there, but they didn't stop us. There was one room I went into and, honest to God, it was the smallest room I'd ever seen. There was nobody sleeping in that room, there couldn't have been and if there was, I can't remember if there was a bed. The children were all sitting, there were about twenty of them, and they were small children and they were all wearing hats. The staff had been told to dress them and they took it literally, dressed them, everything they had they put on the kids and there they were with the hats.

I went around another ward where the children were all disabled and they were in cots and beds. One bed was soaking and I realised there were no people from the charity working there. I discovered they had been ordered from the ward because one of the Romanian workers, one of the people who works for the State, let one of the children fall. The charity people were blamed and the boss came and put them out of there. That's how they run things, and if you try to fight the system you are told to leave.

I was outside then and this teenager, Alan, he was about eighteen, came and sat beside me and asked, 'You are a singer?'

I said, 'Yes, I sing.'

He said, 'You're famous?'

I said, 'Ye-es.'

He says, 'You're rich?'

I said, 'Well . . .'

He asked, 'Do you make a lot of money?'

I said, 'Well . . . enough.'

He asked, 'Do you make a hundred thousand?' I don't know if he understood what a hundred thousand pounds was, because I can't imagine how he would understand what a hundred thousand pounds would be. You could have a handful of notes in their currency and it would only be worth fifty pence.

Anyway, I just looked at him and smiled. And he said, 'Oh, oh, you're a rich man! Are you going to help us?'

Alan was intense. He was asking these questions like, 'What are you going to do?'

I said, 'I'm going to try and help Monica to raise money so that she can bring you out of here.'

He asked, 'All the children?'

I said, 'Yes, all the children.'

And he put his arms around me and gave me a hug.

Another day, this wee girl caught my hand, she was maybe twelve, they are all small for their age. They all look five years younger than they are, and she was walking with me, and she was looking at me, really going at it big time – talking. I hadn't a clue what she was saying. There was a girl from the Irish Embassy there and I said to her, 'What's this one talking about?' I thought it was going to be funny.

The girl from the Embassy turned to me and said, 'She's asking if you'll take her home.' And all I could do was put my arm around her, and give her a hug.

But there was one wee boy that I really loved while I was there, not that I spent a lot of time with him, but when I came out of one of the rooms he got up and hugged me. There was one occasion when some of the children sang a verse from 'My Forever Friend', with Gheorghe playing the guitar, and I could see the wee fellow a couple of children away from me. He manoeuvred until eventually he was beside me and then he was happy. And the day I left he was at the gate and his was the last hand in my mine, he held my hand until I had to let him go – and then he just ran away. Afterwards, I used to see his face and I'd think, 'God, I'd love a picture of him.' And I thought, if I could adopt a child, he would be the one. I came back home and I thought about him, and talked about him and when the cover of the single came out, there he was, sitting right there in front of me. And that was just an incredible coincidence. I knew then that I had more to do in Romania.

I said, 'Monica, what do you want to do?'

She said, 'We want to bring them out of there, we want to build homes, we want to build a halfway house for the children, so that they can live normally and be rehabilitated. We want to build a group of homes for the handicapped, so that they can be allowed to progress, to be educated and taught work skills.'

I said, 'Monica, this is going to take a fortune!'

She said, 'I know.'

I asked, 'Is it going to take a million pounds?'

She said, 'At least.'

I remember thinking, how do you go about raising a million pounds? Then I thought, if I ask a million people for a pound each, then it's not really that big an undertaking. At no time in Romania did I feel hopeless because I knew I was going to do something. I wasn't happy with what I had seen, but I never felt helpless or that it was hopeless. Some of the other people who were with us when we were there had cried.

We visited an old folk's home while we were there and I'll never forget it. What I saw there, the living conditions of the people, was just so shocking that you couldn't describe it. It was the most undignified and degrading situation I have ever seen. People were sleeping in beds that were right up against each other. They had neither top nor bottom to climb out. And it was men and women mixed. There was a girl with us from GMTV and when we came out she just went to pieces. She broke down and she cried and cried. The journalist from *Hello!* magazine who travelled with us was very upset as well. What I thought was, 'I'm going to go for this, I'm just going to go for it.' I decided that the children would be my priority.

From the time I returned home all I did was talk about it, at every opportunity. Everywhere I went, I talked about Romania and the plight of the people there and what was required to give them a chance in life. I haven't done that much really, I suppose, but I've been given a voice and a platform to talk about the situation. And when I speak, many listen because of the position I'm in. I know there are other places in the world that are facing terrible disaster and where there is severe poverty. I know that there are situations in Ireland that need attention. But this is where I found myself. I couldn't even go to Romania and look at their national problem. I couldn't consider the other problems in Siret. I could only look where I was brought. I couldn't even start saying, 'What are we going to do about the old folks' home?' I can't do that. No one man or woman can do everything. I hope there are other people who will go to those other places, give help, be it in Ireland or England or wherever. The children's orphanage has become my mission and I believe strongly that what we are doing is right. What we are doing is helping children that have had absolutely no chance or will have no chance of progressing in life without our help.

When the single, 'Give A Little Love', was released in April 1998 it entered the UK pop charts at number 7. Another thing I did to start the fund-raising was encourage people at my shows to go away and think how they could be a part of this project. The response of people has been incredible. They have organised walks, runs, cycles, marathons, cake sales, coffee mornings, dances, you name it. And it doesn't matter how big or how small the contribution, it all adds up at the end of the day. There was one Down's Syndrome boy who did a sponsored reading to raise money. I've met him and things like that make it all worthwhile.

I've had big cheques, small cheques, medium-sized cheques, every sized donation from the smallest to the largest. Even if it's only twenty pence, if five people give that, it's a pound. And twenty-five people makes five pounds. It all adds up and it does make a difference. So you see, even if you think there is nothing you can contribute, then think again. It doesn't matter how small the contribution, it will be gratefully accepted and you can be a part of the big drive to help those people in Romania.

16. THE PRINCESS, THE PRESIDENT AND *TOP OF THE POPS*

It's a long way from Kincasslagh to *Top of the Pops*, but against all the odds I finally made it on to the famous BBC TV show that so many of us have grown up with, with a song called 'I Want To Dance With You' in 1992. I was on tour in Australia when the word came through that the single was selling very well in the British pop charts, so I was excited by that as it was something new to me. Initially, we heard it was number thirty-eight and then it went up to number thirty, so we decided we should go home a day early to perform on the show. I thought it was just incredible that this was happening. My manager Sean, who was with me on the trip, phoned home when we reached Singapore and we got the news that things were looking good for an appearance. I wanted to shout the news from the rooftops, as it was beyond what I thought I would ever achieve.

I was always being asked in interviews about my ambitions and for a time I answered that I was just happy to be doing what I was doing. But the interviewers grow tired of that, so then I would tell them about some ambition or other, just for a change. One day this reporter asked me out of the blue, 'What's your ambition for the future?' I couldn't think of anything at first, but then I said I wouldn't mind going on *Top of the Pops*. I can still vividly see his reaction, he was astonished by my reply. I don't normally remember people who interview me, but when I do, it's for all the wrong reasons. This fella didn't even bother to write down my reply. He just looked at me and said, 'Would you not need to change your image, change the songs you sing, to get on *Top of the Pops*?' Well, I can tell you, I wasn't very impressed with those remarks. They certainly poured cold water on the interview. But the strange thing about that incident is, it didn't happen long before the call home to appear on the show. At the time, it seemed really star-like that I had to come back from Australia to do *Top of the Pops*. But the call came through and this Kincasslagh kid was only too happy to answer it.

I recall being really anxious as I travelled to the BBC studios on the day. I remember thinking, maybe when I reach the gate they'll ask, 'Daniel who?' I thought I'd feel like a fish out of water, turning up with all the trendy young pop acts. But I didn't experience any problems when I arrived. I must say, everyone was very nice to me. There were lots of popular acts from that period on the show with me, including a group called The Shamen. It was such an unusual experience and it was great, just terrific. Looking back, I still regard it as an unbelievable time in my life. I remember seeing stars like Suzi Quatro on the programme as a kid, but I never thought I'd see the day when I'd be one of the performers on the show. I used to joke about it, but I didn't ever honestly think that my records would sell that much. Getting there is a major landmark in the life of any performer in the music business. The first thing you notice when you go in is that it's a lot smaller than you think. There are several stages and you see all the other performers wandering around the corridor backstage. It was a big deal for me and I was nervous. Even after I finished and went back to the dressing room I was nervous, although maybe it was excitement. And then I went home and the following weekend there was the All-Ireland with my native Donegal bidding for the All Ireland football crown. As I've mentioned, they won and 'I Want To Dance With You' went up to number twenty in the British charts. It was like a double victory for Donegal and for me personally.

One of my regrets is that I didn't write songs. It wasn't a talent I felt I had, nor did I feel driven to do it. As a result, I had to depend on other people for my songs and they came to me in various ways. Some of them were obvious, they're classics or standards and I'd sing them or record them if they were right for me. I was also lucky to be offered good original compositions. I suppose as you gain popularity and you sell albums, there's money to be made, so songwriters pitch their creations to me. But I also think that writers like their 'little babies' to go to people who will respect them. Writing a song must be like giving birth in a way, because it's something you create. I don't do it, but I would imagine that's how the writers feel about their work and I'm sure they want them to be used in the best possible way. I want the writer to be happy with what I've done and how I've interpreted it. I would never sing a song just because somebody tells me it's guaranteed to be a hit record. I have to have a feel for the track and believe in it, and if I felt I couldn't sing it, I could not sing it.

So what's a good song to me? When I'm given something I listen to the melody first and then I listen to the words. I don't like songs that move through different chord sequences a lot. I find them difficult and I think they're demanding to listen to. So I listen to the music first, then I listen to the words and both have to be right. There are songs I love listening to, but that are not right for me to sing because I feel they don't tell a story that I would like to tell.

And when the music and the story come together, I have no hesitation in doing the song. It's a matter of waiting for the right occasion, as sometimes songs grow on me. The first time I heard 'The Last Waltz Of The Evening', I didn't like it at all. But the first time I sang it, I loved it. It was written by an American songwriter, Tom Pacheco, who was living in Ireland, and it came to me when I was doing my TV series *The Daniel O'Donnell Show*, back in 1989. We invited Irish songwriters to write material and we used a song every week as part of the show. 'The Last Waltz' was one of them. I don't instantly dismiss songs, unless they're saying something I wouldn't say, stories I wouldn't tell.

It was Ritz boss Mick Clerkin who found my second number one record, 'My Shoes Keep Walking Back To You', after he came across it in Nashville. Mick has a good ear for the songs that will suit me. The record also featured 'Far Far From Home', which was written by Hugh Donoghue from County Cavan. He's one of my favourite writers as I also recorded another of his songs, 'Eileen', which appears on my

Best Of . . . album. The late Mary Sheridan is another songwriter whose work I like and I put 'Letter From The Postman's Bag' on the *Best Of . . .* album. I'm also keen on the work of John Farry from County Fermanagh. He wrote 'Summertime In Ireland' and 'Lough Melvin's Rocky Shore', both of which I have recorded. Songwriters send me material all the time and, in general, Irish writers have served me well.

'My Donegal Shore' is the most important song of all to me. Without it, I would never have achieved anything. It's also very special to me because it mentions Donegal. But it also has a special place in my heart because it became my first hit in rural Ireland, thanks mainly to the pirate radio stations who picked up on it. Then it travelled over to the Irish in Britain through RTE radio, so it weaved the magic for me. For my album, *The Very Best Of Daniel O'Donnell*, it was the first one to be chosen. That album also features 'I Need You', which helped me to cross over to a wider audience. 'Our House Is A Home' is another of the songs on that album that I always do in concert. It's a very simple song about a simple time in Ireland and it expresses the sentiments that I felt when I was growing up. Anybody who has been to my part of the world will know you're always assured of a cup of tea, and a good welcome when you're visiting an Irish home, and all the other things that are mentioned in the song.

My first number one record in the Irish pop charts was a song called 'Take Good Care Of Her', released back in 1987. It was a double A side, with 'Summertime In Ireland'. It's another of those songs that has a special meaning for me, because your first number one record is always a bit special. I can still vividly recall the excitement of getting to number one in August of that year. I tuned in to the Irish charts show on Radio 2 and listened to the country's top DJ Larry Gogan doing the countdown and finally announcing that Daniel O'Donnell had gone to number one with 'Take Good Care Of Her'. It sent tingles of excitement down my spine. All my hard work and often enormous struggle had paid off.

My first entry into the British Country Chart was with the album, *I Need You*, back in March 1987. When my tour director, Eamon Leahy, told me it had gone in at number fourteen, I was taken by surprise. I must have been very naive at the time because I didn't even know that there there was a British Country Chart. Three months later, my earlier album, *The Two Sides Of Daniel O'Donnell*, made it into the same charts and on October 31 of that year, *Don't Forget To Remember* made it to number one in the UK Country Chart within *one week* of its release.

Videos, of course, are very important nowadays, and I have had to embrace them as they are requested by music shows like *Top of the Pops*. People also want them and there's a demand for them. Recording, photo shoots and videos may not be the favourite parts of my work, but they are important for promotion. 'An Evening With Daniel O'Donnell', the live show recorded in Dundee, Scotland back in 1990 is still my favourite.

I have done a lot of TV in Britain and I would like to do more because I've enjoyed what I've done in the past. *The Mrs Merton Show* is the programme that stands out. She was very irreverent, was that Mrs Merton. But I loved every minute of it. And I suppose I was a wee bit naughty on it. I had never seen the show before I agreed to appear on it. I don't get to see a lot of TV due to the fact that I do so many live shows every year. I do watch *Coronation Street* quite a bit, as it's one of my favourites. I had seen Mrs Merton in a TV advertisement. But I had never seen her show and when I told the audiences at my shows that I was going to be on *The Mrs Merton Show*, there was a shocked reaction. Then I had people writing to me, telling me that I shouldn't go on and to be careful. So I got videos of her show to watch, but then I made a decision not to watch them because I thought I was going to get, not frightened, but I would have an idea of what she was going to be like to me and I would rather not know. So I didn't know and I went on and I must say I enjoyed it immensely. Now, whether it was the fact that her grandmother had warned her to be nice to me, I don't know. Her grandmother lives in Gort, County Galway, and I met her on the evening of the show. I met Caroline before the show as

Caroline, and when she dresses for Mrs Merton she becomes Mrs Merton, even in rehearsal. But there's no rehearsal with the chat. You don't know what she is going to be at.

There was one moment where I was caught on the hop after Mrs Merton introduced 'trumping' into the conversation. I had never heard the term before and I told her as much. But she persisted with the line of questioning, asking me if I trump.

I insisted, 'I don't know what that means. I really don't know if I do that or not.'

So Mrs Merton explained it to me and I forgot myself and said, 'Oh, you mean farting!'

Needless to say, that got a laugh. It's a funny show, but she could tear you to shreds at the same time. But I think she did like me, she gave me a relatively easy time and I survived to tell the tale. I've seen people on it since then who she has really given a good going over. I remember Shane Richie being grilled on it and at one point he said, 'I should have listened to my mother.' He was very funny on it, just terrific. He laughed all the time. I don't think the way to be with her is aggressive or defensive. On a personal level, I thought Caroline herself was nice. I didn't spend a lot of time with her, but in the time I was with her she was very friendly and we got on well.

The people involved in television at home in Ireland are very good to me. Anything that I've wanted to be on, if it's possible to put me on, they've done it. One of the Irish TV chat shows I've always enjoyed doing is the *Late Late Show*, which was hosted by Gay Byrne. In Ireland we all grew up with the *Late Late Show* and with Uncle Gaybo, as he's affectionately known, both on TV and radio. Gay is acknowledged as having had a major influence on Irish society through the programme. He tackled all kinds of subjects. He brought things out in the open, got us to deal with them and helped us to progress. Gay also went into the *Guinness Book of Records* as being the longest running TV chat show host in the world, beating the great Johnny Carson from America. They say a prophet is never recognised in his own land, but that is not true in Gaybo's case. He's idolised and has received the ultimate accolade of being bestowed with the Freedom of the City in Dublin, joining luminaries such as former American President John F. Kennedy. Like everything in life, all good things eventually come to an end and this year he brought the curtain down on his career in radio and TV. Gay will be sadly missed.

Gay was very good to me, whether it's the fact that he has a soft spot for Donegal or just likes me, I don't know, but he has always been more than nice to me and he would never let a word be said against me on air and, I'm sure, off air as well. I loved watching him and listening to Gay as a presenter. I really enjoyed his style of broadcasting. I can't remember what I sang the first time I was on the *Late Late*, but it was, of course, a big deal to be on the show. And then to get an interview, that was a major affair. But I also enjoyed the ultimate honour of being the subject of a special tribute show and that was one of the best I have ever been involved with on television. That was a great year for me, 1996. I performed at The Point in Dublin and it was a tremendous success. At the end of the year I won the 'Entertainer of the Year' award in Ireland. All those wonderful things happened for me over the space of a few weeks. It was a really high point in my life.

I'm glad to say that I have something special in common with Gay Byrne – we both share a love of Donegal. Gay and his lovely wife, Kathleen, have a holiday home in my county. We often meet. I've been round to their home. I do believe I could drop in any time and there would be a welcome. I really think they are very hospitable. Local people have accepted them as part of the area and that's hardly surprising as they've been coming to Donegal for years. Gay is going to be a such a big loss as a broadcaster. It's the end of an era, there will never be another Gay. There will never be anybody like him ever in Irish broadcasting or, indeed, in the world. Gay could go right across the spectrum of topics and I'm sure there are subjects he talked about that he didn't know about, but you wouldn't know what they were. I'll miss Gay, he's the nearest we have to royalty in Ireland.

Speaking of royalty, I was also honoured to be part of a Royal Gala Concert in Birmingham, which took place in June 1996 in the presence of Princess Anne and also featured top entertainers like Cliff Richard, Chris de Burgh, David Essex, Salena Jones, Beverly Craven and Dale Winton. It was a wonderful evening in aid of the Save The Children fund. It was a special occasion for me and the day after I received a Silver Heart award, presented to entertainers for their contribution to charity, and it's one that I really cherish. After the concert in front of the patron, Princess Anne, all the performers were introduced to her, including this fella from Kincasslagh. I was a bit nervous as I stood in line for the 'meet and greet', as it's called. As we waited for the Princess to enter the room, I remember thinking my hand was sweating. It's funny the things that happen like that. I had a tissue and I was wiping my palm every now and then while we waited in line for the big moment. Then Princess Anne came in wearing *gloves!* And there was me fretting for nothing over my hand being sweaty!

Princess Anne had a brief conversation with me about Donegal and how difficult it must have been for me to tear myself away from that lovely part of Ireland. I don't know if she has been there herself or not. But she voiced the opinion that it was a lovely place and that Ireland, in general, is a beautiful country. I absolutely loved being part of that show, particularly as I was sharing the same bill with Cliff and I joined him on stage along with Salena Jones to sing 'Congratulations'.

Well, from a Princess to a President . . . I've been keeping some good company in recent years. During 1998, I was a guest of the Irish President Mary McAleese at Aras an Uachtaráin, the presidential home, in Dublin's Phoenix Park. I really enjoyed that. It was a ceremony for the Gaisce Awards, as they're called, recognising achievements by young people. I had presented them a number of years ago when Mary Robinson was President. You present them on behalf of the President. I felt it was a great honour to be there with the President of Ireland and I find Mary McAleese to be a really warm, down to earth President. She is a President you can call Mary, you don't have to stand on ceremony and be formal. I think it's wonderful that the office of President is held by somebody I can identify with on a personal level. I couldn't always identify with other Presidents. If I see Mary McAleese, I will make my way to her. I would never have done that before. I also had the honour of being asked to sing for the President at a special function organised for her in Australia later that year. That was something wonderful for me on a personal level, to think that so far away from home they thought me worthy of being a part of the evening. I sang a few songs, including her favourite, 'Will You Go Lassie Go', because I had been told that's the first song she and her husband Martin danced to on their wedding day. I love it myself.

But the day in Phoenix Park really stands out in my mind. When you stand in front of Aras an Uachtaráin and sing for the President it is a bit special. It was great, we had tea on the lawn then the President and her husband, Martin, came and sat with us. It was lovely to see her doing ordinary things like sitting eating a bag of crisps. Presidents don't generally do that in public, but Mary McAleese did. I gave her one of my buns, and you don't normally do that with Presidents. I remember saying to her, 'Did you get a bite at all?' because she was so in demand and obviously hadn't had the chance to eat. So I said, 'Here eat this bun.' That's the kind of laidback atmosphere she generates around her. You just forget she's the President. So those are all terrific memories.

17. MARY DUFF AND 'THE FAMILY'

It has often been said that Mary Duff and myself make 'a lovely couple.' People feel that looks-wise, we complement each other. I remember when we first went on tour to Australia, the media and the public were of the mistaken impression that we were an 'item'. So we had to tell them that Mary's husband, Paul, might have something to say about that. I don't think they've made a bed that's comfortable for three yet!

Two nuns went up to Mary one time after a show and said, 'It's a pity you and Daniel didn't get married. You'd be lovely together.'

There's never, ever been a romance between Mary and myself. She was dating Paul when we first started working together. They say you should never mix business with pleasure, so fortunately we've never had that complication in our lives. From our very first meeting, I knew that I would enjoy the partnership with Mary as she's such an easy person to be around. I admire the way she conducts herself and the professional manner in which she approaches her work. It's been a happy marriage, musically speaking. Finding Mary was another great day's work by Sean Reilly.

Mary was working with Meath County Council in Ireland, issuing driving licences, when she entered the Dwans Sunday World Search For A Star contest. Sean was at the final and spotted Mary's huge potential. He was managing me at the time and my career was growing to the point where I needed a full-time support act for the shows. Sean asked Mary if she would be interested in the job, so she packed in her daytime work for the Council and went on the road as a singing star in her own right. This was back in September 1987. She has grown with the Daniel O'Donnell show, as she was there from the very early stages. When we first started working together the shows were often only half full. So Mary wasn't initially thrown in at the deep end. She was part of the whole struggle to get where we are today.

When I'm not touring, Mary goes off and does her own shows. Another very pleasing aspect of our partnership is that many of the people who come to my shows and buy my records, videos and books have also crossed over to Mary. And if husbands and boyfriends are reluctantly dragged along to my concerts, well they always have Mary Duff to take the pain away!

From the very start, Mary and I gelled instantly. She is such a lovely person and we get on great. We don't by any manner or means live in each other's pockets when we're working together and, indeed, the same is true of the rest of the band. It's healthy to give each other a lot of space. But Mary and I would never have any trouble with each other. And, singing-wise, our voices blend together so well, compared to mine and my sister Margaret's, whose range is totally different to mine. Margo and I did one record together – a song called 'Two's Company' (we are the only brother and sister ever to have a number one record in Ireland) – but the key changes more times than a catwalk model. If Margaret and I were able to sing together we would have recorded at least one album.

Mary started singing in a band at the age of twelve. Her father had his own group, so the young Mary would often step out into the limelight. It was a bit like Margaret and myself. I recall how as a twelve year old, I got up on stage with Margo one night in The Palm Court venue in Belmullet, County Mayo, and sang 'Little Cabin Home On The Hill' and 'The Philadelphia Lawyer'. That was a great experience for me. So Mary had a similar background. Through the years she performed at church socials and local dances, performing ballads and *céilí* music. Her first major experience in the business was with a semi-professional band called New Dimension and later she joined Jukebox, a professional rock 'n' roll band.

I have always said that talent shows are a great means of showcasing what you have to offer. And I would say to anyone starting out in the business or dreaming of becoming an entertainer, no matter what it takes or where you get the chance to perform, go for it. Even if it's nerve racking or if you don't win or if it's just a low key event, go for it. It will be worth it for the experience alone. And you never know who might be there watching. Mick Clerkin signed her to Ritz Records after seeing her competing in the Cavan Song Contest in Ireland.

Since that, Mary has gone on to make an impression in Europe, winning the 1989 Euro Country Music Masters competition in Tilburg, Holland. She beat the cream of the business from eleven other countries, so it was a very prestigious win. It was a victory that raised her profile in Europe and led to regular appearances there, including the Floralia Festival in Holland and the Albisquietli Festival in Switzerland. Mary is now a big attraction in Australia, having toured there with me and also in her own right. While she has won many awards as an entertainer, like myself, the one that she holds dear is the 'Meath Person of the Year' in 1990. It was awarded to her by the people of the county that Mary calls home. Just as I have a love affair with Donegal, Mary is a proud Meath woman. She said at the time: 'Being acclaimed by my own folk, in my own county, gave me a great thrill and I am proud to represent them and my county wherever I may be.'

Apart from working with me, Mary also supported American country superstar Garth Brooks when he staged his first show in Britain, playing London's Cambridge Theatre in 1991. From her native Meath to Melbourne, Mary continues to enthral audiences around the globe.

I feel very comfortable with all the people around me and I think that is important in any working environment. If you're not happy with the people you're working with, then obviously you'll be distracted and you won't produce your best work. Naturally, people rub each other up the wrong way every now and then, but that is the normal cut and thrust of any relationship. As long as you can deal with problems and get them out of the way, then that is fine. There are times when I have a short fuse and when my temper blows I have a wild, sharp tongue. There would be no answer to what I might say, even though I'm not always right. It's usually the people I think most of that I lose my temper with, but fortunately that doesn't happen very often.

My band and crew on the road are like a second family to me. Not surprising, considering how long we spend with each other, as I do tour very extensively every year. We all get on very well, but we don't spend all our time in each other's company. That would probably be disastrous. I could end up going anywhere with any of them and I could be with none of them. When I am on tour there are none of them that I wouldn't want to be with, and there isn't anyone that I want to be with. I get on better with some of them, but in general, if we're going out for a meal, any of them could be there.

Ronnie Kennedy, who plays accordion and keyboards, is the longest with me. Ronnie and I have been together since 1984, more or less. Because we are so close, we're the ones most likely to occasionally spark off each other. If there's tension, Ronnie and I will bring it out in each other. A native of the Dublin suburb of Ballyfermot, he was a founder member of my original band, The Grassroots, which lasted two years. Prior to that, he worked for fourteen years with the Irish singer Johnny McEvoy.

Billy Burgoyne from Ballinasloe, County Galway, is the band leader, as I've mentioned, so I rely on him a lot. If there's ever anything troubling me about the show, something I'm not happy with, I would go to Billy and discuss it. Prior to joining me, Billy worked with an Irish band, The Hillbillies, for twelve years and he spent five years with a pop outfit called Jukebox. Mary Duff was a singer in that band, as I mentioned. Billy made one of his earliest appearances with me as a session musician on the album, *The Two Sides Of Daniel O'Donnell*.

I remember going down to the Nashville Rooms in Moate, County Westmeath, to meet my band after I joined Ritz Records. They called it the Nashville Rooms because they were rehearsing there, but it was only a wee room. I think there's a theatre built on the site now. A guy called Pearse Dunne was the other member. We didn't know each other on

▲ Taking a moment to relax before one of my concerts

▲ The 12th of December 2001 and I've reached the ripe old age of 40!

▲ Sealed with a kiss – my wife Majella

◄ I take Majella down to the waiting fans to show off my beautiful bride

▼ We were delighted as the crowds turned out on the streets to see us on our wedding day

▶ Receiving my MBE from Prince Charles in Dublin

▶ Taking a call on Houston PBS with attorney John Raley © Houston PBS (KUHT-TV)

▼ My *Daniel In Blue Jeans* album reached No. 3 in the UK charts in 2003 and here I am receiving a gold disc for it outside the Royal Albert Hall. *Left to right* Ann Clerkin, Adrian Sear (Demon Music Group), Daniel, Michael Niedus (Demon), Michael Clerkin

◀ Getting that cowboy feeling in Texas on my US tour

▼ Receiving the Red Book from Michael Aspel watched by Eddie Rowley and John Brown

◀ The Mary from Dungloe is a festival built around a local legend. The competition to find a lady to represent 'Mary' for the year attracts entrants from all over the world.
In 1994 Sarah Mulholland, who worked in my Viking House Hotel, entered and won. I had the job of crowning the winner and it was an emotional moment as the tears spilled over for both of us.

▶ The award that means most to me is the Donegal Person of the Year, which I won in 1989. My mother was there to share the occasion.

◀ My turn to hold Sam Maguire, the All Ireland football cup, following Donegal's first-ever victory in 1992. Every man, woman and child in the county touched the trophy during the celebrations.

▶ With Gay Byrne, former presenter of Ireland's legendary *Late Late Show*, who has a holiday home in Donegal and shares my love for the county.

▲ I just thought I had died and gone to heaven when Loretta Lynn was the surprise 'belle of the ball' at the 1997 Donegal shore festival.

► A night out with Cliff. He was so down-to-earth as a person.

◀ and ▼ The farm in Siret, Romania, has enriched the lives of the young orphans

sight back then, so it was a strange meeting. I went in and I met another member called Tony Murray and I assumed he was Pearse. Tony didn't know me, but he figured that Ronnie must be the singer Daniel O'Donnell because at the time I looked too young to be singing!

Tony Murray, who plays bass guitar, is from Athlone, County Westmeath. Before becoming a musician, Tony earned his living doing a wide variety of jobs. He worked in a record shop, he was a barman. When he eventually decided to become a full-time musician, Tony joined Jukebox. John Staunton, who is from Ballintubber, County Roscommon, performed with me on my first recording session. He has worked with several bands in Ireland, including the entertainer T. R. Dallas. Billy Condon, who was with me from 1987, left two years ago. His experience ranges from céilí music to orchestras. Billy trained as a teacher before moving in to music. He started out as a classical musician, then joined the traditional Irish group, Napper Tandy. He was also a member of Irish country singer Ray Lynam's Hillbillies for eleven years. John Ryan and Kevin Sheeran joined in 1988 and they were with me until 1992 when I temporarily went off the road due to my illness. John Ryan has produced all of my albums except *The Two Sides Of Daniel O'Donnell* and *The Last Waltz*. I feel comfortable working with him in the studio and he knows how to bring out the best in me.

When I returned to touring, John and Kevin decided to continue working in their own areas. John had gone into production and he's still my producer. After my return, Richard Nelson joined the group on steel guitar. He's a native of Ahoghill near Ballymena, County Antrim. Prior to joining me he worked as a session musician in Belfast and Dublin and was a member of a number of bands, backing performers like Mary Duff and Logue and McCool. Richard left my band in 2002 to work in Ireland and Kevin Sheeran returned. Raymond McLoughlin also joined us on piano at that stage. His parents are from Swinford, County Mayo, but he was born and reared in London. Raymond joined my band straight out of college, and was part of our big show at The

Point in Dublin. So he started at the top! Stephen Milne, who played in Mary Duff's band, is now part of my line-up as well. So that's the band, they are a terrific bunch of people. When we tell people how long we've been together, they are always amazed that we have stayed together that long as a unit.

We have a great road crew, working behind the scenes, and they all play their part in the tours. Without the guys like Joe Dunne, Eddie Marron and Glyn Owen, who drive and set up all the equipment and do all that sort of work, I would be in deep, deep trouble. Padraig Grogan has been doing the sound since the late 80s. I do believe that soundwise he has found what we want. You can listen to it without it demanding anything from you. John Brown is the man responsible for looking after the lighting. I really didn't appreciate the importance of sound and lighting when I started performing. But I have come to realise that you can make the show that bit more effective and more impressive by the lighting, the setting and the mood they create. Gary Warner does the monitor sound, which is the sound I hear on stage. He's a very calm person and just as well because I do test his patience very often. I'm very hard to please where the sound is concerned and Gary has been very accommodating. Once I have a sound I'm happy with I can concentrate on the performance, so Gary is essential to me. Another lady in the 'family' who's well known to the fans is Loretta Terry, formerly Loretta Flynn, who I've mentioned before, from Waterford in Ireland. I first met Loretta when she started coming to my shows in 1984/85 with her sister and cousin. We struck up a friendship, and Loretta started doing the Fan Club in about 1986. It was originally formed by a girl from Galway called Maria Dirrane and then Loretta took over. Tina McMenamin started to do the Irish side of it and Loretta did the rest. Then it got very big and when Ritz moved into offices in Kilburn, Loretta went and worked there. Whenever we did shows in England, from 1986 on, Loretta would come along. I was always ironing shirts and she'd say, 'Give me that, I'll do that for you.' Now I find it a great relief having someone to do that for me, but at the time I didn't see the need to employ someone else to do it. So, eventually, Loretta became a permanent fixture on the road, looking after the stage gear and all kinds of odds and sods. When the Fan Club reached a certain level, it was decided that a couple of people would have to be employed to work on it. So Loretta is on the road with me full-time. She now looks after all the mail that I receive at the theatres. She sorts the letters out in to different piles, ones to be answered or requests. Before shows I then sit down in the dressing room and I try to answer as many letters as possible.

Joe Collum, of course, is like my shadow. Wherever Joe is, Daniel is not far behind, and vice versa. Joe is definitely my right-hand man. I'd be lost without him. But he has become famous with the fans in his own right because they all know him by sight and they have a lot of contact with him. Do you know, there are times when I've been with Joe and people would see him and not me! If I go to Mass on a Saturday evening when I'm on tour, I might have to go through the theatre I'm playing and Joe would be with me. People might see Joe and not see me. So, maybe if I need to get in somewhere without causing a fuss, Joe is not the best person to be with because he would get me caught! But I rely an awful lot on Joe, I really do. He has a great way about him, but at the same time, a lot of people think he's very cross. He has a stern look sometimes. But I think he only puts it on. It's the same with a guard dog, when you rub him down he just melts. It's amazing how you grow accustomed to not being able to do things like walk through a theatre on the night of a show. I can't do it because it would cause all kinds of hassle, so if I need to get something, Joe is the one who would handle it. Over the years Joe has become a very close friend. I'm very lucky to have such good personal friends working with me. If I'm troubled I could go to Joe or Sean or Loretta. There are not many people who have such true friends, people you can totally rely on and trust with your personal business.

Mick Clerkin of Ritz Records is the man who made it all possible for me. He literally saved my career at a time when

I was at my lowest and giving it one more shot to make it or call it a day.

My friend Eddie Rowley interviewed Mick and gave me a transcript of what he said about me for this book, which I now include here:

'The first time I saw Daniel, he was just amazing. Nobody knew who the hell he was. But he was fantastic the way he used the stage. With the exception of Ronnie Kennedy, who is still with him, I wasn't impressed by his backing band, but Daniel's performance had me hooked. And I remember Daniel saying to me when he was going up the steps on to the stage, "Mick, if you don't like what you hear today I'm going to pack it up." I said, "We'll see how it goes." When he came off I said, "Come and see me on Tuesday and we'll talk about a contract" and he said "Oh fantastic, that's great." He came to see me and we negotiated a contract. Then when I had him on my hands, I decided I wanted to control the whole situation as regards management. I had to go looking for a manager and I phoned a couple of people. One of them was Sean Reilly. I asked Sean if he could recommend anybody. John Ryan was with a band called The Hillbillies at the time and he had happened to see Daniel performing. Sean phoned John for advice about a manager for Daniel. John said to him, "Sean, if I was you I would take that gig myself." So Sean phoned me and said he was interested. Sean and myself reached an agreement and we set up a company called Brockwell to run Daniel's operation. It's owned by myself and Daniel and Sean is a director as well. Sean and myself go back many years. I once managed a band called The Fairways from Edenderry in County Offaly and Sean was their road manager. We worked together. We also worked together in Cavan selling washing machines and stuff in the early days.'

Mick first got involved in the music business when he landed a job as a roadie with Larry Cunningham and The Mighty Avons. He told Eddie Rowley: 'I worked for ten years in England. I went over in 1956 when I was sixteen years of age and worked in a pub and then I got a job with Initial Towel Supply as a rep. I was with them a good few years. I knew

Brian Finlay who was the drummer in The Mighty Avons. Whenever they came over on tour I'd go to see them because the members were mostly from my native County Cavan. They were looking for a roadie and a driver for their bus and Brian asked if I would give it a try. So I did it on a three months trial. It all worked out and I stayed with them for two or three years and then Larry left and I left with Larry to manage him.'

Mick continued building his experience in the record business, working with the Dublin-based record company Release Records. They had a big hit at the time with a song called 'One Day At A Time' by an Irish country singer known as Gloria. Mick approached several major record companies in Britain with the single, but they all turned him down. When it was finally released in the UK by Lena Martell it turned out to be the only record to sell one million copies that year. As he'd recognised the potential of that song, Mick decided to set up his own record label in the UK with a partner, the late Peter Dempsey.

Mick told Eddie: 'We promoted The Furey's single, "Sweet Sixteen", from London's Ryan Hotel. We met our pluggers there and we organised our deals. And from there The Fureys ended up on *Top Of The Pops*. We then got a flat in Kilburn and worked from there before eventually moving to offices in Covent Garden.

'Myself and my daughter Anne built up the organisation. We were the only two and then Paddy McEntyre joined us. He's regional promotion (radio). He came from EMI. His boss Kay O'Dwyer told him he was mad going to "those Irish guys – they'll last about six months." So every time I see her I say "It's fifteen years now Kay, now it's seventeen years. Paddy's still here!" Our concert division is run by Eamon Leahy, so we promote all the shows ourselves as well.'

'Daniel's success has been a major contributing factor to the success of Ritz. And his own popularity is down to his stage presence and charisma. The first time I really saw his appeal was when he was thrown in at the deep end. Brendan Shine [a singer] was doing a tour in England and Scotland. After England his voice went down and he still had sold out shows to do in Scotland. The Capital in Aberdeen had two thousand people attending the show and Brendan had to cancel at the last minute. They were desperately looking for somebody and we gave them Daniel. We cleared some dates in Ireland and made Daniel available to do five or six dates in Scotland. I went to the Capital in Aberdeen that night. They had a notice up outside saying, "Due to unforeseen circumstances Brendan Shine is unable to appear tonight." But Daniel O'Donnell was appearing. There were 2,000 people there and no more than a hundred looked for their money back. The rest had come out for the night and said, "Well, let's stick it out and see what this guy is like." Daniel switched it on. He got through to them. He went back and eventually did six nights in the venue to over 2,000 people a night!

'But it has been a tough struggle for all of us in the UK. It wasn't easy to push that type of music. And it still isn't in Britain. We don't get access to Radio One, Capital FM or any of them. We are depending on specialist programmes, middle of the road programmes and television. A lot of it is television driven. And most of it is concert driven. You have to get out there. The first time around in England, Daniel probably played to 300 people, but the next time round it was 600. Then it was a thousand and that's what creates your audience, your communication with the fans. You don't get on MTV or whatever. So you have to do it the hard way, it's a hard slog. We had to battle all the way. But I must say, broadcasters like Terry Wogan and Gloria Hunniford were great to us.'

So that's how Mick and the Ritz organisation developed and eventually grew into a major business. In recent years, the Ritz Record Company went through many changes before eventually being sold. Mick has gone on to form a new label called Rosette Records, with the offices based in Greenford, London, and that's where you'll find me these days. It's a great feeling to have been part of the growth of a major businesss and to see Mick Clerkin achieve so much.

18. AFFAIRS OF THE HEART

At one stage of my life, I had come to the realisation that I may never settle down with somebody. Now that may have been a very sad statement to make, but I really didn't have any great concern about that prospect. I found that I enjoyed life on my own and I didn't need to be with somebody. That didn't necessarily mean I would resist a relationship if the right person came along. Only a fool would do that. But it wasn't something I went searching for and it wasn't uppermost in my mind.

I never shunned romance, even though I've always led a very busy and demanding lifestyle. I had experienced the thrill and the joy of three serious relationships at that point in my life. And, like everyone else who suffers the breakdown of an affair, I'd also had to cope with the heartache that goes with the end of such a personal experience. As the song goes, 'breaking up is hard to do.' But I would not want to have missed out on those experiences, because they are all part of living and it is such a blessing to have had that sort of deep and loving connection with those ladies.

It is not for me to discuss the intimate affairs of the people who have come into my life so I won't mention any names. While I accept, although I may not like it, that the media will focus on what I do in my private life, because I'm a person who is out there in the spotlight, I feel it is unfair on the women who are involved with me. I can handle all the fuss because I'm used to it, but it really is very difficult for someone who has never had to cope with that before. If it was Johnny up the road, no one would be interested in who he was dating, and in that respect there have been times when I wished I was Johnny up the road. But I'm here now in this position, so I just have to get on with it.

My first serious infatuation occurred while I was a member of my sister Margaret's band. The girl who caught my eye was working in the London hotel where we were staying. I thought I had met the woman of my dreams and I was totally smitten. As far as I was concerned, this was the real thing. I would have walked on water for her and it was a wild feeling. But the relationship didn't last and she took up with somebody else. It was painful for me, but with the benefit of hindsight, it would probably have been a disaster. I feel I would have married her if she had stayed with me because I was crazy about her. But I was only twenty-one years old and I was still trying to find my place in life and establish my career. I had no money, no security and had I taken the plunge and married it probably wouldn't have lasted jig time. My life would probably have taken a completely different direction because I doubt that I would have been able to build up my solo career, as I would have had to settle down and get a proper job to pay the bills at the time.

I think a lot of people make the mistake of marrying young. They fall for someone and they are on cloud nine. Their attitude is, 'This is heaven, this is where it's at, this is my ticket to happiness forever.' Often, in those heady circumstances, couples don't consider the harsh realities of life. How are the struggles going to affect their relationship? It is better to wait until the initial flush of a new relationship cools down to really assess how compatible you are with the other person. Having said that, there are many couples who got caught up in the whirlwind and have grown old together, so there are no hard and fast rules. And if that girl had married me, who knows what would have happened. But it wasn't to be, so I had to get over that.

My second serious relationship lasted for eight years. It really was something special and, after all those years, naturally it was very painful when it ended. I really do think I was selfish, even ruthless, in the way I pursued my career and became oblivious to the needs of the person in my life. Being an entertainer at this level demands a lot of your time and you have to be totally focused on everything that goes with it. It is not easy for your partner to have to play second fiddle to your career and that is often the way it is. They have to fit in with your schedule and how many people in life are prepared to put up with that? Not many, I would say. So that relationship, anyway, was lost forever, and I have to be honest and admit that it was something I did regret.

There are always regrets when a romance falls apart. At the very least, it is a huge personal disappointment, because you do feel initially that things are going to work out. It is not easy for anyone to have to face the pain of a break-up, but in my case and for the lady associated with me, there is also the embarrassment and trauma of having the media publicising the sad event.

I was absolutely amazed at the attention my third relationship generated in media circles. And for the first time in my life, I had great problems coping with some of the stories that were written about me, mainly because so many of them were completely made up. It's not easy to read about yourself, especially in cases where the stories are just fiction from some journalist's imagination. But the people who write those stories never stop to think of the hurt they are causing to the people concerned, as well as their families. I suppose it's easy for people to write about you when they don't know you. To them you are just a product, like a well known brand, and it's a laugh to twist a story because it will make it a good read. But they forget that we are flesh and blood, we are normal and it is going to hurt. It's even more stressful and painful for the other person, who is not used to being in the limelight and has no experience of the media.

The other thing is, we may know the stories are untrue, but do the general public believe them? There were some incredible stories about why my last relationship broke down, that my mother objected to it or that I broke it off because it was upsetting the fans. Those reports were just complete lies, they were concocted by newspapers. But when you meet people, you wonder whether they have read those stories and what they think. Those thoughts do cross my mind when I meet people. So that kind of media coverage is something that I really object to, and the downside of my success is having to cope with that.

All I will say is, I had been disappointed that those relationships didn't work out. When I met somebody that I fell for, I went head first into it. It hadn't happened very often, but it's as if I went a bit mad. I just couldn't help it, I fell head over heels in love. I don't think the media affected my third relationship while it was happening. I don't think it really bothered us. But the stuff that was written when my third relationship broke up did hurt. And I felt a sickness in my stomach when I learned in 1998 that two reporters had been making inquiries about me in a bar in Tenerife. I felt that was such an invasion of my privacy. Somebody in one of the bars told me that two different journalists had been in asking questions about me, and you can be sure they were not out for a nice story. I was shocked. It wasn't like they were going to write about buttons and bows. But it's something I have to put up with because as long as people are interested in you, there'll be journalists looking for some kind of story.

When I pondered the future, I did think I would not be surprised if I died on my own without having that long life with a partner. But that didn't mean that my life would have been an unhappy one, because I was happy, even though I wasn't sharing my life with another person. I was very happy with my own company. I got on well with myself. I could go into my home and shut the door and it wouldn't bother me if I didn't see a single person for days. Although I certainly wasn't a closed book where relationships were concerned, I wasn't actively seeking one. I would never, ever have settled down with somebody because it was something you should do, or because I didn't want to be alone. As I have said, I didn't mind being on my own.

When I was 37 years old and single, I had got used to my own ways. I had got used to the freedom of being able to go anywhere at the drop of a hat without having to take anyone else into consideration. I liked the fact that I didn't have to make plans, I could do whatever I liked, when I liked, because it was only me making the decision. That might sound selfish, but it probably had something to do with the fact that most of my time was taken up with working to a schedule, so when I was not working I enjoyed the fact that there were no demands on my time. I can honestly say, that's how I liked my life to be. Having said that, the times I'd had relationships, for the most part I'd enjoyed them. They hadn't worked out for various reasons and maybe the fact that I had got used to being on my own was a factor.

At that stage of my life, I had my little routines and my own way of doing things and I liked to have my own personal space. People who have been on their own for long periods of time tend to be like that. It can be very difficult to get used to another person in your life after being used to doing your own thing. When I got into a hotel bedroom on tour, I spread my things out all over the place. Even in the bathroom, I liked to spread things out. I liked to have the top on the toothpaste and the shampoo. I was finicky about things. If I had a person with me, I wouldn't have been able to take over the place with my own stuff. So in that respect, I was set in my ways.

Contrary to the image that people might have of me, I wouldn't say I was the easiest person to live with. As they say, if you want to know me, come and live with me. I wasn't very talkative. I could be very, very quiet. I could be inconsiderate in that if there is something I didn't like doing, then I wouldn't do it. I was very liberal in a relationship. My partner could go and do whatever she pleased, as long as I didn't have to do whatever it was, if it was something that didn't interest me. I know that wasn't a very good way to be and it was a selfish way to be, but I'm being honest when I say that's the way I was. And it is something that had created friction between me and the people who had been in my life.

So I felt, at the end of the day, I was better off on my own. I didn't see anything wrong or unusual in that, because there were lots of people who have made that choice and it suited them. It certainly suited me and I was very happy in my situation. I did realise that I was lucky because I had a very close family around me. Becoming a father myself wasn't something I longed for. I do like children and have enjoyed my nephews and nieces, but starting my own family was not uppermost in my mind. I had already been given so many blessings in life and I was content.

19. THE GREAT UNKNOWN

If there is one thing I set out to do through my career, it was to have my place in the history of music, and that is something I have achieved. It is something that is personally rewarding for me, as it gives me a sense of worth and well-being. I am eternally grateful to all the people who helped me to get this status. It may be a selfish thought, but there is a feelgood factor in knowing that I have made my mark and, no matter what happens in the future, it is something that can never be taken from me.

I don't set goals. I try to achieve whatever is set up for me to achieve. Sean Reilly and Mick Clerkin are the people who are steering my career and the road that they lay I seem to walk. I rely a lot on Sean to guide me and bring me to wherever I have to be in my career. They draw up the plans, but then it's up to me to build on them. You can lay down foundations, but it's another thing putting that house up. In that respect, I do have a big part to play in it. But a lot of the time I don't set up the goal. I might end up kicking the ball, but I certainly don't set up the vital pass. And my life has been like that for a good while, and I'm quite content with it, I suppose. I don't think I will ever be any different. I'm quite satisfied as a person, although there are times when I wonder if I'm really achieving things on my own merits because it seems so easy. Why is it not a little harder? But then, it's probably the same with any job or career. Once you gain the experience, it comes easier. But I do like a good challenge. And I like it when I'm taking my show to new audiences abroad, to see if I can win them over with my style of entertainment. I know people who've been supporting me for a long time enjoy the show, but I sometimes wonder whether they are coming because they are really used to it and know how to enjoy it. Some nights are better than others and maybe they come for the great night. But then when I go to a place where the audience has never seen me perform before, and it's like melting or breaking something down, it gives me a great sense of achievement, and everybody needs that. Regardless of what you are doing, everybody needs new challenges to keep them stimulated and I'm no different. I think America is one of the territories nowadays that gives me a good challenge, so going to America is important to me from that point of view.

Nobody can look into the future and predict what is going to happen in their lives, that is a very safe statement to make. But some people can say, 'Well, I'm going to try to do this and try to do that.' I cannot say what I am going to do. I've always been very uncertain about the future and I think I always will be. I cannot see me at fifty years old. I've no reason to think I won't be doing what I am doing, but I cannot see where I'm going to be.

As regards what I do as an entertainer, I will be happy to go on for as long as people enjoy what I do. But I am determined not to stay past my 'sell by' date. If there comes a time when the demand is not there, then I would rather retire gracefully than slowly sink away. I couldn't bear to have to go back to singing in smoky pubs again. Now that may never happen, so I may never have to worry about it. But, being realistic, nobody can sustain their popularity at a certain level forever. That's just the way it is in showbusiness. Entertainers have to accept that, no matter how hard it is to swallow. So I'm prepared for that, if the day ever comes. One thing I will have to look at is finding more time for myself. You do really need to live a little as you go along and, while the stage is so fulfilling, it should not be at the total expense of my private life. It would be nice to have more time to relax and enjoy simple pleasures like golf and holidays and time at home in Kincasslagh.

Sometimes I feel like a dog chasing its tail. There is so much to keep up with and a lot of that pressure is self-inflicted because there are lots of things I try to do on a personal basis. I strive to operate at a certain level and adopt a personal approach to things. Things like answering mail, I try to do as much of that as I can. I have set a very high standard for myself on how to do things. But that is something I will have to learn to let go. I will have to delegate more if I am to get extra personal time. It may mean less shows or a reorganisation of my touring schedule so that I can have more freedom. There is no sense in ending up exhausted, so that's something I have to watch. I don't want to get to the point where I no longer enjoy what I do. I do want to have time for normal things at home. Even when I'm there there is business to be attended to and I would like that to change. I don't want to be in a situation where I have to go away to have a holiday to relax, I want to be able to do that at home because I love being there.

I will always wonder what it is that attracts so many people to me because I honestly feel ordinary. I think it's amazing that so many people queue for tickets to my shows and buy millions of my records and videos. But I'm not searching for answers. I know I have had a charmed life so far, I've been blessed with what I've been given and I can only hope that the rest of my life will be as rewarding. But I don't worry about it. There is a lovely saying, which sums up the way I like to live. It goes: 'Yesterday is a memory, tomorrow is a mystery, today is a gift and that's why they call it the present.' I am very much somebody who lives for the present.

20. MY MOTHER, JULIA

While I have had my struggles along the way, they are nothing compared to the hardship endured by my parents in their early years and after they were married. Their work experiences are shocking by today's standards, but they were the norm for most people of their background in those days. My father, Francie, and my mother, Julia, came from an era where there were no mod cons to ease the burden of daily duties. It was a time when tough, physical labour was the order of the day and there was hardship beyond belief in many cases.

When I hear my mother talking about the old days, it is hard to believe that things were so primitive in her lifetime. Thankfully, her twilight years have been good ones, blessed for the most part with good health, and she has been able to enjoy her family and grandchildren. My success has also given her a great deal of joy and I'm delighted that it has added to the quality of her life.

My lifestyle is far removed from that of my parents, as you will learn from my mother's personal story. Eddie Rowley interviewed her for this book and I include here his description of her life and her own account of it as told to him.

'The curse of island life is emigration and at the age of seventeen, Daniel's mother Julia, who was born in to the McGonagle family in 1919, left her little isle of Owey, just off the coast of Donegal, and headed for work in the tattie (potato) fields on Scottish farms. To say it was hard labour would be an understatement. But the living conditions were even more extreme – Julia was forced to sleep on straw mattresses in cow sheds, which had been washed out after the cows had been milked. Her work started at three-thirty in the morning and finished at three in the afternoon. If she joined the tattie pickers at eight o'clock in the morning, she wouldn't get in till five or six in the evening. At the end of the week, Julia's wages were £3.

' "We moved from farm to farm every week," Julia recalls. "They were big farms, you wouldn't see the end of them when you were standing. You'd work for miles and miles on your knees picking the tatties through wet and dry weather, in the stones and clay, and your two knees would be cut off you. There was no machinery. The men would dig the potatoes and we'd gather them on our knees, pulling baskets behind us.

' "At night, when they put the cows out, they washed out the shed and you set up your bed, which consisted of a mattress made of sacks stitched together and stuffed with straw. You'd be given black blankets to keep you warm and that's how you rested. Even though the work was hard, we'd often go dancing at night and get an hour's sleep before getting up to go to the fields again.

' "Apart from the potato picking, I also had to look after the cooking and washing for five men, my own two brothers, the gaffer [foreman] and two other men. I didn't get any extra money for that. I lived that life for three or four years, sending home as much money as I could."

'Julia's childhood memories of life on Owey Island are happy ones. Her father was a fisherman and "a great singer", she says. The family of seven, including her parents, sister Maggie and brothers James, Edward and Owenie, lived in a little cottage, which was partly thatched and partly slated. It had a large kitchen which also served as a living room and a bedroom. The three boys slept in one room, Julia and her sister slept in the second bedroom and their parents slept in the kitchen. There was an open hearth fireplace where all the cooking was done in pots and on grills over the flames and hot coals.

'At that time there were grants available for thatched roofs to be converted to slates. "My father decided to get our roof slated," Julia recalls. "One of the rooms already had slates on it. A condition for the grant aid was that you had to be able to speak the Irish language [Gaeilge]. The grant inspector arrived on the island and he said to my father, 'Do you have any Gaeilge?' My father said, 'Well, I had enough to put a roof on the room, so surely to God I'll have enough to put a roof on the kitchen.' So he got away with that."

'There were around one hundred and seventy people living on the island back in those days. Fishing was the main occupation, but the islanders also grew their own vegetables and were self-sufficient, as they were in Daniel's childhood. Fish and potatoes were the staple diet, with chicken on a Sunday. "We'd boil the fish or roast herring on a grill over the open fire and there would be a big black pot of potatoes bubbling beside it," Julia recalls.

' "Everybody had a wee farm. We had a cow and a donkey. As children we were put to work sowing potatoes. When setting the potatoes we had to dig the ground with an implement like a trowel. You'd have blisters on your hands from the work, but we didn't care because we were happy."

'Childhood games during Julia's youth were simple ones, tailored to the availability of amusing sources. The afternoons were occupied by the local children bringing cows back to the mountain after milking, and along the route they played a game with an egg. "Each one of us would take turns putting on a blindfold and then an egg would be placed three or four yards in front of you on the ground and you had to try to hit it with a stick. Whoever hit it was the winner and an egg might last five days before someone would actually smash it," Julia reveals.

' "We also played a game with wee rabbits that we'd catch out at the mountain. We used to dip them in the lake and when they were wet they couldn't run. Then we'd draw a square on the ground with a stick and place the rabbits in the middle of it. There would be one child at each corner of the square and when a rabbit would run to one of the sides you had to try to catch him. It was harmless fun and we never killed the rabbits, we let them go when they dried off."

'At night-time the women would meet in one house to knit and chat while the menfolk would gather in other houses to play cards. The school on the island was the venue every third

Sunday for music. "Adults and children alike gathered there and the music was a tin whistle, a melodeon and a fiddle. Everybody could dance and it was great craic," says Julia.

'Apart from potato picking, Julia also earned a living in her teenage years by gutting fish. It was while employed in this occupation at Lerwick in the Shetland Islands off Scotland that she met her husband Francie, Daniel's dad, in 1946. "The first time I set eyes on Francie I thought he was lovely looking, a lovely young fella. I was about eighteen years old and I didn't get the chance to go out with him at that time, only observing him from a distance," she reveals. "It was a few years before I met him at the fishing work. I started going out with him and a year later we were married. As soon as I saw him I liked him and I knew that he was the one that I wanted. After we got married I continued working at the fishing, but when my first child, John Bosco, was born I never went away again.

' "During our marriage, we lived all over the place, including Scotland, in rented houses. We didn't have a home in Kincasslagh until Daniel was born. It was a very hard life for us as a family as Francie was away all the time working. He would come home in July for a week or two and then he'd be away again until Christmas. I was always afraid that the children would forget him.

' "There were times when he'd get a job on farms for three or four months at home and those were happy days for us. But once the Spring work was done and the turf cut, dried [the peat was wet when harvested] and taken home, he would be away to Scotland to work again. He was a good worker and a good earner, but there would be some crying the day he went away.

' "Francie was a wonderful man. He was very religious. The morning he died he said to me, 'Do you know, you're some sleeper! I have a rosary said for myself, one for you, one for John Bosco, one for Margaret, one for James, one for Kathleen, one for Daniel, one for all the sick and one for all the dead. And do you see that pile of Novenas, those wee leaflets, I have all those read too.' He made a wonderful impression on anyone who met him and after his death I received some lovely letters written to me by other people who knew Francie.

'"I never remarried after he passed away. I thought too much of him, and him being the father of my children, to put another ring on my finger."

'After Francie's death, Julia ensured that her children were well cared for, despite the fact that times were hard and she had been left without a penny. The family had moved in to their new home in Kincasslagh the year before Francie passed on, and most of their savings had been spent on the new abode. The remainder went on the funeral expenses.

'Julia would deprive herself of little comforts in order to provide for the children. She became the breadwinner, knitting clothing which was sold through contacts in America. "A relation in America wrote to me and asked if I would be interested in knitting sweaters if he got a market for them. He suggested it would be a help for me to rear my family. Well, I wasn't long writing back and telling him that it would," she says.

'"I used to be up at four o'clock in the morning finishing sweaters and parcelling them for posting away to the States. That's how I supplemented my widow's pension to keep bread on the table and shoes on the children's feet. I took care of it myself and that's the way I reared them.

'"But they were all good children. None of them gave me any trouble, I'm happy to say. You bring them up as best you can and you hope for the best and, thank God, I was blessed with my brood. Wonderful, all of them. Daniel was probably closer to me than the rest of them because he was only six when his father died and wherever I went, he went too.

'"Even when his father was alive, Daniel would come with me because he was only a child. Whenever I was going anywhere without him I used to say, 'You can't come with me, Daniel, because I'm going to Confession.' I knew he wouldn't want to come with me if he knew I was going to Confession in the local church. One day Daniel was crossing the road – you didn't have to worry about children on our road at that time as there was only one car in the area – and the dog got loose and was running after him. Daniel was about three years old at the time and he looked back and said to Francie, 'Daddy, call the dog back and tell him he can't come because I'm going to Confession.'

' "He was a very good child. I remember one day on the bus to the local town of Dungloe, the driver asked the school children to stand back and let the adults on. Daniel said to me, 'Mammy, you go on and when all the big people are seated keep a seat for me.' While I was on the bus, I could hear people behind me saying, 'Danny is not getting on.' Then my Daniel got on and I heard them say, 'Oh, Danny is on. Danny is on.' I then realised they were talking about my Daniel. I saw him wheeling a trolley and I thought to myself, where in the name of God did he get the trolley. He left it beside the couple behind me and sat down beside me. The lady said to him, 'You're not sitting beside your girlfriend today.' I then replied, 'But he is sitting beside his girlfriend.' She said, 'Do you know Danny?' I said, 'A good right I should have to know him.' She said, 'Why, do you live near him?' I said, 'I do.' She said, 'Don't tell me, you're not his mother?' I said, 'That's who I am.'

' "She said, 'Well, do you know, you must be the proudest mother in Ireland. Wait till I tell you a story. We came down from the North because we were afraid of the Troubles and we bought a little house down here. Every so often we go to the supermarket in Dungloe for our groceries. Before Daniel came along, the schoolchildren used to kick over the trolley and spill out the groceries. But since the day Danny saw us, he's taken the trolley off us and made us go and get a seat on the bus. Then he brings the trolley in and leaves it beside us. When he gets out at Kincasslagh, he takes the trolley down to the door and leaves it there so that it's handy for us when we reach our stop. Now that's my story about Danny.'

' "All the pensioners on the bus loved my Daniel. The day he left school they were all crying and saying how they'd have no one to help them with their bags on the bus."

'Julia was very concerned about Daniel going into showbusiness. Her daughter Margo had been in the business before him and Julia was aware that it's a tough industry with lots of pitfalls. "My daughter Margaret had a hard life in it," she says, "but I never tried to stop Daniel or any of my children doing what they wanted to do. I used to think to myself, 'If I made them do this or that and anything happens to them, I'll never forgive myself.' I would advise them, but I would let them please themselves.

' "I am delighted the way things worked out for Daniel and I was with him the first night he went on stage at the Ragg in Thurles, County Tipperary. Oh, I thought it was great to see him up on the stage and he was such a great wee singer. When I look at what he has achieved, I sometimes think, 'Did my Daniel do all of that?' It's great and it's wonderful to see the enjoyment he brings to people. It's funny, though, I never play his records in the house. The only time I hear one of his records or tapes is if I'm out in a car and somebody puts one of them on. Most times, I hear them on the radio. I'm not one for playing records or watching TV. The grandchildren are always playing wee tapes of their own in the house, so I just listen to the radio."

'Julia had always prayed that Daniel would find a loving partner to share his personal life. "I would die happy if I had seen that," she once remarked. The prayers of a devoted mother were finally answered when Daniel met a wonderful lady called Majella.'

21. MAJELLA AND OUR WEDDING

It was a lovely balmy evening in the autumn of 1999 as I sauntered along the street past the bars and restaurants on my favourite holiday isle of Tenerife. The mood was relaxed and I was joking and laughing with my little group of friends and quietly contemplating on the lucky hand of cards that had been dealt to me. I had great people in my life, a wonderful career and I was blessed with good health. The only piece of the jigsaw missing at that moment was a partner to share my good fortune. Although I wasn't desperately searching for anyone at the time, nor was it really on my mind, little did I know that my destiny in that regard was just around the corner as I headed for the local bar run by my friends Tom and Marion Roche.

As I have done with many of the Irish people living and working on the island, I had built up a very good relationship with Tom and Marion during my many visits to their bar down the years. It was always one of my ports of call whenever I holidayed on Tenerife. I found Tom and Marion to be warm, hospitable people and I felt totally at ease in their company from the very first moment we met. Tom is a great character, full of wit and wisdom. He is very entertaining and great company to be with. Like myself, he loves people and is always the life and soul of the party wherever a crowd has gathered. Marion is a lady you fall in love with upon first meeting. She is the type of woman who easily endears herself to all and sundry with her friendliness and kindness. I always looked forward to meeting them on my holiday.

Their daughter Majella had been in the restaurant during one of my visits and we were briefly introduced. I remembered that she was attractive, with short, fair hair and a ready smile. But I had thought nothing more of the encounter. Majella was there again this particular night and we got chatting during the course of the evening. She was great company. We laughed and laughed and, on reflection, I have no idea what we found so funny. It was probably silly things that didn't make much sense, but were obviously highly amusing at the time. I felt like we had known each other all our lives.

As the night progressed, there was a sing-song and, as Majella joined in, I discovered that she had a very good singing voice. When I mentioned this to her, Majella laughed and said she'd actually had a dream that she would sing for me.

'Well,' I said, 'now is your chance.'

I watched and listened enchanted as she sang the ballad 'She Moved Through The Fair'. I couldn't believe how good she could sing.

It was a very laid-back evening and I regarded Majella as a woman who was great craic (fun) to be around. She was down-to-earth, funny and very much her own person with an understated self-confidence. Before leaving the Roches' family restaurant that evening I invited Majella to come with us as we set off to continue the fun of the night in the local bars. The thought of developing a relationship with Majella still hadn't crossed my mind as she took up my offer. Later, as we parted company in the early hours of the morning and I got ready to head back to my apartment with friends, Majella and I made an informal arrangement to meet up again. The next night I was back in her family's restaurant and the pair of us again went out on the town together. Well, me bucko, there's something definitely happening here, I thought to myself. By the end of the holiday, after spending endless hours together, I realised that I had become emotionally involved with Majella. And, to tell you the truth, I was that comfortable the way I was, it frightened the life out of me. But I knew I wasn't going to overlook this special relationship. We both had different lives thousands of miles apart, but we agreed to keep in touch by phone when I left to go back to my other life on stage.

It wasn't long afterwards that the profits of the phone companies started to hit an all-time high as we continued our long-distance romance down the line. Doesn't Alexander Graham Bell have a lot to answer for! Majella and I would talk endlessly about nothing on the phone. The communication we had and still have is wonderful. I went back to Tenerife on holiday and we were together again, and then Majella came over to join me on a break from her work.

My life was moving at a very fast pace at this stage and at the back of my mind a nagging doubt about the relationship began to bother me more and more. This was not a simple affair, I realised. It wasn't just about me and Majella, as there were so many other considerations to be taken into account. The most striking problem at that time for me was that Majella had been previously married, although she had by now been separated and was going through a divorce for four years. From a religious point of view, this was something that posed difficulties for me and I was grappling with my conscience over the whole thing. There were also young children involved as Majella was mum to daughter Siobhan and son Michael. I had to consider the fact that I was getting involved in the lives of a lot of other people. Me being me, I began to get cold feet about the relationship. The more I debated it in my mind, the colder my feet became. After agonising over it for what seemed like an eternity, I eventually made the tough decision to step back from the romance.

When I look back and think about that time, I realise more than ever just what a wonderful person Majella is. I had come into her life and we had bonded, now I was breaking that very personal connection. Maybe it's age and experience, and having coped with the trials and tribulations of life along the way, but, whatever the reason, Majella was very mature, calm and understanding in the way she handled my painful decision to end the romantic side of our relationship. There was no screaming and shouting. No tantrums or tears whatsoever. Majella totally accepted my point of view, whether she agreed with it or not. She understood that I had difficulties with her complex personal life. We talked about it and she knew I couldn't see past the complications. Naturally, given the love, affection and esteem I had for Majella, I was very keen to maintain the friendship. Again, Majella was happy to remain friends.

Over the course of another year I holidayed on Tenerife and met up with Majella. There was no denying that I absolutely loved her company. The nagging doubts at the back of my mind were back to bother me once again. This time I was being nagged about whether or not I had done the right thing when I ended the relationship. We seemed so perfect as a couple when we were together, and I missed Majella when we were apart.

Well, I finally came to my senses in April 2001 while taking another break on the island. We were together and I realised that, yes, we were a great couple and we were very happy together. Sometimes you do have to overcome a lot of obstacles in your quest for the best things in life. And only a fool would turn down the opportunity to find true happiness. Without realising it, Majella and I had drifted back into being a couple again. We acknowledged that situation and I told her of my deep feelings. I realised that I wanted to spend the rest of my life with her because I loved her. I told her that she made me totally happy and I accepted how much she cared for me. The beaming smile on Majella's face said it all. She wanted me as well. And she told me how happy she was with me. We decided to try again.

Although I love what I do with a passion, there are times when I wish I was Johnny from up the road. This was one of those times. Because I'm lucky enough to enjoy success as a singer and entertainer, the media obviously take a big interest in everything to do with my personal life as well. Now, I can accept that it's something that goes with the territory of being what is termed a 'celebrity'. Whether you like it or not, people are going to write about you and pass comment on you. And, believe me, it's not always flattering or positive. It's something you learn to deal with when you're in the public eye and you take the good with the bad. The only major problem I have with media coverage is how it affects other people in my life, my family and friends. When we decided to embark on our relationship, I discussed the whole media scene with Majella. I had been through the wars in the newspapers as a result of a previous relationship and, believe me, it's not a very pleasant experience when you're in the eye of the storm. But it's even more horrifying when you're a private person who is not used to being written about in the papers or talked about on the radio. It can be hell on earth. So I discussed all of this with Majella and I tried to make her aware, as best I could, of the rocky road that lay ahead.

There was no doubt in my mind that my relationship with a divorced mother-of-two was going to make newspaper headlines. Because of the 'Mr Perfect' image that has somehow been attached to me through the media, I reckoned they were going to have a field day with this story. It was so totally the opposite of what they expected from Daniel O'Donnell. Well, real life just isn't as clean and tidy as the stuff of fairytales. And, away from the stage and what I do as an entertainer, I'm just a normal person like everyone else. My biggest worry at this time was that the lives of Majella, her children and her former husband, Raymond, were going to be turned over because of Daniel O'Donnell. Fame can be a curse. But what was there to do? We were in love and we had decided to be together; we would have to face the consequences, whatever they might be. We felt that, irrespective of religion or what people might think, if you are going to be happy neither God nor man should deny you that. I prayed to God that no one would get hurt.

At first, I was determined to keep our relationship a secret from everyone, apart from our families and close friends. It's not that I was ashamed of it in any way, but Majella and I wanted to have time to ourselves for the relationship to grow before it went into the public domain. We wanted to be sure that it was going to work between us. Because I live my life like a Nomad, constantly on the move and rarely spending long periods in one place, we did actually manage to keep our personal life under wraps until the time came to tell the world. And that was on the night of the landmark birthday in my life, my big four-O.

The 12th of December 2001 was a momentous night for me in many ways. I had been the boy-next-door for so long; they had even called me 'Ireland's most eligible bachelor' up to that point. But everything was about to change. In what seemed like a flash, I had hit middle age. Well, to my surprise, that didn't bother me one bit. At least I still had my hair and my own teeth. Age was only a number to me. I didn't feel one bit different on the day of that big birthday. I was a little apprehensive all right, but that was because I was going to make a major personal announcement at the charity birthday banquet in my honour before 1,200 people in Birmingham's Hilton Hotel.

It was a day to reflect on my life. As I looked back, a whole sea of mixed emotions swept over me. Like a show reel, so many images were going through my mind. I thought back to my early days growing up in Kincasslagh, walking the country roads to school, my first public performances in the local village hall, a great summer working in a Dublin hotel and then a short term in college before I joined my sister Margaret's band. I thought back to my exciting adventure doing my first solo recordings in Big Tom's Studios and then forming my own band. The early struggles on the road as I tried to make my name in showbusiness were so vivid. I laughed out loud as I remembered some of the hilarious moments, like the whole band, including myself, sleeping in one room along the motorway because it was all we could afford at the time. God, it only seemed like yesterday. But now here I was, twenty-odd years – and some would say very odd years – down the line, having packed so much into my life. There were so many incredible events to remember, not least being a *This Is Your Life* tribute in the year 2000 when Michael Aspel presented me with that famous red book. That was a night to remember, having people I admire, my very own idols, Loretta and Cliff, paying tribute to *me*. I had come a long way indeed.

The *This Is Your Life* TV show was very special to me. I had grown up watching it on television when it was presented by our own Eamon Andrews. I may have had lots of dreams as a youngster, but being the subject of *This Is Your Life* one day in the future was never among them. I'll never forget the moment it happened. I was a guest entertainer, along with Engelbert Humperdinck, on Bruce Forsyth's variety show from the London Palladium when Michael Aspel sprung the surprise. There was an explosion of applause when Michael arrived on the stage at the end of the performance with his famous red book. Thinking that it was heading in the direction of Engelbert, I stepped back to give Michael a clear run at his target. Instead, imagine my confusion as he made a beeline in my direction. People said to me afterwards that the blood drained from my face at that very moment and my mouth fell open. There were no words coming out of my open gob, just a vacant stare and my head shaking. It was just like a car crash. Suddenly everything was happening in slow motion. In the distance, I could hear Michael Aspel saying, 'Tonight, Daniel O'Donnell, this is your life.' But it still wasn't registering with me. 'Are you sure?' I heard myself asking. Then the audience burst into laughter. Michael Aspel pointed to the name on the cover of the red book. 'Daniel O'Donnell' it read. I remember watching the reaction of other stars being surprised on *This Is Your Life* and wondering, did they know? Well, I can tell you, in all honesty, I had no inkling whatsoever that Michael Aspel was going to do a number on me that night. It was the best-kept secret of my life.

It happened on a Wednesday night and I had arrived in London on the Monday after spending two months on a tour of Australia and New Zealand. I didn't go home to Donegal, instead opting to stay over for the Palladium show. When I was on the phone to home, they had told me not to bother ringing any of them on the Wednesday as new phone cabling was being installed in our area. Little did I know that they had all made the trip to London and were in the TV studios waiting for my arrival.

After the initial surprise at the Palladium, I was whisked off to the TV studios where the show is recorded. As I waited in the dressing room, I mentally prepared myself for the emotional rollercoaster that lay ahead. I was determined that I would remain composed no matter what came my way. Needless to say, that didn't work for very long. When the doors opened to reveal the first set of guests, my mother, sisters Kathleen and Margaret and brothers John and James, our emotions just spilled over and we were all tearful. This kind of thing doesn't happen to people like us, I thought. We're a normal family from a small rural area in the north west of Ireland and it was never part of the plan for one of us to be on *This Is Your Life*. And that wasn't the end of the tears. Before the show closed and after I had received so many moving tributes from people that included neighbours at home as well as a whole host of celebrities, there was another surprise in store for me. The show had flown in several Romanian orphans, my young friends from the homes we have set up through the Romanian Challenge Appeal charity. To have those special people in my life around me at that moment made everything I had done up to that point seem really worthwhile.

After the *This Is Your Life* post-show party I returned to my hotel in the early hours of the morning, but couldn't sleep. I sat on the bed and wondered if it had really happened. The following morning a car arrived to take me to the airport. The driver asked me who had been featured on *This Is Your Life* the previous night. 'We-ell, it was me,' I said. But I didn't sound at all certain.

I realised, looking back, on the night of my birthday in Birmingham, that my life up to that point had been full. It was a nice feeling to know that, if nothing else happened in my world from now on, at least I had been fulfilled up to then. Not many people get the kind of opportunities that came my way in those forty years. So I had a lot to be thankful for.

As Majella and I got ready in our hotel suite, I glanced at her and had a feeling of total confidence in what I was about to do. There wasn't one single doubt in my mind, as the lift whisked us downstairs to the lobby en route to the banquet hall, that the announcement I was going to make to the world outside felt totally right for me. In fact, I was more calm and relaxed than Majella, who normally takes everything in her stride. But, as she said, Majella felt it was the calm before the storm. I suppose I had oversold the possible reaction of the media and, in particular, the impact it may have on her family. As we strolled across the foyer, I gave her hand a reassuring squeeze and smiled at her. 'Oh, Daniel, I need a glass of wine to steady my nerves,' she said, laughing.

I'm not sure how many of the 1,200 people in the room that night, other than my family and close friends, were aware that Majella was my girlfriend before I introduced her. Certainly, not everyone would have known, although there had been some speculation in the media. I didn't do the introduction straight away, instead opting to wait until it came to speech time. Everyone at the charity dinner had had a wonderful meal and they were enjoying their drinks; the mood was just perfect as I took to the stage. In the course of thanking everyone for supporting me, not just on the night, but through all my years, I then announced that there was a special lady with me and I wanted to introduce her. Majella was still sitting at the top table as I told the gathering that I had found someone who meant the world to me and I wanted to share the rest of my life with her. There was a hushed silence and I could hear some collective gasps from the tables.

I said, 'I have never been happier and I hope that all of you, the people who have supported me [the fans], will be happy for us and that you will accept Majella as part of my life.' Then I joked with the female fans at the dinner, 'But don't you worry, you're all still my girlfriends, too.'

I called Majella to come over to the stage to join me. To a very enthusiastic round of applause, Majella made her way through the crowd to the podium where I was holding court. I was the proudest man in the hall at that moment as we embraced. The instant reaction in the ballroom that night was totally positive from everyone we met. I lost count of the number of women who came up to me and said that they were delighted I had found someone special and that I wouldn't end up a lonely old man. I reassured everyone that, even though I now had someone else to share my life, it would not change what I did as Daniel O'Donnell the entertainer. I would always be there for my other 'girlfriends' as well.

Everything went so well on the night, but I was still worried about the media intrusion into the lives of Majella's family. To their credit, the newspapers were very kind to us. 'Daniel's divorcée girlfriend' was, of course, in all the headlines. But all of the publicity centred around Majella and myself and the privacy of her family and ex-husband was respected. It was such a relief to both of us. We live in a different world now and that was so evident to me in the way that people accepted my relationship with a woman who was divorced with children. It made no difference to anyone. And why should it? As Majella said, everyone deserves a second chance in life. All that matters is that we weren't hurting anyone. We were happy and our families were happy too.

My mother's story, told in this book, ends with her wish that I would one day meet 'some nice girl who will be as good to him as I was'. She said she would die happy if she saw that day. At this stage, I don't need to reiterate how important my mother is to me. The last thing I would ever want to do is cause her any upset or pain. In an ideal world, it would have been easier if Majella had not been previously married and with children. But you can't live your life for other people. You have to live it for yourself and do what you think is best for you. Once you are happy, you are going to be better to the people around you. But my mother is not someone who lives in the Dark Ages either. All that really matters to her is that Majella is a nice, decent person and someone who makes me happy. They got on very well together right from the start. Majella is a normal country girl with no airs or graces. She fitted right into the O'Donnell clan. And I knew she had won my mother's affection the day I saw her showing Majella how to make my favourite pancakes. That was a sign that my mother was handing over.

As for Majella's young daughter and son, Siobhan and Michael, well, they accepted me right from the start. Majella didn't say anything to them in the beginning about our relationship, but children sense things. They used to ask Majella, 'Is he your boyfriend?' They are two very happy, bright children. And they were happy that their mum was happy.

At Christmas time that year I was on top of the world. I'd had a charmed life, but now I was so much happier with Majella being a part of it. To complete the perfect year, Majella was spending Christmas with me and was joined by Siobhan and Michael at our new home by the sea at Cruit, not far from my native Kincasslagh. We had both looked at the house together and it was now *our* home. The minute we walked through the doors when we went to view it, we both felt comfortable in it. It is a lovely, five-bed bungalow-style house with panoramic sea views. It's like living on a boat. It's right on the edge of the water. As soon as I drive through the gate and walk through the door, I'm in my very own heaven there. I had lived in a lovely big house at Rathcoole, as I described earlier. But I never really settled in it. Now I know the real reason. It was just a house. It was never a home. It takes more than bricks and mortar to make a home. In my case, it was Majella who turned this house into a home. When she's not there it's a house, but as soon as she comes through the door it's a home again.

When Christmas Day came around I was like a hen on a hot griddle. Unknown to Majella I was about to take our relationship to the next stage. Although we had discussed getting engaged, we had not decided on a time or a place. She did know that I had already found what I considered to be the perfect engagement ring. It's a set of two small rings which fit into each other, with a single diamond on one and four little diamonds on the other. I had said to her that I was going to keep it from her eyes until the moment arrived to place it on her finger. It was torture for her knowing that I had the ring, as she wanted to see it, try it on and wear it. But I was determined that when the moment arrived it would be memorable and that seeing the ring for the first time would play a role in that special event in our lives. Now I was waiting for the right moment to pounce.

Before we sat down for Christmas dinner at our home in Cruit with my mother, sister, Kathleen and her husband John and family and a few friends who had joined us, I said to Majella, 'Phone your mother.' She said, 'No, I'll do it later.' I said, 'Would you ever go upstairs and phone your mother on

Christmas Day.' I wanted her to go up to the room. Majella went upstairs to make the call and after a couple of minutes I followed her. They were speaking when I entered the room and I took the phone and said to her mother, 'Marion, do you know what I'm going to do now. I'm going to put a ring on your daughter's finger.'

As I fumbled in my pocket to retrieve the ring, I also put on my song 'Save A Little Lovin' ', which Majella loves. Then I put the ring on Majella's finger and she started to cry and then Marion was crying at the other end of the phone. Then we both went downstairs to break the news to my family. Once again, there were lots and lots of tears. My mother started to cry, then Kathleen got all teary. It was lovely to see that everyone was so happy for us, just as we had wished. It's a Christmas Day neither of us will ever forget. I was extremely happy, unbelievably happy, really. In fact, I was so content and so happy it was almost sickening.

My greatest wish in life was to marry in our little village church in my native Kincasslagh. But, because Majella was divorced, that didn't seem possible at the time. Obviously, as a practising Catholic, I wanted our marriage to be a proper church ceremony. Majella and her former husband, Raymond, had applied for a church annulment. If this was granted, we could marry in the church. It's a decision made in Rome and obviously a very complex matter. We were also both painfully aware that annulments are not granted lightly. The prospect of a positive outcome was something I didn't dare think about during the months that followed. We are both religious and I firmly believe in prayer. I said to Majella, 'Every night we're together and every night we're apart we'll say the Rosary.' I didn't say why we were saying it. When I was on tour, I would often get a text from Majella to say, 'Just gone to bed and finished the Rosary.'

In the end our prayers were answered and the annulment came through, paving the way for our fairytale church wedding. There are some who would say that if you didn't have money you wouldn't get those things. Well, I say to that, if you start praying, God will work his own way. The day we got the news that Majella and Raymond had been successful in their application for an annulment was one of the happiest days of our lives. The tension and stress had been almost unbearable at times. But now we had our answer.

It was now full steam ahead for the wedding and the planning began in earnest. There was a date to be decided, the church to be organised and a venue for the celebrations to be sorted out. And where were we going to start or end with the list of people to be invited? We eventually decided on our date – Monday, 4 November 2002. We were both adamant that it was going to be as normal a wedding as we could possibly make it. It was never going to be a celebrity wedding. One newspaper reporter asked me if lots of big stars would be attending. I told him there was only going to be one star on the day – Majella. Shortly after we announced our wedding date, the celebrity magazines were on the phone trying to tie up exclusive deals to cover our big day. A big sum was mentioned for the rights to our photographs, but it was something that was totally out of the question. I was not going to sell my wedding to any publication. It was something we didn't want to do. We both wanted a lovely, personal day, a solemn and joyous event, and that wouldn't have been possible if there was a commercial aspect to it. Good luck to anyone who goes down that road, but it wasn't for us.

When we sat down to work out our guest list, we decided that our day was going to be with people who made both of us what we are. Where I was brought up, and where Majella and I will live for as long as God leaves us together on this earth, wasn't a childhood growing up with celebrities. I grew up with ordinary people who weren't interested in what I did, but liked me simply as a person. Along the way we had also both encountered people who had made a difference to our lives. Those were the people we wanted to join us on our wedding day. Mind you, as we worked our way through the guest list it was a bit of a shock to discover how many of those special people we had accumulated!

Meanwhile, our lives continued as normal. I had my shows to do and in the daytime I dealt with any arrangements that had to be decided. Majella, of course, played a major role in ensuring that we had taken care of every aspect of the day. As the event drew closer and closer, I could see that Majella was on a real high. While excited myself, I was surprised by the calm way I was dealing with it. I felt really comfortable about the whole thing. To be honest, the most important aspect of the day for me was going to be the ceremony in the church. The spiritual and religious side of it. When we sent out our invitations we included a personal note specifically asking our guests to attend the church as well as the celebrations later at the hotel. We had noticed at some recent weddings we'd attended that many guests didn't go to the church to witness the bride and groom getting married and to share that spiritual side. They just turned up for the hooley. It was important to Majella and I that everyone should be with us as we exchanged our solemn vows in church.

The night before the wedding we observed tradition by spending it apart. I went home to my mother while Majella slept in our new home in Cruit. The church wedding was set for one o'clock the following afternoon and Majella warned me to be there on time. She told me, 'Be there at one because I'm going to be there at five minutes past the hour.'

I smiled. 'God, you really do mean business,' I said.

'I waited this long for my second chance, I've no intention of hanging about,' she said, laughing.

To my surprise, I slept soundly that night and in the morning when I awoke I had a sense of being calm. My pulse wasn't racing. My blood pressure was normal. There were no butterflies in the tummy. I was happy and chirpy – and I'm not a morning person at all. The best men arrived up to the house – my childhood pal P.J. Sweeney, my nephew John Francis Doogan and brother James – all looking dashing in their finery. We talked and laughed as I slipped into my own outfit and we headed off to the church about half an hour before the time. I wanted to have some time to go and meet the fans who had come along to wish us well. But, heeding Majella's warning, I made sure to be in the church by one o'clock.

A strange thing happened to me as I entered St Mary's Church in Kincasslagh that day. Right up to the moment I went through the doors, my emotions were totally under control; I had no feeling of being nervous or upset in any way. But the moment I looked at the sea of faces in the church I broke down. It was just a flood of memories racing around my head, sparked off by the different people I spotted in the congregation. They were people from so many periods of my life and it was so moving to have them there with me on this particular day. There was also the fact that I was in the place where we wanted so much to get married and where we could have the service that we'd dreamed of. No one will know how much that meant to both of us. 'God, I don't know why I'm crying,' I said, a little embarrassed.

I took up my position and the time passed, but there was no sign of Majella. Little did I know that back at our home in Cruit there was a major drama unfolding. There was a technical problem with the electric gates and they wouldn't open. Majella was trapped inside. The news of this catastrophe was relayed by mobile phone to someone in the wedding party at the church and passed on to me.

Ah, well, I thought, sure, I'll go and say hello to the people in the church – all 530 of them – while I'm waiting. I then toured the aisles greeting all my friends, many of whom had travelled from as far away as Australia and America. It was actually a very nice moment for me in the church, making that connection with everyone before the ceremony began.

Meanwhile, poor old Majella was still being held prisoner in our home as locals frantically tried to get the blooming gates open. Even the local Garda Sergeant had received an emergency call to come and rescue the bride-to-be. When all the great minds and handymen got together, the problem was eventually solved and Majella was released to head off for her life sentence. Well, so much for being there on time. She eventually arrived at 1.40 p.m. I'm sure the fans outside must have thought she was a really cool customer to keep me waiting that long. I, on the other hand, didn't care how long it took. Majella was going to be there and that's all that mattered.

When she arrived up at the top of the aisle on the arm of her father Tom, I turned to take her hand and she was just as beautiful as I thought she was going to be, only that she was even more beautiful in her sleeveless pearl-encrusted gown and her veil and tiara. Her face was ablaze with happiness. As if I needed any confirmation that what I was doing was right, when I held her hand after Tom gave her over to me, I felt I was holding on to the rest of the world.

Majella appeared to be completely unruffled by the earlier drama back at the house. We took our places, Majella and myself, her bridesmaids – Siobhan, her daughter, and my nieces Patricia and Fiona Doogan – and the best men – P.J., John Francis and James. As the ceremony began with the celebrants, Father Brian D'Arcy, the Irish showbusiness chaplain who has been such a good friend to me down the years, and our local priest, Father Pat Ward, there was another hitch. The main microphone wasn't working and we couldn't hear the priests. Well, there's not an awful lot you can do in situations like that except stay calm. Father Ward tried to sort out the problem without success. A couple of minutes had ticked by. Then it struck me that a second microphone by the side of the altar was working, so I jumped up from my position, sailed up on to the altar and moved that mic into the main spot. It worked. The experience of showbusiness paid off and it was a light-hearted moment which, in hindsight, helped to put everyone at their ease.

As the ceremony began, I was determined to savour every moment of the spiritual experience. Father Brian's homily was sincere and thought provoking. His words came from wherever is the deepest in his heart and they fell on my ears in the nicest possible way. There were also wonderful hymns sung beautifully by my sister Margaret, Mary Duff and Triona Crawford and Leon, who do backing on some of my records. The music was played by John Staunton, Ronnie Kennedy and Stephen Milne from my band.

The highlight, of course, was the rite of marriage ceremony when Majella and I exchanged our vows, promising to give ourselves to each other for life. We pledged to be true and faithful and to support and cherish each other. There was another light-hearted moment amidst this very serious and solemn part of the proceedings when Majella had difficulty placing the ring on my finger. She laughed and I could hear some chuckles coming from the congregation behind us. The ring eventually slipped on and that was it. After all those years, I was now an old married man in an instant. 'You may now kiss the bride,' said Father Brian. And as I did so there was a thunderous burst of applause from our families and friends in the background. A warm sensation swept through my body and I had a feeling of elation. I glanced at Majella and in that brief moment I realised that I had been lucky in life up to then, but now I had been blessed with more than I possibly deserved. I must have been awfully good in another life to deserve such happiness.

During the Communion procession that followed in the Mass, I turned to Majella and said, 'I need to go to the toilet.'

Majella smiled.

'No, I'm serious, Majella. I need to go and I need to go now,' I stressed.

She nodded. 'Well, nip out the side door there, but don't be long.'

Had Majella thought about what I was suggesting, there was no way she would have allowed me out the door. After all, TV cameras and photographers from the media at home and abroad were all focused on the church at that time. Me doing my business would certainly have been the scoop of the day.

But I had other ideas. It wasn't a call of nature I was responding to. I had hatched a plan to spring a surprise on Majella by singing 'The Wedding Song' to her in the church that day. To do that, I needed to make my way up to the gallery at the rear of the building where the organist was situated. As I arrived up on the gallery I put my finger to my lips to make sure that people didn't respond in any way that would draw Majella's attention. While walking across the gallery I noticed Majella turning her head and I instantly went down on my hands and knees in case she spotted me. As I crawled along the floor I suddenly came up against two legs. Looking up, I discovered it was one of the priests, Father Michael, who had been handing out the Communion hosts.

'What are you doing down there?' he asked.

'Sshhh! Is Majella looking up in this direction?' I asked.

He glanced towards the altar and shook his head. 'No,' he whispered.

'OK, thanks.'

I then raced into position, ready to sing the song. By this time, there was still a trickle of wedding guests filing up the main aisle to receive Communion. When everyone was seated again, I could see Majella shuffling in her seat, obviously a little agitated. Father Brian looked down at her and shrugged his shoulders. What was going on? Where was Daniel?

As my voice filled the church with the opening line, 'You by my side . . .', I got a side view of Majella. She was totally overcome with emotion. She had no idea that I was going to sing to her in the church on our wedding day. Tears rolled down her cheeks as she sat out front, alone. Father Brian actually walked down off the altar and sat beside her for support. But the tears were happy tears, as Majella realised that what I was doing symbolised my love for her.

It was always going to be a long day, our wedding day. But what was the hurry? We had the rest of our lives to take it easy. As we signed the register, lots of the wedding party were keen to capture the moment with their cameras. The church was slow to empty as the well-wishers queued to congratulate us on the way out. But Father Brian soon had people leaving faster than greyhounds in pursuit of a hare. Our church is right by the sea and someone had sent word that the tide was coming in and there was a danger that some of the cars would end up surrounded by water. When Father Brian made the announcement, people left skid marks in their rush to leave the building.

As I have said many times, I have wonderful fans. Their loyalty, patience and understanding never ceases to amaze me. They were still waiting outside the church when we emerged as man and wife. Would you believe it, after all that time. We went over to them and they gave us the most wonderfully warm reception. If proof was needed that the people who follow me would still accept me as a married man, it was there at that moment. There was a total outpouring of love and genuine good feeling for both of us. They even asked me to kiss the bride, and, of course, I was happy to oblige.

The other thing I found quite amazing was the fact that Sky News were broadcasting live from outside our little church in Kincasslagh for fifteen minutes up to the time we emerged. You'd think we were royalty. I must say, all of the media who were there on the day to report on our wedding and to photograph us showed us a lot of respect in the way they behaved. It was a two-way road of course. We posed for their photographs and answered their questions. We were totally open with them and in return they didn't spoil our day in any way.

The journey from Kincasslagh to Letterkenny, where our reception was to be held at the magnificent Holiday Inn Hotel, should have taken an hour. But we stopped off at the Viking House Hotel to greet more fans who were waiting for us there. Since this book was first published, I have sold the Viking because I didn't have enough time in my life to spend in it and I felt that visitors and residents expected me to be there and were disappointed when I wasn't. I still drop in, though, and was happy to do so on my wedding day.

By the time we left the Viking it was dark, and the heavens had opened and the rain was coming down in buckets. But, as our wedding cavalcade snaked its way through the town of Dungloe, people were out on the street waving enthusiastically at us and motorists were beeping their horns. We had our windows rolled down and we were waving back at them. With the whole carry on, you'd have thought we were royalty. But it was a lovely feeling to have the people of my own county of Donegal come out to show their love and support in that fashion, despite the rain. As we drove through the darkness along the country roads we occasionally came upon bonfires that had been lit in our honour.

The staff of the Holiday Inn in Letterkenny deserve sainthoods after my wedding day, there is no doubt about that. It must have been the longest day and night of their lives. But the management and staff of the hotel were absolutely fantastic. With over five hundred people in attendance, it was never going to be a fast-moving affair. When we arrived at the hotel, those who hadn't had the opportunity to congratulate us at the church due to the tidal warning now took the opportunity to do so and to have souvenir photographs taken with Majella and myself. There was a champagne reception for all the guests before the meal and, meanwhile, our photographer, Barry McCall, was trying desperately, but with little success, to organise the official wedding photographs. By the time we eventually sat down for the meal it was 11.30 that night. Can you believe that! And, do you know, not one person seemed to notice the time.

The banqueting hall looked absolutely magnificent, with the tables and chairs bedecked with white linen covers and a blaze of colour created by a generous arrangement of floral displays. We had organised a little raffle for the flowers, which were displayed on stands. The winners would leave that night with their floral souvenirs of our day. We were quite traditional in our selection of food, with the guests offered a main-course choice of beef or salmon.

As I glanced around the room, it was lovely to see everyone enjoying themselves and to see new friendships being formed among people who had met for the first time. One of the familiar faces I spotted was my very dear neighbour Annie McGarvey. She was a big part of my young life as you'll have read earlier in the book. Seeing Annie, radiating goodness with her sunny personality, sparked off images of my childhood in my mind. It was a lovely, fleeting moment of memories from those simple days growing up in Kincasslagh.

When it came to speech time, Majella's father, Tom, warmly welcomed me into their family and recalled how he and Marion had known me for eight years, adding, 'Long before Majella met him.' He said my joining the Roche family 'just seems a progression of our friendship over all the years'. Tom paid me a lovely compliment when he added how he and Marion were so happy for their daughter Majella 'to meet such a wonderful person'.

I felt on the day that I was surrounded by 'family' because all the people at our wedding meant so much to Majella and me for all kinds of reasons. In my own speech at the wedding, I told the gathering that we'd decided our special day was going to be with people who made both of us into what we are, and I added, 'All of you know why you're special to us and all of you know why you're here today.'

Recalling my early trips to Tenerife, I said, 'Little did I think when I started going down to say hello to Tom and Marion in their restaurant that one day I would end up marrying their daughter. I found them to be really genuine. They never wanted me there because I was a singer: they wanted me there because I think they like me. And that's why I went down to them, because I liked them. I found that Tom was a great character and a wonderful man and that Marion was one of the few people who can be called a lady in this world.' I thanked them both for accepting me into their family and told them it was a real privilege to be a part of it.

There were special thanks, of course, to my own family for everything they had done for me. Firstly, there were my siblings, John, Margaret, Kathleen and James. 'I am the youngest,' I pointed out, 'and all of them in their own way have been so good to me. Kathleen has been like a mother to me and Margaret gave me the opportunity to start my career.'

I paid tribute to my own mother, Julia, when I said, 'I was six when my father died and from then on she has been everything to me. She never let me feel that I needed anything I couldn't get. She gave me security; she gave me love; she gave me encouragement to sing, even at the Burtonport festival when I was young. "Go on over there and enter that talent show," she'd say. I never won, but, sure, what did they know.' I laughed. 'When I started singing, it was never ever going to be a part of my plan to get success for being anything other than what I was. My mother was my mother and I was always going to tell the world about how wonderful she was and she will always be that same person, that wonderful woman who was such an influence in our lives.'

Then I turned to the new Mrs O'Donnell in my life, Majella. I told everyone how beautiful Majella was to me when I first caught a glimpse of her in the church that morning. I said, 'I know that it's not easy for her coming into my (showbiz) world. And I know there will be times when it's not going to be easy in the future to stay in this world that we're going to live in. But I know together we're a wonderful team. We're great friends. I know she loves me and I love her. So thank you, Majella, for consenting to spend the rest of your life with me.'

Turning to Majella's children, Siobhan and Michael, I said, 'Everybody is lucky when they get married that they marry someone that they want to be with. Well, I think that I'm extra lucky because Majella has brought with her Siobhan and Michael. They have accepted me more than I think anybody could be accepted. And I just love it when they come home from school to be with us. I know I can say this, and Majella will back me up, they have a wonderful dad and I will never be anything in their lives compared to him. But I will be the most wonderful friend that you'll ever meet and that's all I want to be.'

My thoughts that day were also with all the people in Romania who have become such an integral and a wonderful part of my life. I said, 'One day I'm going to bring Majella to the orphanage so that she can meet *my* children.'

They say that time flies when you're having fun. And I know people are going to find this hard to believe but, by the time we finished the meal and everything that went with it, it was one-thirty in the morning. 'There's a wonderful night's dancing ahead,' I told everyone. 'It will go on forever. As long as you can stay, I want you to stay.' And I meant every word of that.

The local band, fronted by singer Mary B, struck up and Majella and I took to the floor for the first dance, as is customary for the bride and groom. Majella had a twinkle in her eye as we waltzed across the room and I knew that she was plotting something with me in mind. She had hinted in the lead up to the wedding that she would have a little surprise, just so I wouldn't be too shocked on the day. But I had no idea what it was going to be.

After that first dance, Majella and my very good friend Marc Roberts took over the stage to sing a song. It wasn't just any old song. It was one that Majella had written for me with Marc, the man who also turned me into a songwriter – I'll tell you all about that later. I sat and listened intently to the wonderful words and beautiful sentiments, as Majella's lovely voice filled the room, with Marc doing a superb job on backing vocals and guitar. Luckily, I had an inkling that something was afoot because it helped me to keep my emotions in check. It was a lovely, personal moment that I will take with me through life. The song is called 'When I Found You' and it contains the lines, 'I thank God above for making dreams come true/'Cause he gave me all I wished when I found you.' It was the best wedding present I could have received. At the end, I joined Majella on stage, gave her a hug and told her the song was really beautiful. Then I whispered to Marc, 'That's a hit.' He obviously agreed because he later included it on his album *Meet Me Half Way*.

Now that I was on stage, there was no chance of me leaving it without singing a song or two. I could have sung all night, but this was my wedding day and there was lots of dancing to enjoy. I smiled as I thought how this wedding was destined to live through the night. Everyone was in high spirits and it seemed no one wanted to go home.

At three-thirty in the morning, the band made way for a disco and still there were plenty of people on the floor, tripping the light fantastic, as they used to say. They were still dancing at six o'clock in the morning, but by then Majella and I had slipped away as dawn was breaking. We were witnessing the birth of a new day and it was the first day of the rest of our lives together. It couldn't have been more perfect.

Breakfast the next day started at a time when all the other sane people were having their lunch. There was still a lovely atmosphere in the hotel as family and friends came to wish us well and send us on our way. One local journalist asked me if I was going to have a honeymoon. I said, 'Yes, hopefully for the next forty years.' In fact, I was heading off on a working tour of America, with my new wife.

My life is better now than at any other stage because I have somebody to share it with. When I think of the future now I think of what *we'll* do as opposed to what *I'll* do. As an entertainer, I live out of a suitcase a lot of the time. It's an unusual life of constant movement and I'm very fortunate to find a woman who can live with this hectic lifestyle. Majella doesn't have a problem with what I do. She understands it and she doesn't try to change it. Any alteration in my work will be down to me. She knows that this is what I love to do. This is me. My career is a part of me and I'm a part of it. To take one from the other would not be me, and I would not be fulfilled. Majella has bought the whole package and I've bought hers, too. We all have packages, I suppose. I feel a calmness when we're together. There is a great feeling of comfort between us, for Majella as well as for me. We get on really well. We have our discussions and, like everyone else, there are things we disagree about, but that's normal.

To be honest, married life hasn't been a dramatic shock to the system. I haven't noticed big changes. In the first edition of this book, before Majella came into my life, I had talked about being used to my own ways and enjoying the freedom of being able to go anywhere and do anything at the drop of a hat without having to take another person into account. The main difference in my life now is that I *do* have to think about somebody else. I used to go out and play eighteen holes of golf and then I'd play another eighteen if I felt like it. Now I have to take Majella into consideration. That's been the only change for me, but that's normal for me now.

Seeing me so happy in my married life, people have asked me if I regretted not going down that road earlier. Well, I can honestly say that I have absolutely no regrets. This is our time – Majella's and mine. We met at the right time. We're good together. I'm not one for regrets over anything that has passed. I don't look back and say, 'I wish I had this or that.' I'm just grateful that now is when it's happening.

22. MY SONGS AND MEDJUGORJE

Curled up on a couch, totally transfixed by the magnificent sea views from my new home in Cruit, I was sure that any moment now I was going to be inspired to create a wonderful song. It's true I was a virgin at this kind of thing, songwriting that is. It was my first time embarking on such an adventure. But, when I set my mind to something, one way or another, I always get to where I want to go.

I sat and I contemplated for ages and ages, but there was no sign of any creative inspiration. I paced up and down the room, thinking that, any moment now, it would come to me. I was going to become a songwriter and that was that. But, sure, the more I thought about it, the more my mind drew a complete blank. Maybe I should stick to the singing and let the songwriters get on with their business, I thought eventually.

The reason I was suddenly focused on the notion of penning an original song of my own was all down to an old friend called Marc Roberts, who at that moment was on his way over to me from Galway city. We had arranged that we would sit down and write together. Marc, for some reason, had great faith in my ability to produce a set of words that would mean something in the context of a song. I wasn't so sure myself.

I had known Marc for fifteen or sixteen years, since I first came across him when he was a contestant in a Search For A Star talent competition on the RTE TV show *Live At Three*. I was watching the afternoon programme and he struck me as being a very talented performer. We later met when we were both appearing at a charity concert in Carlow. I was standing at the back of the hall while Marc was performing on stage. I thought he had real star quality. He had Latin good looks and at the time his hair was long, which made him look uncannily like the British pop singer David Essex. He had a lovely, laid-back, soothing voice in the James Taylor mould and it was complemented by a warm and friendly personality which instantly endeared him to the audience. To me, Marc had the complete package and the crowd that night obviously thought so too, judging by the spontaneous round of applause he received at the end of his set.

When we met backstage afterwards, I had an intuition that we were going to become good friends. Marc was friendly, unaffected and very entertaining. He's a funny, quick-witted guy. Ireland is a small circuit and we met again along the way on many other occasions. He's a country boy like myself, as he originally comes from Crossmolina in County Mayo. So we had that background in common. The more I got to know him the more I realised that Marc is one of life's sincere guys with great qualities. He is genuinely interested in people and he's a fantastic listener. Songwriters wear their heart on their sleeve, which makes them very vulnerable. As a result, people empathise with them and they become a good 'ear' to folk who sit down and talk about their problems. I instinctively felt that Marc could be a very loyal friend. That has been affirmed time and again with the passing years.

In 1997, Marc really made an impact when he represented Ireland in the Eurovision Song Contest with a song called 'Mysterious Woman', written by another Irish songwriter, John Farry. Marc was the toast of the country, a household name overnight. The Eurovision was held in Dublin that year and Marc was one of the favourites to win. I really thought he was going to do it. His performance on that big stage in front of an estimated TV audience of 300 million was the stuff that scoops awards. But would it win the Eurovision? The voting that night was a nail-biting experience. Marc was in contention right up to the winning post, but Catriona and The Waves eventually surfed home with their song, 'Love Shine A Light'.

A home bird, Marc has continued to perform all over Ireland and one of his most notable successes has been a John Denver tribute show. He also does brilliant interpretations of big, emotive songs and there are those who feel he could be a huge star in musicals in London's West End. In fact, after his performance in the Eurovision, Marc appeared on the Richard and Judy TV show and the company behind *Blood Brothers* in the West End contacted his record company to see if he would be interested in doing a lead role. Unfortunately, Marc was working on an album at the time and 70s heart-throb David Cassidy ended up landing the part.

One of Marc's greatest pleasures in life is writing songs and he's not precious about them. I know he would have loved me to have recorded some of them. But, while I regard them as first-class songs, they just don't suit my style of singing. What Marc writes is always too off-centre for what I do, which is more middle of the road. He sent me numerous songs over the years and, even though we are best friends, I have to do what I feel is right for me as a singer. I used to say to him, 'Marc, I love your songs, but I'd rather listen to you singing them.' Then one night Marc's manager, Don Collins, suggested that the two of us should get together and write a song. The seed was sown.

This was the day we had chosen to co-write, but I hadn't an idea in my head as I waited for Marc to arrive. Even the beautiful scenery outside my window failed to inspire me. If it was anyone else other than Marc I wouldn't have put myself in this position. He was a friend and I could trust him. I knew that if I came up with something stupid he wouldn't laugh. Marc arrived and we chatted and I did everything except settle down to the job we'd set out to do. I was up and down, doing this and that, talking to people on the phone and generally putting off the moment. Marc knew how to play me. He took out his guitar, slipped off his shoes and put his feet up on the couch. Then he started strumming the guitar and was ignoring me as I went about my business. Eventually he said to me, 'What's in your head?'

'Nothing.'

'There must be something in your head.'

I thought to myself, 'You don't know my head.'

And then he asked, 'What are you thinking?'

I said, 'Well, the only words that come to mind are When you're feeling sad and lonely think of me.'

'Write it down,' Marc said.

'But it sounds corny,' I pleaded.

'Write it down, it mightn't by the end of the song if it makes sense.'

I had neither a notebook nor even a piece of paper, that's how organised I was for this songwriting experience. At the time I had just moved into the house in Cruit and so I knew there were cups and mugs still wrapped up in white tissue paper, so I went to investigate. I returned to the room with a huge piece of wrapping paper and Marc joked, 'We're not going to write that much!'

I sat down and I wrote the line, 'When you're feeling sad and lonely think of me.' Then we figured out what the song was going to be about and where it was going to go. I'd come up with a line and then Marc would say, 'Well, what about this?' By the end of the night we had a song called 'I Will Think Of You'.

Well, you'd think I was after having a baby I was so excited. As soon as it was finished I rang my friend Josephine Burke, and Marc and I sang it down the line to her, even though it was midnight. Then I rang Majella in Tenerife – this was before we got married – and I said to her, 'This is not a proposal so don't get excited, but I've just written this song with Marc and I want you to hear it.' And I sang it to her. Majella knew I was like a child at Christmas. If someone had given me a Rolls Royce I wouldn't have been half as excited. It was the most wonderful sensation and a great sense of achievement. This was something I never thought I had in me. We sang the song about ten times that night.

The next morning as soon as I woke the words were swirling around in my head and I began to sing it again. This was *my* song. It sounded like nothing else anybody had done before.

As I was preparing breakfast I suddenly heard Marc laughing in the background. He had just got up and found me in the kitchen humming, 'When you're feeling sad and lonely . . .' Marc strolled over to the corner, took his guitar off the stand where he had left it propped up overnight and began to strum the tune. Then we sang the song again.

'We've done one, there has to be more in you,' Marc later urged me.

I was at the sink washing up. Marc started strumming his guitar again, working out a new tune and obviously trying to get me motivated. To my surprise, I found myself saying, 'I see you there across the room and I wonder who you are. That would fit there, wouldn't it?'

'It would,' said Marc. 'Write it down.'

Would you believe that twenty-five minutes later we had another song finished. It turned out to be 'All I Want Is You', which also features on the *Live, Laugh Love* album.

Not all songs, of course, came so easily. 'Yesterday's Memories' took hours and hours. It's a story song, so we had to go through the whole family tree to make sure that it made sense. Things like, 'How could somebody who was already dead have a daughter?' We stayed up till two o'clock in the morning working on it and when we finished the song I went and sang it to Majella. I'm sure there were times she wished I didn't value her opinion so much. 'Yesterday's Memories' ended up as the title track of my next album.

Marc has been the key to opening up a whole new creative outlet for me and it has given me so much pleasure. There is a great sense of achievement when a song is finished and it turns out well. It means a lot more to me to sing my own songs and the fans tell me that they love it too because they feel they're getting more of me. Many of the people who attended my 40th birthday charity night in Birmingham went up to Marc and said things like, 'Thank you so much for helping him to write so that we can get to hear what goes on in his head.' It was like they had a different part of me that they didn't have before.

I don't think I could have started songwriting with anyone other than Marc. We were friends and I was totally comfortable working with him. I didn't worry about making an eejit of myself because I knew Marc wouldn't laugh. There's a huge element of trust in songwriting. You can end up saying something that you might think is corny and you don't want the person opposite to laugh at you. You want them to say, 'No, that won't work, but what about this?', and give you another idea back.

Listening to the way I talk and the way I phrase my sentences gave Marc the idea that I had songwriting potential. He used to say to me, 'There's a lyrical quality to the way you speak and you craft words so well. You're an ideal candidate to write songs.' He liked the Donegal sense of humour and the colloquialisms like, 'Nobody knows where the shoe is hurting only the person that's wearing it', which is a phrase that can be applied to so many situations. I don't play a musical instrument, so I needed someone to sit down and work with me and bounce ideas back and forth. Marc was that guy and it has become a very successful partnership. Now, in case some of you think that Marc does most of the work when we're writing, let me tell you that he is a friend, but by God does he make me work. When he writes with someone, they have to contribute as much as he does to the song. Marc composes the music, but we do the lyrics between us because I know what works for me.

When Majella and I were getting married, she wanted to tell the world how she felt about me in a song. There was only one problem: Majella isn't a songwriter. So she turned to Marc for his help. One day Marc and I had been writing, but I had to leave the house to go to a funeral. While I was gone, Majella discussed her idea with Marc and the pair of them plotted how they were going to work together without me discovering what they were up to. There was no way they could meet up and spend time working on it without me becoming suspicious. So they agreed that Majella would write down everything she wanted to say to me in a letter and Marc would then compose a song using her words. Marc told me later that the opening line of the letter was: 'How can I put into words the way you make me feel?' He thought it was a lovely introduction and that's how the song began.

Some time later, when I was doing a show at the Leisureland in Galway, Majella came with me and we both went to visit Marc at his apartment. I had to leave early to go to the show and Majella stayed behind. It was then that Marc played her the song and she loved it. Her gave her a tape to take away, so that she could learn it herself.

The day before our wedding, Marc called at our house in Cruit. It was full of people, including many relatives from abroad who were over for the big shindig. With all the fuss that was going on, Marc slipped down to a room with Majella and she quickly sang the song for him. He said it was absolutely perfect. She had picked it up straight away. Majella is very musical. They decided on a key and Majella had arranged that after the first dance the band would call her up. It was a wonderful highlight of our wedding day and it was a lovely progression of my foray into songwriting. Little did Marc realise the impact he was going to have in my life when we first met all those years ago at that charity event. Fate works in mysterious ways.

In June 2002, I wrote two hymns in strange circumstances while on a pilgrimage to Medjugorje, a small mountain village in southern Bosnia. For those who are not aware of the story of Medjugorje, it is a place where the Blessed Virgin Mary appeared to six young visionaries in June 1981, and has continued to do so to this day.

It was about six o'clock in the evening back in 1981 when two girls, Ivanka Ivankovic, aged fifteen, and Mirjana Dragicevic, aged sixteen, were returning home from a walk. Looking towards a hill called Crnica, Ivanka saw a bright silhouette of a woman with a child. She said to Mirjana, who also saw the vision, 'It's Gospa!', the Croatian for Our Lady. Surprised and scared, they did not approach her. The following day, the two girls felt strongly drawn to the place where they had seen the apparition and were accompanied by four others, Vicka Ivankovic, Ivan Dragicevic, Maria Parlovic, all aged sixteen, and Jakov Colo, aged ten. All of a sudden there was a flash of light and the children looked up and saw Our Lady, this time without the child. They say she was smiling and joyful and indescribably beautiful. Our Lady called them forward with her hands and they went up to her, fell on their knees, and began to pray. She told them: 'I am the Queen of Peace and God has sent me here to help you. I have chosen this parish in a special way and I wish to lead it.' The six visionaries were given many messages relating to peace, faith and prayer and have said that they are ecumenical in nature, meant for people of all religions and all faiths, not just for Catholics. The visionaries have also each been given ten secrets. They say the secrets will remain secrets until an appointed time. Only the visionaries know the day and time the messages will be revealed. Ivanka, Mirjana and Jakov have received all ten secrets and they no longer see Our Lady, except on special occasions. The remaining visionaries have each received nine of the ten secrets and they still see Our Lady almost every day.

The credibility of the six visionaries has been tested medically and scientifically and they have undergone scrutiny by the Catholic Church. When the apparitions first began, thousands of people started to gather on the hill where the Blessed Virgin was appearing. It alarmed the local Communist authorities and, fearing a political uprising, they wanted to jail the children and prove they were emotionally unstable or medically ill. But, by insisting that the young people be tested medically and psychologically, they unwittingly established the soundness and stability of the visionaries and created wider acceptance of their messages. Since then, millions of pilgrims have been flocking to Medjugorje since news of the apparitions spread around the world. Among those making the pilgrimage to the place of apparition have been people suffering from all kinds of illnesses. Some were at death's door, and there are many who claim to have been cured at Medjugorje.

For a long time, I had been planning to go to Medjugorje. I've been to Knock in County Mayo, where Our Lady appeared, and I've been to Lough Derg, a penitential island in Ireland. But I'd never been to any of the other shrines, like Lourdes. I just never had any urge to go to them. Medjugorje is somewhere I felt I would like to go one day. People say that you are invited to go to Medjugorje. You don't go by chance. It's not that *somebody* invites you, but *something* compels you to go there.

A cousin of mine, Annette, called me one night. 'You know,' she said, 'I got a message for you to go to Medjugorje.'

Now let me stress, before I tell you this story, that my cousin Annette is not some kind of religious fanatic. Far from it. She said to me on the phone that night, 'I want to tell you my story of Medjugorje.' Annette told me that she got a call one day from a woman who said there was a flight to Medjugorje the following day; someone had just cancelled and would she like to take her place. So she accepted. 'At that time,' she said to me, 'I had a question.' She never told me what it was, but it was obviously something major in her life.

She said, 'In Medjugorje one night I left the house where I was staying to go to Mass and, instead, I found myself turning left to go in the direction of the Blue Cross [a place of many apparitions of Our Lady] and it began to rain. I had this question in my head and I started to cry.'

Now, you may not be aware of this, but sometimes if people cry like that they are being cured of something if it's a religious kind of experience. She was walking at a great pace to the Blue Cross when she spotted a pair of Rosary beads on the path and she said to Our Lady, 'Mother, you're the only mother I have in this world. My own mother is dead. You know the question I'm asking. I know it's unfair to do this, but you're the only one who can give me an answer. I'll know if the answer is yes if I find another Rosary beads before I go back home. I know I have no right to do this, but it's the only way I know how.'

It was getting dark and eventually she reached her destination. She heard somebody saying, 'Hello, come over here.' She got a fright, looked around and there was a woman underneath a bush, sheltering from the rain. The woman said to her, 'Come over here and we'll say the Rosary together.' It was a woman from Camden Town in London.

As they were praying, an old, weather-beaten man with the appearance of a local arrived at the area. After a while, the two women noticed that he was disrupting the rocks around the Blue Cross. The London woman said to Annette, 'Look at that fella, he is destroying the cross.'

He bent down, searched with his hands and picked up something. Then he walked from the cross over to my cousin, opened her hand and placed a pair of Rosary beads in it. She was startled and then she looked into his face and she said, 'Why are you doing this?' All he said to her was, 'Santa Maria', meaning Holy Mary, Our Lady. He never looked at the woman from London; he just walked away without saying another word. And Annette had got her answer.

Later, Annette got a message and it was to tell me to go to Medjugorje. She told me that she was reading and praying and what came into her mind were thoughts that she should tell Daniel O'Donnell to come to Medjugorje. When she told me I didn't think she was mad or anything like that. It was a place I'd felt drawn to myself, so I decided at that point to go and my friend Josephine Burke accompanied me. There were about twenty people in our travelling party and they were from Waterford. There are no hotels in Medjugorje; the people who go there on a pilgrimage stay in houses. There could be as many as thirty rooms in those houses and each house is run by a family.

The first morning at breakfast, I overhead a lady saying to someone, 'Is that Daniel?' I knew by her accent that she was from Donegal, close to the area where I come from.

'Yes, it's Daniel,' I said.

'Oh, I can't believe this, I'm going to get weak,' she replied.

Well, I didn't know I had that effect on people. We got chatting and it turned out I knew their families, but I didn't know them. They were Peter and Breege, a husband and wife.

'We have been praying for you,' Breege said to me.

I thought to myself, Oh, here we go. At that time, Majella and myself weren't married and I assumed that here were people who disapproved of our relationship and now I was going to get nailed.

'We have been praying for you since last September,' she continued.

Thanks be to God, I thought. Nobody knew much about Majella in September 2001, so it couldn't have been that she was praying about.

'What is it?' I asked.

'Oh,' she said, 'I'll tell you another time.'

'Tell him now. Tell him now,' Peter insisted.

So we went over to a corner of the room and we settled ourselves down at a table. By this stage, the curiosity was killing me.

Peter and Breege, it transpired, go to Medjugorje on a yearly basis, sometimes twice a year. Talking with them, I knew instinctively that these people weren't religious freaks. They came across as a very normal couple, lovely people. I feel the general impression of people who go to places like Medjugorje is that they are Holy Marys. Some may be a bit over the top, but Peter and Breege are not.

Breege told me why she had been so shaken to see me in Medjugorje. 'The last time I was here I was praying in the chapel one day and I heard this voice in my head, "Tell Daniel O'Donnell to come to Medjugorje." I thought to myself, He's too busy to be coming to Medjugorje.'

It was a very unsettling incident for her. She came out of the church and told Peter what had happened. He didn't know what to think of it either. Eventually they shrugged it off and went about their business. But the next time Breege was in the chapel, she had the same experience, 'Tell Daniel O'Donnell to come to Medjugorje.' She came out and said to Peter, 'It's happened again. I can't believe this.' She was really troubled by it.

Then another day Peter was in the chapel and he got the same thought to tell me. He came out and said to Breege, 'I got the same message as you.' Breege said, 'Oh well, thanks be to God, it's you that has the responsibility for it now. I don't have to bother thinking about it anymore. It's in your hands.'

Still, they now both felt obliged to give me the message. They just didn't know how they were going to get it to me. They told a group of people who go to Medjugorje that they had a message to deliver, but they didn't feel they were able to do it and they asked for a group prayer to help them.

There had been a celebration function for me in my local hall in Kincasslagh after I was awarded an honorary MBE, and Brid came along to give me the message. But there were too many people around and she couldn't do it. Peter came down to my home in Cruit another day and rang the bell, but there was no reply. Then she spoke to a priest who knew me and he suggested that the best way of getting a message to me was through a cousin of mine – Annette who had got the same message when she was in Medjugorje. Breege and Peter never actually talked to Annette to pass on the message they had received because they felt it was too personal. Stranger still is the fact that I had been thinking about going, but only made my decision after Annette called me.

This was my first morning in Medjugorje and I thought things were a wee bit crazy. Peter and Breege had also told me that they had been staying in a different house, but they weren't comfortable there. They had asked to be moved and where should they end up, but in the same house where I was staying. It really was a strange affair.

That first day I visited the local St James's Church and it was beautiful. I felt a great sense of peace there. Later, I headed off to climb the hill of Apparitions at Podbrdo with our group. There was a nun among the party and she wasn't good on her feet, so I said to her, 'I'll help you up the hill.' Medjugorje isn't a trip for people who aren't good at walking. You need to be in decent shape. On the journey up the hill we were all reciting the Rosary, walking past images depicting the mysteries of the Rosary, and the further we went up the heavier the nun was getting. At one point she was going to give up, but I encouraged her to hang in there, as we were nearly at the top.

Upon arrival there was no denying that the effort to get there was certainly worth it. This was the place where Our Lady first appeared to all of the children. There's a big area where you can sit down on rocks. I sat there and I stared down over Medjugorje, which means 'the village between the hills'. It was a beautiful day and the atmosphere was still and peaceful. It was a little piece of heaven on earth at that moment. All of a sudden, I found my head full of words and I remember thinking, God, I have to write these down. I had no paper with me. I had a prayer book that Josephine had given me and, to be honest, I had never opened it. I scoured the book for a blank page and discovered one near the back, with just a small amount of print on it. I started to write and the words just flowed. I found it very odd that I was writing without thinking about it. The words were just appearing on the paper and they were about Medjugorje. When I had finished I had a verse of a hymn.

The next day Breege and Peter were going up the hill with their two sons and one of their girlfriends, and I decided to go with them. So off we went and again we sat down. The same thing happened. Suddenly there were words going around in my head and I jotted them down and it was the chorus of a hymn. I thought, When I go home I'll get Marc to do the music. I knew there was more to be written. Then I thought, No, just sing it yourself. This was me talking to me. So I sang it there and then on the spot.

Breege came over to me and asked, 'What are you doing?'

'I'll tell you what I'm doing. I'm writing a hymn about Medjugorje,' I said.

Breege was delighted and she told the rest of the family. They asked me to sing it for them, which I did. And when I'd finished, Breege said, 'That's why you had to come here.'

And I did think it was another very strange experience.

Another evening we were on our way up another mountain, Cross Mountain, where pilgrims do the Stations of the Cross along the way. It's quite high and a difficult climb as well. There are numerous crosses to be found at the top. The ritual here is that people bring their 'cross' – whatever is troubling them – to the top of this mountain and leave it behind them. We all sat down again and I had my back to Medjugorje. I was looking out over a beautiful landscape, mountains everywhere, and again the words started to come into my head. There and then I wrote the second verse of the hymn. Just as I was finished, someone called, 'Daniel, are you ready?'

I said, 'Yes, I'm ready now.' I said it as if I realised that I had done whatever I had come to Medjugorje to do.

Before climbing Cross Mountain that evening, it had been several days since I'd written the first verse and chorus and I hadn't taken out the book to try to finish the hymn. But in that moment, I had written the second part. And, I said to our priest, Father Pat, 'Call the people back who are with us and I'll sing this.' And I sang it all for the first time at the top of Cross Mountain.

Earlier, after I had written the first verse, my friend Josephine had asked me what I was going to call it. 'Are you going to mention Medjugorje in the hymn?' she asked.

'No, it'll be too difficult,' I said. 'But people will know it's about Medjugorje because I will have told them.'

Then the second verse came along. It says:

'She tells us to reach out to one another
To never turn our back on those in need
And when our world is dark and full of worry
She'll hurry to our aid and intercede
I know she'll never leave us or forsake us
And from our side she never will be far.'

And when I wrote the word far I realised that it was going to rhyme with Medjugorje. And I continued:

'And with her son she will protect and keep us
Sweet Queen of Peace of Medjugorje.'

And I realised in the last line I had the title and I had also mentioned Medjugorje in the verse. That hymn is now 'Sweet Queen Of Peace'.

Back in the village, word got around among the people that I had written a hymn. We were in a restaurant which is frequented by Irish people and some said to me, 'You've written a hymn. You should sing it.' But, strangely, when I tried to sing it, I couldn't remember it. David Parkes, an Irishman who was cured of Crohn's Disease in Medjugorje many years ago – he claims that his greatest cure was his spiritual renewal – was there at the time and he offered me a mini-disc to record the song. I got the idea that what I needed to do was to go back up the hill where I had started to write it and sing it there.

As I thought about this hymn that I had written and considered the prospect of recording it, I began to think how I would like the proceeds to go to charity. And I thought, if I write another hymn, that would be even more to go to charity. 'I will write another one,' I said to myself. I was getting a bit cocky at this stage.

There's an apparition every day in Medjugorje. Our Lady appears to the visionaries once a day, in the evening. One evening I was there with one of the women when she had her apparition and it was the most incredible experience. It took place in a little church at her house and there was a very small group of people present. We were saying the Rosary when she came in. She was a very normal-looking woman, no different to anyone else in the village where she comes from. If you saw her on the street and didn't know her, there would be nothing strange about her. She began praying and then she walked up to the front of the little church where she continued her prayers in front of a statue of Our Lady. Suddenly, she stopped and looked up. I was behind her and to the side and I could see her talking. You couldn't hear her speak, but she was talking and smiling and listening. I remember getting butterflies in my stomach and I had a feeling of fear, but a nice kind of fear, and I believe that I was in the presence of Our Lady. She was actually there and I was close to her. I'm probably just as close to her now, wherever I am. But I was conscious that she was there at that moment. It was both exciting and humbling and certainly unforgettable.

It was late at night when I had made the decision to go up to the hill of Apparition to sing the hymn 'Sweet Queen Of Peace'. I had a rucksack on my back and I had a flash lamp and a Rosary beads. So off I tottered up the hill, me and myself, and I was saying the Rosary along the way. It was dark, but it was a really calm night and the sky was full of stars. It was so quiet and, as I was walking and praying, these words came to me: 'Somehow when darkness falls I feel you close to me.' And I realised immediately that this was the start of the second hymn.

I remember thinking, Now, listen here, I have a pair of Rosary beads in one hand, a flash lamp in the other, how in God's name can I write down what I'm getting into my head? I'm going to leave it until I get home to Ireland and then I'll write it.

When I returned to Ireland, I went into the studio in Dublin on the Monday to record my album *Yesterday's Memories*. I started to sing and I was hoarse. I tried a second song. Sometimes when you sing different songs it clears it. I went through five songs and I couldn't do it. I was working on the album with my producer, John Ryan, and I decided to tell him about 'Sweet Queen Of Peace'. Now, I didn't go into all the details because it's a story that does sound like I have gone a bit mad. I didn't want to frighten John off. So I told him in a way that I thought would be acceptable, leaving out all the really strange events that had unfolded out in Medjugorje. John wouldn't be religious in the same way that I am, but he is a spiritual man.

Then I said to John, 'I think I'm going to have to come back another day to work on the album, but while I'm here I think I'll record the Medjugorje hymn.'

I started to sing it for John and then he said, 'Well, I'm going to tell you something very strange now: your voice is clearing up.'

I recorded 'Sweet Queen Of Peace', and then I recorded five more songs after that for the *Yesterday's Memories* album. It was like I had to give the first indication that I was going to do something with 'Sweet Queen Of Peace' before anything else could happen.

Then I said to John, 'I'm going to write another hymn.'

'The worst thing you could do, Daniel, is write a bad song,' he replied in his slow Mayo drawl.

'Why would I write a bad song? Sure, I'd never do that. If it's not good, I won't bother with it,' I replied, a bit peeved.

I was staying at Josephine's house outside Dublin that week while working on the album. The band was due in the studio at one o'clock on the Thursday afternoon. At ten minutes past midday, I got a brown envelope and I went into Josephine's sitting room and I wrote down, 'Somehow when darkness falls I feel you close to me.'

At twenty minutes to one I called Majella on the phone and I said, 'Listen to this.' I had written the second hymn in half an hour with the air and everything, and I went into the studio to John and I recorded it that same day.

As I work on this book, those two songs are set to feature on an album of hymns, which I plan to release in the autumn of 2003. I'm recording this particular album because of those two hymns. They are recorded with a full orchestra and they are just beautiful, even if I say so myself. I intend to give a donation to Romania and to an orphanage in Medjugorje from the profits of those two songs.

On reflection, I can say I loved Medjugorje and it was a most incredible experience in my life. I didn't see Our Lady and the sun didn't spin, but I felt a wonderful peace and the two hymns are so beautiful. Sometimes I feel I didn't write them at all. I'm not mad. I'm not crazy. I'm very happy that I'm a Catholic, but I'm not pumping out religion. I love singing Gospel songs and I think it's important for us to realise that we would be nothing without God in our lives, well, I certainly wouldn't be. People need to realise that to be religious doesn't mean you need to be crazy. A lot of people think that if people are religious they are on a different level. You're not on a different level. You have something lovely in your life. My religion helps me to make sense of life and it's comforting for me to know that there is a life after our time here and that we will meet our dearly departed loved ones again at some time in the future. I do believe that there's a greater world than ours, and I'll be fiercely disappointed if there's not.

23. AN MBE AND THE AMERICAN DREAM

December 2001 had been an eventful month for me, with my fortieth birthday celebrations and my announcement to the world that I had found someone special to share my life, when I'd introduced Majella for the first time at my big party in Birmingham. Reflecting on the twelve months of that year, I had many things to be thankful to God for. I had enjoyed good health; the tours had sold out at home and abroad; that year's album was successful and everything was rosy in my personal life. Twenty years had passed in a flash – it seems the older you get the faster time goes by – but I still had the most wonderful career. Now, when I say career, I mean *life* because, let me stress again, singing, entertaining and meeting people is by no means a job to me. At the age of forty, I was lucky to still regard it as a gift that is personally totally fulfilling and rewarding. It is a way of life for me, a magical one, but one I wouldn't have without the people who support me at home, in the UK and in Australia, New Zealand and America. The foundation for my success is in Ireland and the UK where the fanbase grew at a rate that was beyond anything I could have imagined when I set out on this road. It started off as a breeze here at home and around England, Scotland and Wales and before long it had become a whirlwind, picking up more and more people along the way. They have sustained my career at a very high level to this day, flocking to the theatres and arenas when I tour and sending my albums shooting up the charts.

As I was contemplating all of this at home on the morning of New Year's Eve, there was a phone call from my sister, Kathleen.

'We've had some of the papers on to us, Daniel. They're saying that you're going to get an MBE and they want a comment from you,' said Kathleen.

'Sure, that couldn't be right,' I said.

'Well, they seem very sure that you're to get the MBE,' Kathleen insisted.

I was certain this was a wild rumour as I had heard nothing about it from my management or from any official quarter. I was Irish; why would they give *me* an MBE? Still, I thought I'd better make some phone calls and have it checked out, so that I could have an answer for the papers. To my surprise, the word came back that, yes, I was going to be honoured with an MBE. I found it difficult to comprehend. I have been lucky to be the recipient of many awards during my life, and one of my greatest personal honours was to receive the Donegal Person Of The Year. I'm not one to get terribly excited about things and I'm normally laid back, but when my home county of Donegal honoured me I was jumping with joy. It was the same with the MBE, for many reasons.

I was delighted, not just for myself and my family, but also for the people of the UK who have supported me through the years. In a way, I felt that this was recognition for them. They had made me a huge part of their lives, poured their love into me and my music, and now this was *their* big moment, an affirmation of what they believed in. Their Queen was recognising me, paying me a tribute and that's the greatest honour they could have given me, that their sovereign would recognise me in that way. A large number of my English fans had written to the Queen, explaining how they enjoyed my music, describing the impact of my shows on them, how I had enriched their lives, which was lovely to hear. I wasn't aware that people were doing that. The fact that it was coming from my fans as well as the Queen made it an award to treasure all the more.

It's an honorary MBE because I'm outside the Commonwealth and, initially, I was told that it would be presented to me at the British Ambassador's residence in Dublin. Then the word started filtering through that Prince Charles was coming to Dublin and that while he was here he would do the honours. I was even more delighted. It would have been wonderful, of course, to have gone to Buckingham Palace to receive it. But Prince Charles in Dublin was the next best thing and it was going to be a lot more relaxed by all accounts. I was allowed to take eight or nine people with me to the ceremony, whereas at the Palace you can only have two, as the security is a lot more strict. So I was accompanied on the day by my mother, Julia, Majella, my sister Margaret, brother John, friends Josephine Burke and Evelyn Sheehan and my manager Sean Reilly.

Prior to the Prince coming in, we were given a crash course in royal etiquette. We were shown where to step up when the time came for the presentation. It seemed to be very formal. But when Prince Charles came into the room the atmosphere was more jovial. The Prince exudes a warmth that instantly puts people at their ease. There was no sense of someone who is totally distanced from us, a person so precious that it's almost a sin to look at him. No, he came across as a lovely human being and he seemed to be a people person, embracing everyone from all walks of life. He was smaller than I had imagined, but he looked fit and he is obviously a man who does his best to enjoy his life as, like the rest of us, he battles the dwindling sands of time.

Charles and I had a mutual friend called Derek Hill, a well-known and highly regarded artist who lived in Donegal. He has since died, God rest him. Derek occasionally used to give Charles my albums to pass on to the Queen Mother as, apparently, she enjoyed my music. He was a great friend of the Queen Mother as well, and had introduced her to my songs and albums. I doubt if what I do would be Charles's cup of tea, but, although I hadn't met him, I had performed before him at the BBC One *Songs Of Praise* first broadcast of the millennium in January 2000. He was accompanied by his sons, Prince William and Prince Harry, at that special event in the magnificent Millennium Stadium, Cardiff, which had an audience of 66,000 people and also featured my good friend Sir Cliff Richard, Welsh baritone Bryn Terfel, Andrew Lloyd Webber and the Band of the Welsh Guards.

Later Derek told me that on speaking to Charles after the show he had asked, 'Isn't that the chap whose music you gave me for my grandmother?' So he had an awareness of me.

Charles mingled with us at the MBE presentation in the Ambassador's residence and he came across as being very witty. He was constantly cracking jokes. I felt so fortunate that my mother had lived to see the day and to be a part of it. Mind you, her presence there that day had me on edge because she's a very straight-talking woman, you know. She doesn't hold her fire if she has something to say to you, good or bad. She speaks her mind. There's no talking behind anyone's back with my mother. She'll let you know to your face what she thinks. My mother was a big fan of Diana, so I was worried about what she might say to Charles. I was conscious of the time that Loretta Lynn came over to Dublin to appear on an Irish TV show, which I hosted in the early '90s and my mother had words with her husband, Doolittle, over the way he had treated her during their married life together. Mother had been to see the film *The Coalminer's Daughter*, based on Loretta's life, and in it Doolittle had been portrayed as a husband who had given her a hard time. When my mother met him at the TV studios in Dublin she said in a very formidable fashion, 'You were a right boy!' Well, the poor man withered right there in front of her.

Now here she was, about to meet Charles and God knows what she thought of him and his relationship with Diana. I could bet that if she had a view it was going to be in Diana's favour because she loved her so much. Before Charles came into the room I had said to her, 'Now, Mother, don't you be saying anything.'

As we chatted informally with him, I heard my mother saying, 'I sent a card to your two boys when Diana died.'

'That was very nice of you,' Charles replied.

I held my breath and thought, Oh my God, don't say a word about anything else, Mother, or I mightn't get the MBE after all. My mother, I'm glad to say, was on her best behaviour that day. Maybe it was something to do with the fact that she took a shine to Charles.

His aunt Margaret had just died and we spoke about that. I told him that I had given his assistant CDs for his grandmother, the Queen Mother, who was alive at the time. It was that kind of conversation, quite normal really.

Then there was the formal presentation and, when I stepped forward to receive my Honorary MBE, an extensive citation was read out, outlining the reasons why I had been chosen for the award. It referred to my charity work and my contribution to the music industry. As I listened to the lengthy tribute I thought, God bless us and save us, is that me at all? It made me feel very important.

I had on a lovely suit at the presentation, but after the ceremony I was heading on to the airport, as I was flying to England to start a tour the next day. My car was parked in a field near the Ambassador's residence and I changed out of my good suit and into my casual clothes right there behind the car in the open air. I remember standing in the cold, with my trousers off (fortunately it was dark), and thinking, Well, I'm back down to earth again. Nothing changes.

There's no chance of me ever writing my name with MBE after it, but I do get letters addressed to me as Daniel O'Donnell MBE . . . and I chuckle. That said, it's an award I genuinely do treasure.

I do stop and take a long, hard look at my life sometimes when I find myself in situations that are such a long way from my humble background in Kincasslagh. I mean, at the MBE presentation, I was a guest of honour in the company of Prince Charles. That is a long way from the summer I spent working in the local graveyard or, during another summer, washing dishes in a Dublin hotel. But now I never know from day to day what doors are going to open and who I'm going to meet. It could be the President of Ireland or a member of the British Royal Family. If you started taking those kinds of incredible experiences for granted your head would end up in serious trouble. So I always stop and remind myself of where I've come from, and I enjoy the moment without letting it affect me in a negative way.

In June 2003, I had one of those wonderful experiences while on tour in America. I met Charley Pride and Loretta Lynn, two of my favourite American singers (as I have already revealed), and spent time in their company. I had the pleasure of sharing time with both of them in the same week. Before we set off for Dallas, my manager Sean got a call to see if Majella and myself would have lunch with Charley and his wife, Rozene and Charley's manager, John Daines. We met up on Wednesday, 4 June, and it turned out to be a very pleasant afternoon in their company, two very hospitable and easy people to be around. We had such a good time, Majella and me, that it seemed to pass in a flash, like all of the best experiences in life. There was nothing spectacular about the afternoon; we just enjoyed some lovely food and chatted like old pals. It's the people who make the experience and Charley and Rozene leave a lovely after-glow and great memories to take away.

The following Saturday we went to Loretta Lynn's show and she invited me up on stage to sing with her, which was a personal thrill in itself. I also sang, 'I'll Take You Home Again Kathleen', which is one of Loretta's favourite Irish songs, as her mother used to sing it to her. Loretta's grandmother was Irish. We went backstage while she was on a break and we chatted with her. She then invited us to her home the following day, and we spent a couple of hours in her company.. When I reflect on those few days, they are amazing to me. That might seem strange to some people because of the business I'm in, but I'm just human like everyone else and I'm a fan, just like all fans.

We then went on to the Grand Ole Oprey in Nashville. We had bought tickets and I saw that George Hamilton, another American country singer I've got to know over the years, was the star attraction. I left a note for George to say that we were there and during the show he introduced us and we took a wave. Later, the manager of the Oprey came over and said, 'Lovely to have you here. You must come and perform sometime.' So, meeting two of my all-time favourite singers in the period of a few days and having that experience at the Grand Ole Oprey, things that are quite incredible from my point of view, stopped me in my tracks and made me question how in God's name I got to where I am today.

While in Nashville, Majella and myself took a trip out to Memphis to do the tour of Elvis's home, which I had never visited. I enjoy Elvis's music and have included some of his songs in my shows and recorded them for my albums, but Cliff was my number one, so I wasn't hugely excited and I didn't have any high expectations of my journey to Graceland. It wasn't a kind of religious outing, as it is for the real Elvis fans. Boy, did I get a surprise. It turned out to be one of the greatest experiences of my life. I even have a shiver as I write about it now.

We bought our tickets at ten o'clock in the morning and we didn't get going on the tour until half-past twelve in the afternoon because of the huge crowds waiting to take the trip. When we lined up there were probably a hundred or more people in front of us. Now, I know people are thinking, Why did Daniel have to queue? Surely he could have organised VIP treatment. Well, as the people who know me will attest, I always like to buy tickets and do things as normally as possible to have the same experience as everyone else. I bought the tickets for Loretta's show and she was annoyed, but that's just the way I am.

So anyway, I was on the tour and we were in a group of twenty people. It was while travelling up the driveway and standing outside the house among all the other visitors that I finally had an awareness of the incredible impact Elvis made during his short life. I found it amazing that a singer could still command such respect and such adoration so many years after his death, which occurred on 16 August 1977. He was only forty-two years old and it's a shame that the world didn't get to see more of him. The quality of the tour is second to none, being both personal and informative, with Elvis's own voice interspersed throughout the commentary as you wander through the interior.

The house itself is gorgeous and decorated in 70s style. I recall the gracious living room, with a piano in the background and there was a very striking portrait of Elvis lining the stairs. We were reminded of his sad death when told that we couldn't go upstairs. That part of Graceland is forever closed to the public. Not even the tour guides have been there.

We sauntered out by the pool and around the garden before we finally ended up at the grave, where he's buried with his parents and his grandmother. I was disappointed that the Elvis tour ended on that poignant note. Obviously he's dead, but while I was in the house I had a feeling, strange as it may seem, that he was still around. I wondered, when I came out of the mansion, if all the love and good feeling that people have for him in the house brings his spirit back. I was upset when I got to the grave because it's the last memory you take away from the visit. I feel that I made a connection with Elvis on the tour for the first time in my life. Since then, whenever I sing an Elvis song it has a deeper meaning for me and I hope that that is reflected in the performance.

It may not be on a grand scale like Elvis's Memphis mansion, but Majella and I now have a place to call our own home when we're in America. I had been looking at houses for quite a long time without success. Majella and I had viewed several beautiful homes, but there was always some ingredient missing. Eventually we both fell in love with a lovely four-bedroom, single-storey residence in Orlando, Florida, last year. They say that a house welcomes you and this particular one instantly won our hearts. There were pillars at the entrance, which is a feature I personally like, and as soon as we stepped over the threshold it was like meeting an old friend. We felt totally at ease. There was a warmth to the atmosphere. We knew instinctively that it was going to be a comfortable home. It has the essential pool for the heat of Florida and, although it's in a development, it's very private. A management company looks after it for us and, like the apartment in Tenerife, as soon as we arrive and turn the key there's a feeling of home away from home. My mother came out to holiday with us in June 2003, and she loved it too. No home, of course, will ever surpass Donegal, but I quite like having roots in other places. I'm a big child at heart and in Orlando I love the fact that our home is just fifteen minutes from Disneyworld and I've been there numerous times to savour the thrills of all the attractions.

After many years knocking on the door career-wise, America is also finally opening up for me. I always enjoyed doing shows in the States, but I never shared my manager Sean Reilly's confidence that I could build up a large following in that vast territory. Bigger guys than me have tried and failed. It is so daunting. You could be big in one state and nobody would have heard of you in the next one. I did believe there was a market in the US and Canada, but I just didn't know how I was going to reach the people. I had tried shows in different cities down the years, but it didn't amount to anything major.

From 1997 on, we'd started concentrating on Branson and stopped going to other places in the States. Logistically, it was too difficult to tour and it didn't make economic sense because the audience wasn't there to support it. A certain amount of people came to our shows all the time, but not enough to tour. It didn't make financial sense going to Branson either, but it was slowly building and there wasn't the enormous expense of touring because we were based in a theatre. But, through every adversity, Sean Reilly never lost his focus. He was determined to make it work because he had a gut instinct that if I got the break I could make the same connection with people in the States that I have done at home, in the UK, in Australia and in New Zealand. Sean was definitely the driving force behind America for me. If it wasn't for him, I would have been happy to give up on it years ago. Like all good showbiz stories, I eventually got lucky. I was in the right place at the right time and the key to the door came my way through a lady called Diane Bliss.

Diane works in the Public Broadcasting Service (PBS) community TV in Detroit. There are PBS stations all over America and they are financially supported by the public. Diane had heard about me and felt that I was someone who might make an impact on PBS in Detroit. She came over to see me perform in London's Royal Albert Hall in 1999 and my show confirmed her instinct. Diane was accompanied by a male colleague who wasn't as enthusiastic, but she kept on pushing to get me on air.

Eventually, I got the call to go to Detroit and we did a test. They showed one of my concerts, which had been recorded in Limerick, and I did an interview. Then it was shown in three or four other areas in the States through PBS. There was such a good response that they decided to air another of my video recordings, this time a show from Killarney, and that was shown on seventy per cent of the PBS stations around the States. That got a great reaction and it has taken off from there. My office back home in Dublin knew that it was working when the letters started to come in from fans around the US.

The type of exposure you get through PBS cannot be bought. The shows are shown over and over again, so it creates a huge awareness of someone like me. And if people like what they see, well, then, you are on to a winner. Viewers are asked to pledge sums of money for gifts that could include a copy of the Daniel O'Donnell show, which they have been watching. The video is a 'thank you' gift in return for, maybe, a $100 pledge. So, the idea is to broadcast shows that will capture the imagination of people and encourage them to make financial donations in return for the videos, CDs or books of the artists they enjoy watching.

Through the exposure I've enjoyed on PBS, my shows in Branson now sell out and crowds are coming to my concerts in venues right across the States. At this point I can now say that Canada and America are definitely opening up for me, something I didn't think would happen. Thank you, Sean, for believing in it and for ignoring 'Doubting Thomas'. I'm glad I was wrong. Where it will take me in the future I don't know, but right now I intend to enjoy every moment of the wonderful opportunities that are starting to come my way in America.

Reflecting on the day in 1983 when I recorded the song 'My Donegal Shore', I never imagined that 21 years later I would be accepting a Lifetime Achievement Award in England. But in September 2004, I was honoured with exactly that distinction at a ceremony in London's Sheraton Hotel. The fact that it was voted by the fans, in a poll conducted through the *Irish Post* newspaper in Britain, made it all the more special. I certainly owe an enormous gratitude to the people who contributed to that poll and for your continuous support. A Lifetime Achievement Award doesn't mean it's the end of the road for me. I intend to go on. And I can honestly say that it gets better as it goes on.

In the early 70s, I became aware of the songs of one of country music's legends: the late Jim Reeves. The velvet style of Gentleman Jim, as he was known, really appealed to me. I was only a child when he was killed in a plane crash on a flight back to Nashville from Arkansas on 31 July 1964. Jim and his manager, Dean Manuel, reported their single engine plane had been encountering heavy rain while crossing remote hills a few miles from Nashville's Berry Field Airport. The light aircraft was making its approach to land at 5 p.m. when it disappeared from the radar screen. Two days later the wreckage and bodies were found amid dense forest. Jim Reeves was just 41 years old.

Jim Reeves lived on through his music, and his songs were tremendously popular during my teens. I always found them very easy to sing and, later, when I established my career, I recorded several of them. One of my ambitions was to record an entire album of Jim Reeves songs. In October 2004, during the year that marked the fortieth anniversary of his untimely death, I finally got to realise that dream. I had a chart hit with *Welcome To My World*, a tribute album featuring twenty classic songs of Jim Reeves, including 'Adios Amigo', 'He'll Have To Go', 'Distant Drums', 'You're The Only Good Thing' and the title track, 'Welcome To My World'.

So what lies ahead of me in my world? Well, as you get older you realise more and more how important it is to just live in the moment. I have already been blessed with so much, thanks to the support of each and every one of you. You continue to allow me to follow my dream, but who knows where it will take me in the future. May our paths cross along the way.

DISCOGRAPHY

DANIEL O'DONNELL ALBUMS

TITLE	TRACKS
The Boy From Donegal (1984)	Donegal Shore
	Home Is Where The Heart Is
	Galway Bay
	Shutters And Boards
	Forty Shades Of Green
	My Side Of The Road
	5,000 Miles From Sligo
	The Old Rustic Bridge
	The Old Bog Road
	Slievenamon
	Noreen Bawn
	Ballyhoe
The Two Sides Of Daniel O'Donnell (1985)	The Green Glens Of Antrim
	The Blue Hills Of Breffini
	Any Tipperary Town
	The Latchyco
	Hometown On The Foyle
	These Are My Mountains
	My Donegal Shore
	Crying My Heart Out Over You
	My Old Pal
	Our House Is A Home
	Your Old Love Letters
	21 Years
	Highway 40 Blues
	I Wouldn't Change You If I Could
I Need You (1986)	I Need You
	Sing An Old Irish Song
	From A Jack To A King

My Lovely Rose Of Clare
Stand Beside Me
Irish Eyes
Dear Old Galway Town
Three Leaf Shamrock
Veil Of White Lace
Kickin' Each Other's Hearts Around
Medals For Mothers
Wedding Bells
Snowflake
Your Friendly Irish Ways
Lough Melvin's Rocky Shore
I Love You Because

Don't Forget To Remember (1987)

Don't Forget To Remember
I Don't Care
Old Love Never Dies
I Wonder Where You Are Tonight
Don't Be Angry
Roses Are Red (My Love)
Before I'm Over You
Take Good Care Of Her
Pretty Little Girl From Omagh
Green Willow
Don't Let Me Cross Over
The Good Old Days
Pat Murphy's Meadow
I Just Cannot Make It On My Own

From The Heart (1988)

The Minute You're Gone
It Doesn't Matter Anymore
Mary From Dungloe
Bye Bye Love
The Old Rugged Cross
Wasting My Time
Kelly
Things
Act Naturally

	Honey Wooden Heart It Keeps Right On A-Hurtin' My Bonnie Maureen I Know That You Know (That I Love You) The Old Dungarven Oak Danny Boy
The Last Waltz (1990)	Here I Am In Love Again We Could Last Waltz Of The Evening When Only The Sky Was Blue Heaven With You I Still Love You Talk Back Trembling Lips The Shelter Of Your Eyes When We Get Together Ring Of Gold A Fool Such As I Memory Number One Look Both Ways A Little Patch Of Blue Marianne (CD only)
Thoughts of Home (1989)	My Shoes Keep Walking Back To You The Mountains Of Mourne London Leaves Blue Eyes Cryin' In The Rain Old Days Remembered Send Me The Pillow You Dream On Moonlight And Roses A Little Piece Of Heaven Far Far From Home The Isle Of Innisfree My Heart Skips A Beat I Know One I'll Take You Home Again Kathleen

	Second Fiddle My Favourite Memory Forty Shades Of Green
Daniel O'Donnell Favourites (1990)	Bed of Roses Forever You'll Be Mine Excuse Me (I Think I've Got A Heartache) My Wedding Band Is A Halo Of Gold Streets Of Baltimore Geisha Girl Life To Go That's A Sad Affair Bringing Mary Home Home Sweet Home Banks Of My Own Lovely Lee Home Is Where The Heart Is Rare Old Times The Green Hills of Sligo
The Very Best Of Daniel O'Donnell (1991)	I Need You Never Ending Song Of Love Don't Forget To Remember A Country Boy Like Me She's No Angel Stand Beside Me Eileen Pretty Little Girl From Omagh Danny Boy Wedding Song My Donegal Shore A Letter From The Postman's Bag The Three Bells Our House Is A Home A Loved One's Goodbye Home Is Where The Heart Is The Old Rugged Cross You Send Me Your Love

	Take Good Care Of Her Standing Room Only
Follow Your Dream (1992)	Follow Your Dream Welcome Home Not Until The Next Time Cryin' Time Back In My Baby's Arms Again My Claim To Fame Is You Sweet Memories I Just Want To Dance With You The Love In Your Eyes You're The Reason Belle Of The Ball Galway Ball Destination Donegal How Great Thou Art
A Date With Daniel O'Donnell Live (1993)	I Need You My Shoes Keep Walking Back To You Pretty Little Girl From Omagh The Love In Your Eyes My Irish Country Home My Donegal Shore Follow Your Dream Whatever Happened To Old Fashioned Love I Just Want To Dance With You Our House Is A Home The Rose Of Tralee Never Ending Song Of Love The Wedding The Mountains Of Mourne The Little Things Somewhere Between I Need You It's A Long Way To Tipperary

	Stand Beside Me
	How Great Thou Art
Christmas With Daniel (1994)	An Old Christmas Card
	Snowflake
	Pretty Paper
	I Saw Mommy Kissing Santa Claus
	White Christmas
	Christmas Long Ago
	When A Child Is Born
	Santa Claus Is Comin' To Town
	Christmas Time In Innisfree
	Silver Bells
	Rockin' Around The Christmas Tree
	Christmas
	A Christmas Story
	Silent Night
	The Gift
Especially For You (1994)	Singing the Blues
	Leaving Is Easy (When Loving Is Hard)
	She Goes Walking Through My Mind
	Happy Years
	Broken Hearts Always Mend
	Guilty
	Travellin' Light
	Come Back Paddy Reilly To Ballyjamesduff
	Whatever Happened To Old
	Fashioned Love
	Sweet Forget Me Not
	You're The First Thing I Think Of
	It Comes And Goes
	Silver Threads Among The Gold
	Someday (You'll Want Me To Want You)
	Lover's Chain

	Never Be Anyone Else But You
The Classic Collection (1995)	World Of Our Own Love Me The Minute You're Gone My Forever Friend Follow Your Dream The Old House A Little Piece Of Heaven The Old Dungarven Oak Walk Right Back Distant Drums Little Cabin Home On The Hill Lover's Chain The Little Things Mary From Dungloe Just Walkin' In The Rain Old Photographs Moonlight And Roses I'll Take You Home Again Kathleen
Timeless: Daniel O'Donnell and Mary Duff (duets)	Timeless We Believe In Happy Endings I Won't Take Less Than Your Love Whispering Hope Have You Ever Been Lonely I Heard The Bluebirds Sing Eileen McManus Secret Love Vaya Con Dios Walk Right Back A Girl I Used To Know Jeanie's Afraid Of The Dark Somewhere Between Will The Circle Be Unbroken
Irish Collection (1996)	Pretty Little Girl From Omagh The Isle Of Innisfree An Old Irish Song

Forty Shades Of Green
Three Leaf Shamrock
Dublin In The Rare Old Times
The Blue Hills Of Brefini
The Green Glens Of Antrim
The Old Dungarven Oak
My Donegal Shore
Home Is Where the Heart Is
The Mountains Of Mourne
Far Far From Home
Danny Boy
Any Tipperary Town
Irish Eyes
Our House Is A Home
Galway Bay
Come Back Paddy Reilly To Ballyjamesduff
I'll Take You Home Again Kathleen

Songs Of Inspiration (1996)

Footsteps
It Is No Secret
You Needed Me
I Saw The Light
One Day At A Time
My Forever Friend
When I Had You
You'll Never Walk Alone
What A Friend We Have In Jesus
Why Me
The Old Rugged Cross
Yes I Really Love You
How Great Thou Art
This World Is Not My Home
He Took Your Place
Amazing Grace
Family Bible
In The Garden

	Children's Band
	Standing Room Only
I Believe (1997)	Everything Is Beautiful
	I Believe
	Any Dream Will Do
	I Can See Clearly Now
	I Have A Dream
	The Greatest Love
	A Little Peace
	The Way Old Friends Do
	Rivers of Babylon
	What a Wonderful World
	Even On Days That It Rained
	Beyond the Great Divide
	Our Special Absent Friends
	Love, Hope And Faith
	Desiderata
Love Songs (1998)	The Magic Is There
	Then You Can Tell Me Goodbye
	For the Good Times
	Halfway to Paradise
	The Way Dreams Are
	Let Me Be The One
	Spanish Eyes
	Sealed With A Kiss
	Hello Darlin'
	Smooth Sailing
	Somewhere
	Lay Down Beside Me
	Love Me Tender
	Give a Little Love
Greatest Hits (1999)	I Just Want To Dance With You
	Whatever Happened To Old Fashioned Love
	Make The World Go Away
	I Need You

	The Magic Is There
	Secret Love
	Four In The Morning
	My Donegal Shore
	Take Good Care Of Her
	The Way Dreams Are
	Danny Boy
	When Hope Dawns At Sunrise
	Home To Donegal
	Footsteps
	Save The Last Dance For me
	My Shoes Keep Walking Back To You
	Uno Mas
	Stand Beside Me
	There Goes My Everything
	Timeless
	Singing The Blues
	Beyond The Sunset
	The Love In Your Eyes
	Give A Little Love
	The Gift
	How Great Thou Art
Faith & Inspiration (2000)	Softly And Tenderly
	Here I Am Lord
	Morning Has Broken
	Marriage Of A Lifetime
	Be Not Afraid
	Light A Candle
	Annie's Song
	Nearer My God To Thee
	Abide With Me
	Wind Beneath My Wings
	I Watch The Sunrise
	Make Me A Channel Of Your Peace
	Let There Be Peace
	The Rose

	Battle Hymn Of The Republic Panis Angelicus
Heartbreakers (2000)	Don't Forget To Remember Old Loves Never Die I Wonder Where You Are Tonight Before I'm Over You Take Good Care Of Her Don't Let Me Cross Over Crying My Heart Out Over You Excuse Me (I Think I've Got A Heartache) That's A Sad Affair Your Old Love Letters You Know I Still Love You A Fool Such As I Singing The Blues Leaving Is Easy (When Loving Is Hard) She Goes Walking Through My Mind Broken Hearts Always Mend Whatever Happened To Old Fashioned Love Sweet Forget Me Not It Comes And Goes Someday You'll Want Me To Want You
Live, Laugh, Love (2001)	Live, Laugh, Love Somewhere Under The Sun Green, Green Grass Of Home On the Other Hand Waltz Across Texas Among the Wickow Hills Only This Moment Is Mine All I Want Is You Don't Say Love One More Time

	I Can't see Me Without You Rosa Rio I Will Think Of You Thank You For Loving Me Roads Of Kildare Belfast
Yesterday's Memories (2002)	Sing Me An Old Fashioned Song Walk Through This World With Me Help Me Make It Through The Night Tonight Will Never Happen Again Coat Of Many Colours Tennessee Waltz Blackboard Of My Heart Even If It's Only For A Minute I Can't Help It (If I'm Still In Love With You) Then The World Will Know My Dreams Just Came True The Way That You Are When Two Worlds Collide Yesterday's Memories
The Irish Album (2002)	Pretty Little Girl From Omagh The Isle Of Innisfree Sing An Old Irish Song Forty Shades Of Green Three Leaf Shamrock Dublin In The Rare Auld Times Blue Hills Of Breffni Green Glens Of Antrim The Old Dungarvan Oak My Donegal Shore Home Is Where The Heart Is The Mountains Of Morne Far Far From Home Danny Boy Any Tipperary Town

	Irish Eyes Our House Is A Home Galway Bay Come Back Paddy Reilly To Ballyjamesduff I'll Take You Home Again Kathleen An Exiles Dream Heaven Around Galway Bay Hometown On The Foyle Lovely Rose Of Clare Roads Of Kildare Cutting The Corn In Creeslough An Irish Lullaby Dear Old Galway Town The Banks Of My Own Lovely Lee Pat Murphy's Meadow Destination Donegal Lough Melvin's Rocky Shore Mary From Dungloe The Green Hills Of Sligo The Rose Of Mooncoin Your Friendly Irish Way Limerick You're A Lady These Are My Mountains Home To Donegal Belfast
The Daniel O'Donnell Show (2002)	Stand Beside Me Home To Donegal Medley: You're The First Thing I Think Of I Don't Care Back In My Baby's Arms Again Waltz Across Texas The Old Dungarvan Oak Medley: Act Naturally Excuse Me (I Think I've Got A Heartache)

Forever And Ever (I Love You)
I Heard The Bluebird Sing
Vaya Con Dios
Belfast
You're The Reason
I Can't See Me Without You
An Irish Lullaby
Galway Bay
My Shoes Keep Walking Back To You
Our House Is A Home
Among The Wicklow Hills
My Irish Molly
Hello Darlin'
Only This Moment Is Mine
Green, Green Grass Of Home
Medley: When You Walk In The Room
Ob-la-di, Ob-la-da
Blueberry Hill
Let's Dance
Somewhere Between
Top Of The World
Roads Of Kildare
I Just Want To Dance With You
Rivers Of Babylon
How Great Thou Art

Dreaming (2002)

I Just Want To Dance With You
The Love In Your Eyes
Send Me the Pillow You Dream On
I Love You Because
Home Is Where The Heart Is
Pretty Little Girl From Omagh
Moonlight And Roses
I Need You
Veil Of White Lace
Wedding Bells
Follow Your Dream

	Sweet Memories Green Glens Of Antrim My Donegal Shore Far Far From Home Irish Eyes Welcome Home A Little Piece Of Heaven Old Days Remembered My Favourite Memory
Daniel In Blue Jeans (2003)	Singing The blues Teenager In Love Never Be Any Else But You Love Me Tender Halfway To Paradise Blueberry Hill Bye Bye Love It Doesn't Matter Anymore Travellin' Light A Fool Such As I Roses Are Red Save The Last Dance For Me Donna Send Me The Pillow That You Dream On Wooden Heart Young Love Twelfth Of Never Honey Green, Green Grass Of Home Sealed With A Kiss
At The End Of The Day (2003)	Sweet Queen of Peace You Raise Me Up Only the Shadow of Your Love Sweet Heart of Jesus Holy God We Praise Thy Name Going Home

	Hail Glorious Saint Patrick
	Lady of Knock
	When Darkness Falls
	Queen of the May
	God be With You Until We Meet Again
	Let It Be
	In Bread We Bring You
	Surely the Presence of the Lord/ May God's Blessing Surround You Each Day
	At The End Of The Day
The Jukebox Years (2004)	Hello Mary Lou
	Oh Boy
	Do You Wanna Dance
	All Shook Up
	Three Steps To Heaven
	When
	Girl Of My Best Friend
	Come On Over To My Place
	When You Walk In The Room
	Daydream Believer
	Sweet Caroline
	Wonderful Tonight
	Walk Right Back
	Beautiful Sunday
	Ob-La-Di Ob-La-Da
	Is This The Way To Amarillo
	Knock Three Times
	I'm A Believer
	Let's Dance
	That'll Be The Day
	Bonus Track: Living Next Door To Alice
Welcome To My World (2004)	Welcome To My World
	Anna Marie
	I Love You Because

When Two Worlds Collide
Am I losing You
Adios Amigo
How Can I Write On Paper
I Won't Forget You
Guilty
There's A Heartache Following Me
He'll Have To Go
It Hurts So Much
Moonlight & Roses
Blueside Of Lonesome
This World Is Not My Home
Rosa Rio
Distant Drums
Four Walls
Don't Let Me Cross Over
Is It Really Over
I Missed Me
Not Until The Next Time
You're The Only Good Thing

DANIEL O'DONNELL VIDEOS

TITLE	TRACKS

Live In Concert (1988)	Intro: Stand Beside Me
	Stand Beside Me
	Our House Is A Home
	Veil Of White Lace
	Medley:
	  Fräulein
	  Red River Valley
	  Black Hills Of Dakota
	Pretty Little Girl From Omagh
	My Donegal Shore
	I Wonder Where You Are Tonight
	Don't Forget To Remember
	The Old Rugged Cross

	The Irish Rover
	Wooden Heart
	Take Good Care Of Her
	Roses Are Red
	Medley:
	Fräulein
	I Won't Forget You
	Anna Marie
	He'll Have To Go
	Adios Amigo
	Medley:
	Bye Bye Love
	It Doesn't Matter Any More
	Things
	Play On: Danny Boy
	Danny Boy
	Play Off: Danny Boy
Thoughts Of Home (1989)	My Shoes Keep Walking Back To You
	Forty Shades Of Green
	Our House Is A Home
	Dublin In The Rare Auld Times
	The Mountains Of Mourne
	Far Far From Home
	I'll Take You Home Again Kathleen
	Moonlight And Roses
	Mary From Dungloe
	Send Me The Pillow You Dream On
	The Isle Of Innisfree
	The Rose Of Tralee
	Donegal Shore
TV Show Favourites (1990)	I Don't Care
	Lovely Rose Of Clare
	Geisha Girl
	Take Good Care Of Her
	From A Jack To A King
	I Wonder Where You Are Tonight

	Dear Old Galway Town
	History Of Country Music Medley:
	Miss McLeod's Reels
	Streets Of Laredo
	Your Cheatin' Heart
	He'll Have to Go
	Forever And Ever Amen
	Sing Me An Old Irish Song
	I Need You
	Bed Of Roses
	Elvis Medley:
	That's Alright Mama
	Love Me Tender
	Are You Lonesome Tonight
	Don't Be Cruel
	Home Is Where The Heart Is
	Walk Right Back
	Life To Go
	Lough Melvin's Rocky Shore
	Stand Beside Me
An Evening With Daniel O'Donnell (1990)	I Need You (Intro)
	Stand Beside Me
	Geisha Girl
	Medley:
	Paper Roses
	From Here To There To You
	Please Help Me I'm Falling
	London Leaves
	Galway Bay
	The Last Waltz Of The Evening
	Summertime In Ireland
	We Could
	Second Fiddle
	The Road And Miles To Dundee
	Westmeath Bachelor
	The Old Dungarven Oak
	My Shoes Keep Walking Back To You

	Medals For Mothers
	Memory Number One
	Home Sweet Home
	Heaven With You
	I Need You
	Wooden Heart
	Danny Boy
	Talk Back Trembling Lips
	Fiddle Solo (Boil Em' Cabbage Down)
	Accordion Solo (Alpine Slopes/The Jacqueline Waltz)
	Take Good Care Of Her
	Roses Are Red
	Medley:
	Isle Of Innisfree
	Mountains Of Mourne
	Forty Shades Of Green
	I'll Take You Home Again Kathleen
	Medley:
	Love's Gonna Live Here Again
	Open Up Your Heart
	Before I Met You
	Medley:
	It's A Long Way To Tipperary
	Pack Up Your Troubles
	If You're Irish Come In To The Parlour
	Jig
	Stand Beside Me
	Wild Wood Flower (Play Off)
	Our House Is A Home
	Danny Boy (Play Off)
Follow Your Dream (1992)	I Need You (Intro)
	Stand Beside Me
	Eileen
	Pretty Little Girl From Omagh
	Destination Donegal

Medley:
 Paper Roses
 Not Until The Next Time
 Cryin' Time
Medley:
 A Country Boy Like Me
 Home Sweet Home
 Summertime In Ireland
The Wedding Song (Ave Maria)
Irish Country Home
Ramblin' Rose
I Just Want To Dance With You
Medley:
 Jail House Rock
 Hound Dog
 Blue Suede Shoes
Medley:
 That's Alright Mama
 Love Me Tender
 Are You Lonesome Tonight
 Don't Be Cruel
White River Stomp
Our House Is A Home
Never Ending Song Of Love
Rockin' Alone
Standing Room Only
Welcome Home
The Love In Your Eyes
You Send Me Your Love
Turkey In The Straw (Reel)
I Need You
Medley:
 It's A Long Way To Tipperary
 Pack Up Your Troubles
 If You're Irish Come In To The
 Parlour
 The Black Thorn Stick/
 Kennedy's Fancy (jigs)

(Reprise) Stand Beside Me
(Playoff) The Mockin' Bird (Reel)
How Great Thou Art

Daniel O'Donnell & Friends Live (1993)

Daniel O'Donnell:
Follow Your Dream
Whatever Happened To Old Fashioned Love
The Wedding Song
The Love In Your Eyes
You're The Reason
Somewhere Between (Duet with Mary Duff)
Walk Right Back (Duet with Mary Duff)

Mary Duff:
You're One And Only
A Picture Of Me Without You
Yellow Roses

Sean O'Farrell:
Eighteen Yellow Roses
The Way Love Ought To Be
Nobody's Child

Dominic Kirwan:
Someone Had To Teach You
Almost Persuaded
She's A Heartache

Sarah Jory:
Wind Beneath My Wings

Dominic Kirwan:
If Tomorrow Never Comes
The Young Ones

Tracy Elsdon:
Half The Moon
You Were My Lover

Daniel O'Donnell:
Never Ending Song of Love
My Donegal Shore

	Medley: Rose Of Tralee Dublin In The Rare Auld Times Galway Bay I Just Want To Dance With You Our House Is A Home (Duet with Dominic Kirwan)
Just For You (An Intimate Musical Journey) (1994)	Danny Boy Overture/I Need You/Stand Beside Me Whatever Happened To Old Fashioned Love I Need You/Mary From Dungloe/How Great Thou Art My Irish Country Home How Great Thou Art Irish Dance Medley Dublin In The Rare Auld Times I Need You Come Back Paddy Reilly to BallyJamesDuff Our House Is A Home I Just Want To Dance With You Singing The Blues Follow Your Dream Sweet Forget Me Not Ramblin' Rose The Old Rugged Cross Moonlight And Roses How Great Thou Art
The Classic Concert (1995)	Stand Beside Me Someday You'll Want Me To Want You Just Walking In The Rain Guilty The Boys Of Killybegs

Leaving Is Easy (When Loving Is Hard)
Little Cabin Home On The Hill
The Old House
World Of Our Own
Happy Years
Medley:
- Knock Three Times
- I Can't Stop Loving You
- Blueberry Hill
- Do You Want To Dance

The Little Things
Limerick You're A Lady
It Comes And Goes
Eileen McManus (Duet with Mary Duff)
Secret Love (Duet with Mary Duff)
Will The Circle Be Unbroken (Duet with Mary Duff)
Whispering Hope (Duet with Mary Duff)
You're The First Thing I Think Of
Lovers Chain
Medley:
- It's A Long Way to Tipperary
- Pack Up Your Troubles
- If You're Irish Come In To The Parlour

Stand Beside Me (Reprise)
Oh Boy
How Great Thou Art

Christmas With Daniel (1996)	Christmas Long Ago An Old Christmas Card Christmas Story Pretty Paper Snowflake I Saw Mommy Kissing Santa Claus

	White Christmas Winter Wonderland A Christmas Childhood (poem narrated by Daniel) The Gift Santa Claus Is Coming To Town Silver Bells Rockin' Around The Christmas Tree C.H.R.I.S.T.M.A.S. My Lovely Island Home (poem narrated by Julia O'Donnell) When A Child Is Born Christmas In Innisfree Silent Night
The Gospel Show (1997)	Kumbaya What A Friend We Have In Jesus Everything Is Beautiful Put Your Hand In The Hand Of The Man It Is No Secret Rivers Of Babylon Why Me Lord Medley: Open Up The Pearly Gates We Shall Not Be Moved Whispering Hope (Duet with Mary Duff) Will The Circle Be Unbroken (Duet with Mary Duff) Amazing Grace (Mary Duff) He's Got the Whole World In His Hands (Mary Duff) In The Garden I Saw The Light How Great Thou Art Footsteps You'll Never Walk Alone

	Any Dream Will Do
	Children's Band
	Silent Night
Give A Little Love – Daniel O'Donnell & Mary Duff (1998)	Give A Little Love
	Eileen McManus
	Wounded Hearts
	Just Walking In The Rain
	Timeless
	The Power Of Love
	Limerick You're A Lady
	Homeland
	Whispering Hope
	Singing The Blues
	Goin' Home
	I Just Want To Dance With You
	Strangers
	Never Be Anyone Else But You
	Will The Circle Be Unbroken
Peaceful Waters (1999)	I Can See Clearly Now
	The Way Old Friends Do
	Cutting The Corn In Creeslough
	An Irish Lullaby
	I Believe
	I Have A Dream
	Beyond The Great Divide
	When Hope Dawns At Sunrise
	The Rose Of Mooncoin
	Even On Days When It Rained
	Everything Is Beautiful
	Heaven Around Galway Bay
	Home To Donegal
The Daniel O'Donnell Show (2001)	Stand Beside me
	Home To Donegal
	Medley:
	You're The First Thing I Think Of
	I Don't Care

	Back In My Baby's Arms Again
	Waltz Across Texas
	The Old Dungarvan Oak
	Medley:
	Act Naturally
	Excuse Me (I Think I've Got A Heartache)
	Forever And Ever (I Love You)
	I Heard The Bluebird Sing
	Vaya Con Dios
	Belfast
	You're The Reason
	I Can't See Me Without You
	An Irish Lullaby
	Galway Bay
	My Shoes Keep Walking Back To You
	Love Sick Blues
	Our House Is A Home
	Among The Wicklow Hills
	My Irish Molly
	Hello Darlin'
	Only This Moment Is Mine
	Green, Green Grass Of Home
	Medley:
	When You Walk In The Room
	Ob-La-Di, Ob-La-Da
	Blueberry Hill
	Let's Dance
	Somewhere Between
	Top Of The World
	Roads Of Kildare
	I Just Want To Dance With You
	Rivers Of Babylon
	How Great Thou Art
Shades of Green (2002)	Together Again
	Stand Beside Me
	Sing Me An Old Irish Song

Help Me Make It Through The Night
Tennessee Waltz
Pretty Little Girl from Omagh
My Happiness
Blackboard Of My Heart
The Mountains Of Mourne
Then The World Will Know
Coat Of Many Colours
Medley:
  Day Dream Believer
  Come On Over To My Place
Medley:
  Sweet Caroline
  There Goes My Everything
Medley:
  All Shook Up
  Show Me The Way To Amarillo
Medley:
  Forty Shades Of Green
  I'll Take You Home Again Kathleen
Medley:
  I Wonder Where You Are Tonight
  The Little Things
  Bed Of Roses
Will You walk With Me
Isle Of Inishfree
Sing Me An Old Fashioned Song
I Will Think Of You
Old Fashioned Dance:
  Shoe The Donkey
  The Hornpipe
  The Boys Of Bluehill
  Reprise – Shoe The Donkey
You're My Best Friend
Danny Boy
Wooden Heart
Medley:
  When Irish Eyes Are Smiling

	Green Glens Of Antrim
	The Homes Of Donegal
	Boys From The County Armagh
	The Rivers Of Babylon
	How Great Thou Art
Songs of Faith (2003)	Softly and Tenderly
	Sweet Victory
	Here I Am Lord
	Make Me A Channel Of Your Peace
	Put Your Hand In The Hand
	Nearer My God To Thee
	Only A Shadow Of Your Love
	I Saw The Light
	God Be With You Till We Meet Again
	You Raise Me Up
	Will The Circle Be Unbroken
	Sweet Queen Of Peace
	The Wind Beneath My Wings
	Footsteps
	I Watch The Sunrise
	My Forever Friend
	He's Got The Whole World In His Hands
	Let There Be Peace
	When Darkness Falls
	Open Up The Pearly Gates/We Shall Not Be Moved
	Lady Of Knock
	Surely The Presence Of The Lord Is In This Place/May God's Blessing Surround You Each Day
	One Day At A Time
	Panis Angelicus
	At The End Of The Day
	The Rivers Of Babylon
	Battle Hymn Of The Republic

DANIEL O'DONNELL DVDS

TITLE	TRACKS
Shades Of Green (2002)	Together Again Stand Beside Me Sing Me An Old Irish Song Help Me Make It Through The Night Tennessee Waltz Pretty Little Girl from Omagh My Happiness Blackboard Of My Heart The Mountains Of Mourne Then The World Will Know Coat Of Many Colours Medley: Day Dream Believer Come On Over To My Place Medley: Sweet Caroline There Goes My Everything Medley: All Shook Up Show Me The Way To Amarillo Medley: Forty Shades Of Green I'll Take You Home Again Kathleen Medley: I Wonder Where You Are Tonight The Little Things Bed Of Roses Will You walk With Me Isle Of Inishfree Sing Me An Old Fashioned Song I Will Think Of You Old Fashioned Dance: Shoe The Donkey The Hornpipe

	The Boys Of Bluehill
	Reprise – Shoe The Donkey
	You're My Best Friend
	Danny Boy
	Wooden Heart
	Medley:
	When Irish Eyes Are Smiling
	Green Glens Of Antrim
	The Homes Of Donegal
	Boys From The County Armagh
	The Rivers Of Babylon
	How Great Thou Art
The Daniel O'Donnell Show (2002)	Stand Beside me
	Home To Donegal
	Medley:
	You're The First Thing I Think Of
	I Don't Care
	Back In My Baby's Arms Again
	Waltz Across Texas
	The Old Dungarvan Oak
	Medley:
	Act Naturally
	Excuse Me (I Think I've Got A Heartache)
	Forever And Ever (I Love You)
	I Heard The Bluebird Sing
	Vaya Con Dios
	Belfast
	You're The Reason
	I Can't See Me Without You
	An Irish Lullaby
	Galway Bay
	My Shoes Keep Walking Back To You
	Love Sick Blues
	Our House Is A Home
	Among The Wicklow Hills

My Irish Molly
Hello Darlin'
Only This Moment Is Mine
Green, Green Grass Of Home
Medley:
- When You Walk In The Room
- Ob-La-Di, Ob-La-Da
- Blueberry Hill
- Let's Dance

Somewhere Between
Top Of The World
Roads Of Kildare
I Just Want To Dance With You
Rivers Of Babylon
How Great Thou Art

The Gospel Show (2003)

Kumbaya
What A Friend We Have In Jesus
Everything Is Beautiful
Put Your Hand In The Hand Of The Man
It Is No Secret
Rivers Of Babylon
Why Me Lord
Medley:
- Open Up The Pearly Gates
- We Shall Not Be Moved

Whispering Hope
Will The Circle Be Unbroken
Amazing Grace
He's Got The Whole World In His Hands
In The Garden
I Saw The Light
How Great Thou Art
Footsteps
You'll Never Walk Alone
Any Dream Will Do

	Children's Band
	Silent Night
Peaceful Waters (2003)	I Can See Clearly Now
	The Way Old Friends Do
	Cutting The Corn In Creeslough
	An Irish Lullaby
	I Believe
	I Have A Dream
	Beyond The Great Divide
	When Hope Dawns At Sunrise
	The Rose Of Mooncoin
	Even On Days When It Rained
	Everything Is Beautiful
	Heaven Around Galway Bay
	Home To Donegal

CHART SUCCESSES (UK NATIONAL POP CHARTS)

SINGLES

Date of Entry	Title	Highest Position
12/2/92	I Just Want To Dance With You	20
22/1/93	The Three Bells	71
8/5/93	The Love In Your Eyes	47
7/8/93	Whatever Happened To Old-Fashioned Love	21
16/4/94	Singing The Blues	23
26/11/94	The Gift	46
10/5/95	Secret Love	28
9/6/96	Timeless (duet with Mary Duff)	32
28/9/96	Footsteps	25
1/6/97	The Love Songs EP	27
30/3/98	Give A Little Love	7
5/10/98	The Magic Is There	16
8/3/99	The Way Dreams Are	18
19/7/99	Uno Mass	25
18/12/99	A Christmas Kiss	20

15/4/00	Light A Candle	23
16/12/00	Morning Has Broken	32
16/12/04	You Raise Me Up	21

ALBUMS

15/10/88	From The Heart	56
28/10/89	Thoughts Of Home	43
21/4/90	Favourites	61
17/11/90	The Last Waltz	46
9/11/91	The Very Best Of Daniel O'Donnell	34
21/11/92	Follow Your Dream	17
6/11/93	A Date With Daniel O'Donnell Live	21
22/10/94	Especially For You	14
3/12/94	Christmas With Daniel	34
11/11/95	The Classic Collection	34
6/4/96	Timeless	11
21/10/96	Songs Of Inspiration	11
3/11/97	I Believe	11
26/10/98	Love Songs	9
2/10/99	Daniel O'Donnell Greatest Hits	10
28/10/00	Faith And Inspiration	4
1/12/01	Live, Laugh, Love	27
2/11/02	Yesterday's Memories	19
28/3/03	Daniel In Blue Jeans	3
19/10/03	At The End Of The Day	11
13/3/04	The Jukebox Years	3
23/10/04	Welcome To My World	6

VIDEOS

1989	Thoughts Of Home	5
1990	TV Show Favourites	6
1990	An Evening With Daniel O'Donnell	9
1992	Follow Your Dream (Live)	1
1993	A Date With Daniel O'Donnell And Friends Live	1
1994	Just For You	2
1995	The Classic Live Concert	3

1996	Christmas With Daniel	3
1997	The Gospel Show – Live	2
1998	Give A Little Love	5
1999	Peaceful Waters	
2001	The Daniel O'Donnell Show	
2002	Shades of Green	2
2003	Songs of Faith	1

INDEX